Sault S...

Adventures b...

MW00624356

Sault Ste Marie
PURE MICHIGAN®

Book your rooms today!

1-800-647-2858 • saultstemarie.com • #ilovethesoo

1

Ship Watcher's Paradise
Located in Beautiful Duluth, Minnesota

Whirlpools • Fireplaces • Private Balconies

*Awarded
'Property of
the Year 2013'
by the Minnesota
Lodging Association*

SOUTH PIER INN
on the canal

(800) 430-7437 • SOUTHPIERINN.COM

@ALGOMACENTRAL
#sailwiththebear

STEP INTO MY OFFICE.

ALGONET.COM

Watch the ships up close
from your balcony!

1.877.465.6257
905.227.6177

info@innatlock7.com
www.innatlock7.com

24 Chapel Street South
Thorold, ON L2V 2C6

KNOW
YOUR SHIPS

ISBN: 978-1-891849-24-4 © 2019

No part of this book may be published,
broadcast, rewritten or redistributed
without permission.

Marine Publishing Co. Inc.
317 S. Division St. #8
Ann Arbor, MI 48104

knowyourships@gmail.com
734-668-4734

Editor/Publisher: Roger LeLievre
Crew: Sam Hankinson, Kathryn Lau, Nancy
Kuharevicz, Matt Miner, John Philbin, Neil
Schultheiss, William Soleau, Wade P. Streeter,
John Vournakis and George Wharton

Founder: Tom Manse (1915-1994)

The information in this book was obtained from
the U.S. Army Corps of Engineers, the U.S. Coast
Guard, the Lake Carriers' Association, Lloyd's Register,
NOAA, Transport Canada, The St. Lawrence Seaway
Authority, Great Lakes Tugs & Workboats, Shipfax,
Tugfax, BoatNerd.com and vessel owners / operators.

KNOWYOURSHIPS.COM

Serving the Marine Industry from the Port of Detroit Since 1874

The J.W. Westcott Company
In Business to "Deliver"

Ship Reporters and Vessel Agents
12 24th Street, Detroit, MI 48222
FM Channel 10   (313) 496-0555
Fax (313) 496-0628

Providing Shore-to-Ship and Ship-to-Shore
Delivery Service at Your Request
24 Hours a Day – 7 Days a Week
Throughout the Navigation Season

Specializing in Marine Delivery, Crew Changes and Passengers, Pilot Transfers,
Nautical Charts and U.S. Government Publications, Maritime Textbooks and
Licensing Materials. Grocery and Hardware Orders Filled Upon Request.

M/V J.W. Westcott II

M/V Joseph W. Hogan

www.jwwestcott.com

Contents

Know Your SHIPS
60 Years

DEDICATION 7
PASSAGES 9
VESSEL INDEX 19
FLEET LISTINGS 33
LAKER LONGEVITY 92
ENGINES...94
  Major Great Lakes & Seaway vessels
SALTWATER FLEETS...................................99
  MARINE MUSEUMS 119
STACKS / FLAGS...................................... 131
EXTRA TONNAGE 139
  *Ports, cargoes, whistle signals,
  locks and canals, features, maps*
SPOTLIGHT 157
  Ships, sailors and adventures
HISTORIC GALLERY 173
  Images of lakers from the past
ADVERTISER INDEX 196

THIS PAGE
Mesabi Miner upbound into Lake Huron from the St. Clair River.
(Marc Dease)

FRONT COVER
Wilfred Sykes passing DeTour, MI. (Dan Vaught)

THIS SEPTEMBER...

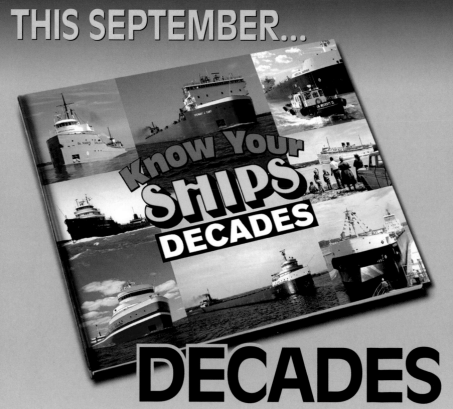

DECADES

An editor's choice of some of the best images that have appeared in *Know Your Ships* since its founding in 1959.

The book includes a year-by-year timeline of important events and also the major fleet stack markings and house flags from the past 60 years.

Large Format • 11" x 8.5"
240 pages • Hardcover • $49.95

Pre-orders begin June 1
Books will ship September 16

Pre-ordered books will be autographed and include a free commemorative reprint of the original *1959 Know Your Ships*

A limited number of books will be printed based on pre-orders

PREORDER JUNE 1 AT KNOWYOURSHIPS.COM

6

Tom Knew His Ships

And we're glad he did!

In these days of digital publishing, it's hard to imagine someone launching a project such as *Know Your Ships* with little more than a drafting table, an old camera, a damp basement darkroom and a dream. Yet in 1959, Thomas Manse compiled the first issue of this familiar guide book to boats on the Great Lakes and St. Lawrence Seaway in his Sault Ste. Marie, MI, basement with just those basics. You hold in your hand the descendant of that early effort, bigger and more colorful than Tom could ever have imagined.

Armed with an old Kodak camera (the kind with a fold-out bellows in the front) that used large-format film to yield black-and-white, post card-sized negatives, Tom Manse began shooting pictures of the passing freighter parade through the Soo Locks in the late 1940s, following in the footsteps of his father, John Manse, who was a well-known marine maritime photographer a few decades earlier. Today you might call Tom a Boatnerd.

The book rose from modest beginnings. That first issue of *Know Your Ships* was just 44 pages. Staple-bound, it sold for 50 cents. Yet it contained listings for more than 600 American and Canadian lakers as well as a full-color stack and flag guide, impressive for the time. It was conceived not as a publication aimed at those working in the shipping industry, but for tourists at the locks, ship fans and people who lived along the water and wanted basic information about the ships that passed their shores.

Now there are more than 100 outlets from Duluth to Montreal selling *Know Your Ships*. The 44 pages have grown to 200. Black and white has given way to color. Film has yielded to digital. The Internet brings customers from around the world. Tom would surely be astonished at today's technology!

Covers then and now: 1959 (above) and 2019.

Know Your Ships **wasn't all** Tom accomplished. He was instrumental in establishing the retired laker *Valley Camp* as a first-class marine museum at Sault Ste. Marie, MI. He was inaugurated into the Great Lakes Marine Hall of Fame in 1983. On Feb. 11, 1986, declared by Sault Ste. Marie as "Tom Manse Day," the local paper wrote, "He's talked ships and shipping every day of his life, and what he's forgotten is more than what most people could know in a lifetime."

Tom was fiercely proud of his Italian-American heritage and was a dedicated family man who, with his wife, Mabel, raised two daughters, Cindy and Judy. He died on April 27, 1994, just as the 35th anniversary edition of *Know Your Ships* was rolling off the press. Because of his vision, *Know Your Ships* has been able to continue on for new generations of lake boats and the fans who follow them. Thanks, Tom! – *Roger LeLievre*

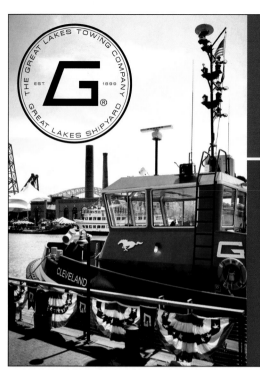

CELEBRATING

120

1899-2019

YEARS

- HARBOR TOWING
- CARGO TRANSPORTATION
- NEW CONSTRUCTION
- MAINTENANCE & REPAIR
- CUSTOM FABRICATION
- EMERGENCY ASSISTANCE

216-621-4854
www.thegreatlakesgroup.com

Congratulations

KNOW YOUR SHIPS
60 Years

You have been there...
Every wheelhouse...
Every voyage...

PORT OF MONROE

www.portofmonroe.com

Passages

Victo (American Victory) scrap tow from tug Cheyenne. *(Joe Cioletti)*

A season of comings and goings

Arriving

Algoma Central Corp. saw two bulk carriers enter service in 2018, *Algoma Innovator* and *Algoma Sault*. *Algoma Conveyor* was expected early in 2019. Other new construction previously announced has been canceled due to the bankruptcy of the overseas shipyard where they were to be

The new Algoma Innovator upbound at the Soo Locks on her first trip to Lake Superior, April 2018. (Michelle Briggs)

built. The fleet's Algoma Tankers Ltd. purchased the saltwater tanker *Ramira*, built in 2008, and rechristened her *Algonorth*, the second vessel in the company's history to bear that name. ... Turkey's Besiktas Shipyard launched two more tankers in 2018 for the Canadian company Desgagnés. *Rossi A. Desgagnés* and *Paul A. Desgagnés* can be powered by any of three types of fuel – heavy fuel oil, marine diesel or liquefied natural gas. Desgagnés also purchased the small cargo vessel *Jan* in 2018 and renamed her *Miena Desgagnés*. ... *Cleveland Rocks*, rebuilt as the cement barge *Commander*, enters service in 2019 for Port City Marine Services of Muskegon, MI. ... McKeil Marine Ltd. has acquired two Turkish-built tankers for Seaway service. New names for *Topaz I* and *Turquoise I* weren't available at press time.

Tug Evans McKeil tows Algoway to the scrapyard. (Jeff Cameron) *Inset shows Algoway and Algorail awaiting the torch.* (Matt Miner)

Departing

Algoma Central Corp.'s self-unloaders *Algoway* of 1972 and *Algorail* of 1968 were towed to Port Colborne, ON, for scrapping during summer 2018. Algoma's *Algowood* and *Capt. Henry Jackman,* both built at Collingwood Shipyards in 1981, were laid up at the end of 2018 and were likely to be towed overseas for scrapping in 2019. The fleet's *Algoma Olympic* and *Algolake* were also towed from Montreal in 2018, headed for Aliaga, Turkey, to be scrapped.

Continued on Page 12

Paul A. Desgagnés can be powered by any of three fuels. (Groupe Desgagnés)

Cement carrier English River on Lake Ontario. (Jeff Cameron)

The retired cement carrier *English River,* built in 1961, arrived at the Port Colborne scrapyard under her own power in July 2018, joining the cement carrier *Paul H. Townsend,* which was brought there in September 2017 and was still awaiting the torch in early 2019. Another cement carrier, *Stephen B. Roman* (built as *Fort William* in 1965 for Canada Steamship Lines), sailed under her own power to the scrapyard at Aliaga, Turkey, on Nov. 14, 2018. Their runs, mostly on lakes Ontario and Erie,

NACC Argonaut arrives at Cleveland on June 24, 2018, for her first visit, loaded with cement. (Ed Bansek)

were taken over by the converted saltwater vessels *NACC Argonaut* and *NACC Quebec* of the new company NovaAlgoma Cement Carriers, as well as the McKeil fleet's *McKeil Spirit.*

When the former laker *American Victory* arrived at Aliaga, Turkey, Sept. 3, 2018, the career of one of the most distinctive and historic vessels to ever sail the Great Lakes came to an end. A 1942-built U.S. Navy veteran decorated for service in World War II as *USS Neschanic* before being converted for Great Lakes use in 1961, she sailed most of her career as the *Middletown* for the Oglebay Norton fleet. In 2006, she was sold to the American Steamship Co., which gave her a fitting name, *American Victory.* She entered long-term lay-up in 2008, a victim of that year's economic downturn, and never raised steam again. In late December 2017, she was sold to the Algoma Central Corp. of St. Catharines, ON, and was resold for scrapping overseas in the spring of 2018.

Continued on Page 14

Stephen B. Roman was among several vessels retired in 2018. (Jeff Cameron)

STEPHEN B. ROMAN

The now-retired Capt. Henry Jackman, built in 1981 as Lake Wabush, above Port Huron/Point Edward. (Marc Dease)

CAPT. HENRY JACKMAN

Manitoba on the St. Clair River in 2011. She was towed to Aliaga, Turkey for scrapping in 2018. (David Michelson)

MANITOBA

MANITOBA

The former Bob-Lo Island passenger steamer *Ste. Claire* was a total loss after flames engulfed the vessel the morning of June 6, 2018, while she was undergoing restoration at a Detroit River dock. As bystanders looked on, firefighters labored in vain to save the 1910-vintage, Frank E. Kirby-designed vessel. She and her running mate, *Columbia,* last operated in 1991, with *Columbia* currently at Buffalo, NY, awaiting restoration.

A slice of Detroit history went up in smoke when the passenger steamer Ste. Claire burned on June 6, 2018. (Detroit Fire Inspector Joseph Cartledge)

After languishing for nearly two years in lay up at Montreal, Lower Lakes Towing Ltd.'s grain carrier *Manitoba* (formerly *Mantadoc, Teakglen* and *Maritime Trader*) arrived at Aliaga, Turkey, on Nov. 18, 2018, for scrapping.

Changing

As the 2018 shipping season began, Algoma Central renamed its two new acquisitions from American Steamship Co., *Buffalo* and *Adam E. Cornelius*, *Algoma Buffalo* and *Algoma Compass* respectively. ... Lower Lakes Towing Ltd.'s barge *James L. Kuber* was renamed *Maumee* early in 2019, the second vessel of the fleet to bear that name.

Lay ups

CSL Tadoussac returned to service in 2018 after three years idle at Thunder Bay, ON. American Steamship Co.'s *St. Clair* returned to service in 2018 after a year's lay up. The fleet's *American Courage* will be back out in 2019 after two years in the barn. The future is not so certain for Great Lakes Fleet's *Arthur M. Anderson*, which has been laid up at Superior, WI, since the end of the 2016 season. Time will tell if this classic receives needed hull repairs and returns to service soon. The same goes for *Edward L. Ryerson*, in long-term lay-up at Superior. *American Valor, Sarah Spencer* and *Manistee* remain sidelined at Toledo. *Manistee* and *Sarah*

Continued on Page 16

Algoma Compass on the Calumet River, South Chicago, IL. (Philip and Emily Kirman)

Algowood stuck in Straits ice in January 2018. *(Jacob Northup)*

Reactivated CSL Tadoussac downbound at the south end of Lake Huron. *(Marc Dease)*

Algoma Buffalo arriving at Lorain, OH. *(Roger Durfee)*

Spencer are expected to be scrapped eventually, while *American Valor*'s future is still uncertain. Interlake Steamship Co.'s long-idle *John Sherwin* remains tied up at DeTour, MI, waiting for her services to be needed, as does *McKee Sons*, docked at Muskegon, MI.

Museums

The retired U.S. Coast Guard cutter *Bramble*, which most recently served as a museum at Port Huron, MI, has been sold and was to leave the lakes in 2019. ... The veteran tug *Ohio* has been donated to the National Museum of the Great Lakes at Toledo by the Great Lakes Towing Co. The *Ohio* was built in 1903 as the fire tug *M.F.D.S. No. 15*, rebuilt as a tug in 1953 and renamed *Laurence C. Turner*. She was renamed *Ohio* in 1973.

The museum ship *William A. Irvin* was moved from her longtime berth at Duluth's Minnesota Slip in Canal Park by tugs in late fall 2018 so contaminated sediments in her slip could be capped and stabilized. Over the winter of 2018-19, the 1938-built *Irvin,* which sailed her entire career for the U.S. Steel fleet, was drydocked for hull maintenance and fresh paint.

The Thunder Bay, ON-based tug *Peninsula,* built in 1944 for the Canadian navy as *HMCS Norton*, was relocated to Marathon, ON, in 2018 for use as a marine museum under the auspices of The Marathon & District Historical Society.

Victo (American Victory) scrap tow in the Rock Cut, St. Marys River, on June 19, 2018. (Roger LeLievre)

Museum ship WIlliam A. Irvin at Superior, WI, in late 2018. Tim S. Dool is in the background. (Ethan Rentschler)

On the horizon

VanEnkevort Tug & Barge of Escanaba, MI, is building a 740-foot-long barge at Bay Shipbuilding Co., Sturgeon Bay, WI, for Great Lakes service. *Michigan Trader* is expected to be completed by mid-2020, and will be pushed by *Laura L. VanEnkevort*, a former saltwater tug.

Central Marine Logistics

Vessel Management & Steamship Agency • Griffith, Indiana

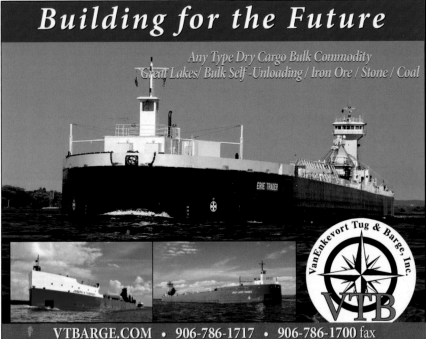

Building for the Future

Any Type Dry Cargo Bulk Commodity
Great Lakes/ Bulk Self-Unloading / Iron Ore / Stone / Coal

VTBARGE.COM • 906-786-1717 • 906-786-1700 fax
vtbarge@vtbarge.com • 909 N. Lincoln Rd., Escanaba, MI 49829

18

Vessel Index

Joseph L. Block departs Duluth, MN, with ore chips as Great Republic leaves with coal. (Gus Schauer)

Great Lakes Fleet

TRANSPORTERS OF BULK CARGOES

The Art of Logistics.

Your business and today's supply chains expect more than haphazard dependability, cryptic scheduling, and a sea of broken promises. Avoid the runaround. Our accomplished staff and premier vessels are at the ready to deliver, backed by more than 2 billion tons worth of cargo experience. Bulk may be our business, but unsurpassed service is what we sell. Leave the art of logistics to the industry leader - Great Lakes Fleet.

cn.ca/greatlakesfleet

Vessel Name	Page #	Vessel Name	Page #	Vessel Name	Page #	Vessel Name	Page #

A

A-390	37	Algoma Transport	35	Anuket Ruby	109	Bayfield	64
A-397	37	Algonorth	36	Appledore IV	40	Bayship	38
A-410	37	Algonova	36	Appledore V	40	BBC Alberta	101
Acacia	123	Algoscotia	36	Aquastar	72	BBC Austria	101
Acadia Desgagnés	52	Algosea	36	ARA Rotterdam	100	BBC Balboa	101
Active	100	Algoterra	36	Archipelago	38	BBC Campana	114
Adanac III	72	Alina	106	Arctic	104	BBC Carolina	107
Adfines Sea	100	Alouette Spirit	65	Arcticus	52	BBC Elbe	101
Adfines Sky	100	Alpena	58	Argentia Desgagnés	52	BBC Europe	101
Adfines Star	100	Alphonse-Desjardins	77	Arizona	51	BBC Florida	114
Adfines Sun	100	Amarant	113	Arkansas	51	BBC Fortune	111
Adriaticborg	114	Amazoneborg	114	Armand-Imbeau	77	BBC Fuji	101
Agassiz	68	Amber Mae	75	Armand-Imbeau II	77	BBC Georgia	114
Aiden William	41	Americaborg	114	Arneborg	115	BBC Germany	101
Alamosborg	114	American Century	36	Arni J. Richter	86	BBC Hudson	101
Alan K. Luedtke	63	American Courage	36	Arsland	116	BBC Kansas	106
Alaskaborg	114	American Girl	79	Arthur M. Anderson	51	BBC Kibo	101
Albanyborg	114	American Integrity	36	Arubaborg	115	BBC Kimberley	107
Albert	38	American Mariner	36	Ashland Bayfield Express	38	BBC Kwiatkowski	101
Alder	83	American Spirit	36	Ashtabula	62	BBC Maine	114
Aldo H.	67	American Valor	35	ASI Clipper	38	BBC Manitoba	107
A. LeBlanc	43	Americo Dean	46	Askholmen	100	BBC Mississippi	101
Alexander Henry	120	AML Alize	45	AS Omaria	111	BBC Mont Blanc	101
Alexandria Belle	82	AML Cavalier Maxim	45	Atlanticborg	115	BBC Olympus	101
Algocanada	35	AML Grand Fleuve	45	Atlantic Huron	41	BBC Plata	114
Algoma Buffalo	34	AML Levant	45	Atlantik Miracle	100	BBC Polonia	101
Algoma Conveyor	34	AML Louis Jolliet	45	Atlas	38	BBC Rushmore	101
Algoma Dartmouth	36	AML Suroît	45	Audrie S.	41	BBC Switzerland	101
Algoma Discovery	34	AML Zephyr	46	Avataq	69	BBC Thames	103
Algoma Enterprise	34	Amstelborg	115	Avenger IV	72	BBC Utah	101
Algoma Equinox	34	Amundsen	43	Avonborg	115	BBC Vesuvius	101
Algoma Guardian	34	Amurborg	115	Ayane	116	BBC Volga	101
Algomah	80	Amur Star	111	Azoresborg	115	BBC Weser	101
Algoma Hansa	36	Anchor Bay	52			BBC Xingang	101
Algoma Harvester	34	Andean	108			BBC Zarate	114
Algoma Innovator	34	Andesborg	115			Beatrix	115
Algoma Integrity	35	Andrea Marie I	46	**B**		Beauforce	114
Algoma Mariner	35	Andrew J.	47, 71	Badger	60	Beaver Delta II	67
Algoma Niagara	35	Anet	116	Bagotville	67	Beaver Gamma	67
Algoma Olympic	35	Anglian Lady	72	Baie Comeau	42	Beaver Islander	40
Algoma Sault	35	Anna May	80	Baie St. Paul	42	Belasitza	109
Algoma Spirit	35	Annie M. Dean	46	Barbara Andrie	37	Bella Desgagnés	54
Algoma Strongfield	35	Ann Marie	63	Barnacle	109	Benjamin Elliot	70
		Anthony J. Celebrezze	45	Barney Drake (The)	49	Benjamin Ridgway	57
				Barry J	59		
				Basse-Cote	54		

Lake Superior
MAGAZINE

Subscribe for Ships Tall & Small
at the Festival of Sail Duluth ...

and get Big Lake Info all year long
+ The 2019 *Lake Superior Travel Guide*

www.LakeSuperior.com • 888-BIG LAKE (888-244-5253)

Vessel Name	Page #	Vessel Name	Page #	Vessel Name	Page #	Vessel Name	Page #
Bert Huffman	57	Cantankerus	49	Cheyenne	72	CSL St-Laurent	42
Bessie B	87	Cape	111	Chicago's Classic Lady	44	CSL Tadoussac	42
Beverly M I	65	Cape Chaillon	43	Chicago's Fair Lady	44	CSL Welland	42
Bide-A-Wee	78	Cape Commodore	43	Chicago's First Lady	44	CTC No. 1	62
Billesborg	116	Cape Dawson	100	Chicago's Leading Lady	44	C.T.M.A. Vacancier	46
Biscayne Bay	83	Cape Discovery	43	Chicago's Little Lady	44	C.T.M.A. Voyageur	46
Blacky	109	Cape Dundas	43	Chi-Cheemaun	72	Curtis Randolph	47
Blain M	65	Cape Hearne	43	Chief Shingwauk	74	Cuyahoga	61
Bluebill	109	Cape Lambton	43	Chippewa	44, 80	C. West Pete	38
Blue Dog	77	Cape Mercy	43	Chippewa III	79		
Blue Heron	84	Cape Providence	43	Chris E. Luedtke	63	**D**	
Blue Heron 8	40	Cape Rescue	43	Christopher Wheatley	44	Daldean	40
Blue Heron V	40	Cape Storm	43	Cinnamon	110	Damia Desgagnés	52
Bluewing	110	Caporal Kaeble V	43	City of Algonac	86	Daniel E	57
BMT 3	41	Cap Streeter	77	City of Milwaukee	123	Daniel Joncaire	70
Boatman No. 3	67	Captain George	87	Cityview	77	Dara Desgagnés	54
Boatman No. 6	67	Captain Molly Kool	43	Claude A. Desgagnés	52	Dartmouth III	81
Bobby Bowes	47	Captain Paul II	45	Cleveland	51	Dauntless	67
Bowditch	34	Capt. Keith	64	Clinton	45	David Boyd	52
Bradshaw McKee	75	Capt. Matthew Flinders	65	Clinton Friendship	45	David E	58
Brant	109	Capt. Shepler	76	CLI Pride	101	David Hornell VC	81
Breaker	70	Caribou Isle	43	Clyde S. VanEnkevort	85	Debbie Lee	64
Bright Star	77	Carlee Emily	59	Coastal Titan	81	Debbie Lyn	63
Bristol Bay	83	Carl M	67	Cobia	125	Defiance	50, 62
Bro Agnes	102	Carol Ann	59	Cod	125	Delaware	46
Bro Alma	102	Carolus Magnus	102	COE Leni	103	Demolen	82
Bro Anna	102	Cason J. Callaway	51	Cojak	79	Denis M	69
Brutus I	81	Catherine-Legardeur	77	Col. James M.		Denis Sullivan	47
Buckley	59	Cedarglen	42	Schoonmaker	123	Derek E	58
Buckthorn	83	Celsius Mumbai	102	Colleen McAllister	75	Des Chenaux	57
Bulldog	40	Cemba	44	Coloma L. Warner	86	Des Groseilliers	43
Burns Harbor	36	CGB-12001	83	Colorado	51	Detroit Princess	45
Buxton II	59	CGB-12002	83	Colorado Star	111	Diamond Belle	47
		Challenge	52	Columbia	37, 123	Diamond Jack	47
C		Champion	44, 48	Commander	75	Diamond Queen	47
Cadillac	80	Channel Cat	68	Constable Carrière	43	D. J. Angus	50
California	51	Charlie E	64	Coregonus	87	D. L. Billmaier	82
Calumet	62	Chas. Asher	74	Cornelia	100	D.L. Stanyer	67
Calusa Coast	46	Chembulk Kobe	102	Corporal Teather C.V.	43	Donald Bert	63
Calypso	111	Chem Hydra	100	Corsair	38	Donny S	76
Cameron O	76	Chemical Aquarius	107	Cove Isle	43	Dorothy Ann	58
Canada Spirit	74	Chem Norma	100	Croaker	120	Dover	64
Canadian Empress	79	Chem Polaris	100	CSL Assiniboine	42	Dover Spirit	65
Canadian Jubilee	47	Cheraw	82	CSL Laurentien	42	Dowden Spirit	67
Candace Elise	38	Chestnut	109	CSL Niagara	42	Drawsko	110

LIGHTHOUSE DIGEST

The Lighthouse News & History Magazine

Request a free sample copy!

♦ Colorful & Vintage Lighthouse Photos
♦ Stories of Lighthouse Keepers, Past & Present
♦ Restoration projects, Nautical Antiques, Keeper's Korner Events Calendar
♦ Subscribe at $5 off regular rates. Just $29⁹⁵!

PO Box 250, East Machias, ME 04630 ☎ (207)259-2121 ☎ www.LighthouseDigest.com/ships

Vessel Name	Page #	Vessel Name	Page #	Vessel Name	Page #	Vessel Name	Page #
Dr. Bob	48	Empress of Canada	48	Federal Baltic	104	Federal Yukon	106
Drummond Islander II	63	Endeavour	37	Federal Barents	104	Felicity	76
Drummond Islander III	48	Enterprise 2000	71	Federal Beaufort	104	Felix-Antoine-Savard	77
Drummond Islander IV	48	Environaut	50	Federal Bering	104	Ferbec	42
DS Brazil	107	Epinette II	86	Federal Biscay	104	Fervent	77
Duc d'Orleans II	47	Erich R. Luedtke	63	Federal Bristol	104	Finnborg	115
Duga	54	Erie	51	Federal Caribou	104	Fionia Swan	113
Duluth	50	Erieborg	115	Federal Cedar	105	Fischer Hayden	50
Duzgit Dignity	103	Erie Explorer	71	Federal Champlain	105	Fivelborg	115
Duzgit Endeavour	103	Erie Trader	85	Federal Churchill	105	Fjord Éternité	74
Dylan Cooper	74	Erik	107	Federal Clyde	105	Fjord Saguenay	74
		Erika Kobasic	70	Federal Columbia	105	Flevoborg	115
E		Erin Schulte	100	Federal Danube	105	Flevogracht	112
Eagle	76	Ernest Lapointe	123	Federal Dart	105	Floragracht	112
Ebony Ray	103	Erria Swan	113	Federal Dee	105	Florence M	65
Ebroborg	115	Escort	70	Federal Delta	105	Florence Spirit	65
Eco Maris	48	Escorte	54	Federal Elbe	105	Floretgracht	112
Ecosse	69	Espada Desgagnés	54	Federal Ems	105	Florida	51
Edelweiss II	68	Esta Desgagnés	54	Federal Hudson	105	Florijngracht	112
Edenborg	115	Ethan George	50	Federal Hunter	105	Flowerpot	40
Edgar B. Speer	51	Evans McKeil	65	Federal Katsura	105	Flowerpot Express	40
Edith J.	68	Evans Spirit	65	Federal Kivalina	105	Fortunagracht	112
Edith M. Becker	75	Eva Schulte	100	Federal Kumano	105	Frances	70
Edna G.	120	Evening Star	77	Federal Kushiro	105	Fraserborg	115
Edson [DD-946]	123	Everhard Schulte	100	Federal Leda	105	Fred A. Busse	61
Edward H	57	Everlast	65	Federal Mackinac	105	Frieda	107
Edward L. Ryerson	44	Exeborg	115	Federal Margaree	105	Frontenac	42
Edward M. Cotter	40	Explorer II	71	Federal Mayumi	105	Frontenac Howe	
Edwin C. Busch	41	Eyrarbakki	86	Federal Mosel	107	Islander	68
Edwin H. Gott	51			Federal Nagara	105	Frontenac II	68
Edzard Schulte	100	**F**		Federal Nakagawa	105	FSY II	49
Eeborg	115	F.-A.-Gauthier	77	Federal Oshima	105	FSY III	49
Eemsborg	115	Fagelgracht	112	Federal Rhine	105	FSY IV	49
Eemsgracht	112	Fairchem Charger	104	Federal Rideau	105	Ft. Dearborn	44
Elbeborg	115	Fairchem Colt	104	Federal Ruhr	107	Fuldaborg	115
Elevit	116	Fairchem Friesian	104	Federal Saguenay	106	Furuholmen	100
Elisabeth Schulte	100	Fairchem Steed	104	Federal Sakura	106	FWN Bonafide	106
Elizabeth	86	Fairlane	107	Federal Satsuki	106		
Ella G. Cooper	45	Fairlift	107	Federal Schelde	106	**G**	
Ellie	59	Falstria Swan	113	Federal Seto	106	G3 Marquis	36
El Zorro	109	Favorite	51	Federal Shimanto	106	Ganges Star	111
Emanuel S.	103	F. C. G. Smith	43	Federal Welland	106	Gardno	110
Emerald Isle	40	Fearless	110	Federal Weser	106	Gaylord Nelson	87
Emita II	56	Federal Alster	107	Federal Yoshino	106	General	48, 76
Empire Sandy	69	Federal Asahi	104	Federal Yukina	116	General Brock III	80

THE BEST EYE IN THE SKY

Best Aerial Images LLC

906-290-1632
bestimagesllc@gmail.com

Vessel Name	Page #	Vessel Name	Page #	Vessel Name	Page #	Vessel Name	Page #
Genesis Victory	50	Gregory J. Busch	41	Harbour Star	69	Huron Lady II	57
George Gradel	50	Gretchen B	63	Harriett	108	Huron Maid	60
George N. Carleton	60	Griffon	43	Harvey	82	Huron Spirit	61, 66
G.L.B. No. 2	72	Grue-des-Iles	77	Heemskerkgracht	112		
Glenada	80	G.W. Falcon	45	Helena G	106		
Glenora	68			Helen H	57	**I**	
G. L. Ostrander	37	**H**		Herbert C. Jackson	58	Ida	107
Glovertown Spirit	67			HHL Amur	106	Idaho	51
GM 6506	50	Hack Noyes	87	HHL Elbe	106	Ida M.	74
Golden Oak	100	Haida	120	HHL Mississippi	106	Ida M. II	74
Good Fortune	69, 80	Halit Bey	114	HHL Tyne	106	Île Saint-Ours	43
Goodtime I	60	Halton	59	H. H. Misner	52	Illinois	51
Goodtime III	50	Hamburg	103	Hiawatha	78	Imke	111
Gotland	108	Hamilton Energy	56	H. J. Schwartz	82	Ina	110
Grande Baie	86	Hamilton Harbour		H. Lee White	36	Indiana	51
Grande Caribe	101	Queen	56	Holandia	111	Indiana Harbor	36
Grande Mariner	101	Hammond Bay	82	Holiday	78, 81	Indian Maiden	40
Grandes Eaux	61	Hamp Thomas	57	Hollyhock	83	Industrial Charger	107
Grand Island	72	Hanse Gate	107	Hon. James		Industrial Eagle	107
Grandon	71	Happy Ranger	101	L. Oberstar	58	Industrial More	102
Grand Portal	72	Happy River	101	Hope (The)	76	Infinity	58
Grant Beattie (The)	74	Happy Rover	101	Houghton	59	Inland Seas	58
Grasse River	79	Harbor Lady	68	Houston	113	Innisfree	45
Grayfox	50	Harbor Queen	40	Howard W. Fitzpatrick	87	Innovation	38
Great Blue Heron	40	Harbor Seagull	68	Howe Islander	45	Integrity	38
Great Lakes	38	Harbour Fashion	112	Huron	80, 123	Intense	77
Great Lakes Trader	85	Harbour Feature	112	Huron Belle	60	Intrepid III	69
Great Republic	51	Harbour First	112	Huron Explorer	70	Intrepid Republic	107
Greenstone II	84	Harbour Fountain	112	Huron Explorer I	71	Invincible	62
Greenwing	110	Harbour Pioneer	112	Huronic	45	Iowa	51
		Harbour Progress	112			Irma	110

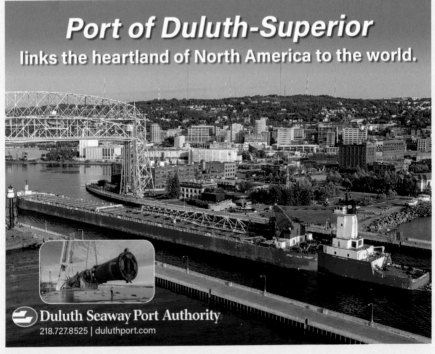

Port of Duluth-Superior

links the heartland of North America to the world.

Duluth Seaway Port Authority

218.727.8525 | duluthport.com

Vessel Name	Page #	Vessel Name	Page #	Vessel Name	Page #	Vessel Name	Page #
Iron Guppy	81	Jan van Gent	115	John Sherwin	58	Kaministiqua	61
Iroquois	68	Jarrett M	66	Joliet	80	Kansas	51
Iryda	110	J.A.W. Iglehart	58	Joncaire II	70	Karen Andrie	37
Isa	110	J.B. Ford	38	Jos-Deschenes	78	Karfi	86
Isabelle G.	106	Jeanette M.	46	Josee H.	54	Karl E. Luedtke	63
Isadora	110	Jean-Joseph	56	Josef	106	Katanni	58
Island Belle I	60	Jet Express	74	Jos-Deschenes	78	Kathy Lynn	75
Island Clipper	86	Jet Express II	74	Jos-Deschenes II	78	Katie G. McAllister	75
Island Duchess	82	Jet Express III	74	Joseph H. Thompson	86	Katmai Bay	83
Islander	38, 68, 70	Jet Express IV	74	Joseph H. Thompson Jr.	86	Kaye E. Barker	58
Island Princess	38	J.F. Whalen	67	Josephine	50	Keenosay	71
Island Queen	64	Jiimaan	68	Joseph J. Hogan	59	Keewatin	120
Island Queen III	60	Jill Marie	44	Joseph L. Block	44	Kelso	43
Island Queen V	81	Jimmy L	76	Joseph-Savard	78	Kenosha	82
Island Wanderer	82	J-Krab	87	Joyce L. VanEnkevort	86	Kenteau	49
Isle Royale Queen III	72	Joey D.	68	J.R. Rouble	48	Kentucky	51
Isle Royale Queen IV	59	Johanna C	102	J. S. St. John	44	Kimberley A. Cooper	45
Isolda	110	Johanna G.	106	Jubilee Queen	59	Kimberly Anne	47
Ivan-Quinn	77	John B. Aird	35	Judge McCombs	56	Kimberly Selvick	41
Iver Bright	114	John D. Leitch	35	Jule	111	Kim R.D.	54
		John Francis	50	Julie Dee	59	King Fish 1	56
J		John G. Munson	51	Juliet Alicia	59	Kirkeholmen	100
		John Henry	59	Juno	110	Kitikmeot W.	103
Jacqueline C	102	John J. Boland	37	Juno Marie	76	Kivalliq W.	103
Jacquelyn Yvonne	76	John J. Carrick	65	J. W. Cooper	45	Kiyi	52
Jacques Cartier	46	John Marshall	41	J. W. Westcott II	59	Klancy II	65
James J. Versluis	44	John Michael	71			Kowie	113
James R. Barker	58	John M. Selvick	41	**K**		Krista S	63
Jamie L	67	John Purves	120			Kristen D	72
Jana Desgagnés	54	John R. Asher	75	Kaho	52	Kristin J.	50
Janice C. No. 1	45			Kajama	52		

Georgian | Centre for Marine Training and Research

Steer toward superior marine education and training.
Recognized as central Canada's marine centre of excellence.

Cadet programs
GeorgianCollege.ca/marinestudies

Certification and training
marinetraining.ca

Vessel Name	Page #	Vessel Name	Page #	Vessel Name	Page #	Vessel Name	Page #
Kristin Joelle	75	Laurentian	70	Lubie	110	Manitoulin	61
Krystal	70	LCM 6	64	Lucia	86	Manitowoc	62, 82
Kurt Paul	102	Leanne Auerbach	100	Lucien-L.	78	Maple City	81
Kwintebank	110	Le Cageux	74	Ludington	120	Maple Grove	71
		Le Champlain	103	Ludogorets	109	Maple Lea	100

L

Vessel Name	Page #	Vessel Name	Page #	Vessel Name	Page #	Vessel Name	Page #
		Lee A. Tregurtha	58	Lugano	108	Margaret	38
Labrador	109	Leo A. McArthur	65	Lyulin	109	Margot	70
Lac Como	67	Leona B.	68			Maria Desgagnés	54
Lac Manitoba	56	Leonard M	66	**M**		Maria G.	106
Lac Vancouver	67	Lettie G. Howard	79	Macassa Bay	87	Marilyn Bell I	81
Lady Doris	108	Le Phil D.	54	Maccoa	109	Marlyn	77
Lady Kate	72	Le Voyageur	78	Mackinac Islander	80	Marquette	45, 80
Lady Michigan	36	Lily North	69	Mackinaw	83	Marsgracht	112
Lady of the Isles	80	Lime Island	38	Mackinaw [WAGB-83]	120	Martha L. Black	44
Lake Char	68	Limnos	44	Madeleine	46	Martigny	108
Lake Explorer II	83	Linda Jean	70	Madeline	64	Martin E. Johnson	74
Lake Express	60	Linnea	86	Madison	63	Mary Ann Market	68
Lake Guardian	83	Lisa E.	58	Madison R.	47	Mary E. Hannah	41
Lake Ontario	112	Lisanna	106	Maid of the Mist VI	64	Mary Ellen I	61
Lakeside Spirit	68	Lita	107	Maid of the Mist VII	64	Marysville	86
Lake St. Clair	112	Little Rock	120	Maine	51	Massachusetts	51
Lake Trader	41	Lois M	66	Maisonneuve	69	Matt Allen	59
Lambert Spirit	66	Lokholmen	100	Malden	72	Maumee	62
L'Anse du Moulin	44	Lolland	108	Malmo	104	McKee Sons	75
La Prairie	54	Lomer-Gouin	78	Mamry	110	McKeil Spirit	66
Larsholmen	100	Louie S.	75	Manatra	64	McLane	120
LaSalle	80	Louisiana	51	Mandarin	110	Med Arctic	108
Laura L. VanEnkevort	86	LS Evanne	107	Manistee	62	Mega	54
Lauren A.	87	LST-393	125	Manitou	64, 81	Mehmet A.	102
Laurentia Desgagnés	54	LT-5	120	Manitou Isle	64	Menier Consol	81

watch

THE SHIPS COME IN

VISIT DULUTH

VISITDULUTH.COM/SHIPPING

LIVECAMS • PHOTOS • HISTORY • FUN FACTS • SHIPPING SCHEDULES

Vessel Name	Page #	Vessel Name	Page #
Menominee	62		

N

Meredith Ashton 50
Merwedegracht 112
Mesabi Miner 58
Meteor 125
Metis 49
Mia Desgagnés 54
Michigan 38
Michigan Trader 86
MMichipicoten 61
Middle Channel 44
Miedwie 110
Miena Desgagnés 52
Mighty Jake 50
Mighty Jessie 50
Mighty John III 50
Mike Donlon 82
Milwaukee Clipper 125
Miners Castle 72
Minervagracht 112
Minnesota 51
Miseford 80
Mishe Mokwa 64
Miss Edna 59
Mississagi 61
Mississippi 51
Mississippiborg 115
Mississippi Star 111
Miss Jamie Lynn 47
Miss Kim Simpson 81
Miss Libby 48
Miss Margy 76
Miss Midland 68
Miss Munising 69
Missouri 51
Miss Superior 72
Miss Wisconsin 68
Mister Joe 67
Misty Jean 87
Mitiq 69
MM Newfoundland 67
Mobile Bay 83
Mohawk 63
Molly M. I 66
Momentum Scan 102
Mona Swan 113
Morgan 59
Morgenstond I 116
Morgenstond II 116
Morro Bay 83
Motti 54
Mottler 109
M.R. Kane 81
Mrs. C. 45
MTM Antwerp 108
MTM Southport 108
Muntgracht 112
Muskie 52
Mystic Blue 69

NACC Alicudi 71
NACC Argonaut 71
NACC Quebec 71
Nancy Anne 48
Nancy J. 57
Narew 110
Nassauborg 115
Nathan S 41
Nautica Queen 69
Neah Bay 83
Nebraska 51
Ned Hanlan II 45
Neebish Islander II 48
Neeskay 84
Nels J. 57
Neptune III 47
New Beginnings 81
New Jersey 51
New York 51
Niagara 120
Niagara Guardian 57
Niagara Queen II 72
Niagara Spirit 66
Niagara Thunder 57
Niagara Wonder 57
Nichevo II 64
Nickelena 70
Nicolet 82
Niki S 41
Nilufer Sultan 114
Nipigon Osprey 72
Njord Clear 109
Njord Cloud 109
No. 55 63
No. 56 63
Nokomis 78
Nomadic Hjellestad .. 109
Nomadic Milde 109
Nordic Mari 109
Nordika Desgagnés 52
Nordik Express 54
Nordisle 111
Norgoma 125
Norman G 50
Norman McLeod 65
North Carolina 51
North Channel 44
North Dakota 51
Northern Lighter 38
Northern Spirit I 65
North Star 44
Northwestern 52
Nunalik 69
Nunavik 104
Nunavut Spirit 66

O

Oakglen 42
Oborishte 109

GLLKA
Great Lakes Lighthouse Keepers Association

Preserving Lighthouse History
Lighthouse Restoration & Preservation
Education Programs
Great Lakes Lighthouse Excursions
Publishers of **The Beacon**, a quarterly
magazine of Great Lakes Lighthouse
History & News

PO Box 219
Mackinaw City, MI 49701
(231) 436-5580 **www.gllka.com**

Visit our gift shop at 707 N. Huron Ave.
right across the street from Old Mackinac
Point lighthouse in Mackinaw City, Mich.

http://LeeMurdock.com
630.557.2742

Vessel Name	Page #	Vessel Name	Page #	Vessel Name	Page #	Vessel Name	Page #
Obsession III	46	Océan Jupiter	55	Ontario Explorer	72	Pelee Islander	68
Océan Abys	54	Océan K. Rusby	55	Oriole	65	Pelee Islander II	68
Océan A. Gauthier	54	Océan Lima	55	Oshawa	68	Peninsula	123
Océan Arctique	54	Océan Maisonneuve	55	Osogovo	109	Pennsylvania	52
Océan A. Simard	54	Océan Nigiq	55	Osprey	74	Pere Marquette 41	72
Océan Basques	54	Océan Pierre Julien	55	Ottawa	80	Performance	79
Océan Bertrand Jeansonne	54	Océan Raymond Lemay	55	Ouilmette	86	Peter-Fraser	78
Océan Bravo	54	Ocean Raynald T.	55	Ovation	58	Peter Ronna	102
Océan Cape Crow	54	Océan Ross Gaudreault	55	Owen M. Frederick	82	Petite Forte	80
Océan Cartier	54	Océan Sept-Iles	55			Petroqueen	65
Ocean Castle	111	Océan Serge Genois	55	**P**		Philip R. Clarke	51
Océan Catatug 1	55	Océan Traverse Nord	55	Pacific Dawn	106	Pia	107
Océan Catatug 2	55	Océan Tundra	55	Pacific Huron	106	Pictured Rocks	72
Océan Charlie	55	Ocean Uannaq	55	Paddy Miles	57	Pictured Rocks Express	72
Océan Clovis T.	55	Océan Yvan Desgagnés	55	Palabora	106	Pierre Radisson	44
Océan Comeau	55	Odyssey II	71	Palmerton	106	Pioneerland	50
Ocean Cote-Nord	55	Ohio	51, 123	Pantanal	106	Pioneer Princess	72
Ocean Crescent	107	Ojibway	61, 78	Papoose III	60	Pioneer Queen	72
Océan Echo II	55	Oklahoma	52	Pathfinder	58, 81	Playfair	81
Oceanex Avalon	110	Old Mission	59	Patras	106	PML 2501	74
Oceanex Connaigra	110	Olive L. Moore	62	Patricia D.	49	PML 9000	74
Océan Express	55	Olza	110	Patricia Hoey	49	PML Alton	74
Oceanex Sanderling	110	Omni-Atlas	55	Paul A. Desgagnés	54	PML Ironmaster	74
Océan Georgie Bain	55	Omni-Richelieu	55	Paul H. Townsend	64	PML Tucci	74
Océan Golf	55	Onego Haren	107	Paula M.	68	PML Tucker	74
Océan Guide	55	Onego Rio	110	Paul Bunyan	83	Pochard S.	100
Océan Henry Bain	55	Onego Rotterdam	107	Paul L. Luedtke	63	Point Valour	81
Océan Intrepide	55	Ongiara	45	Paul R. Tregurtha	58	Point Viking	45
Océan Iroquois	55	Ontamich	40	Pearl Mist	110	Point Vim	61
		Ontario	52	Pelagos	68	Polaris	59

We know our ships!

CAPTAIN SPICER'S
Fine Gifts & Gallery

TITANS OF THE GREAT LAKES
ONTARIO | ERIE | HURON
MICHIGAN | SUPERIOR

315-686-3419
www.captainspicers.com
40467 NYS RT. 12 Clayton, NY 13624

Vessel Name	Page #	Vessel Name	Page #	Vessel Name	Page #	Vessel Name	Page #
Portofino	72	Reestborg	115	Rt. Hon. Paul J. Martin	42	Sedna Desgagnés	52
Prairieland	50	Regalica	110	Ruddy	109	Segwun	69
Prentiss Brown	75	Reggeborg	115			Selandia Swan	113
Presque Isle	51	Reliance	74	**S**		Selasse	111
Pride	87, 108	Resko	110	Sacré Bleu	76	Senja	108
Pride of Michigan	84	R. F. Grant	55	Saginaw	61	Serendipity Princess	68
Primrose	67	Rhode Island	52	Salarium	42	Service Boat No. 1	55
Princess Wenonah	38	Rike	106	Salvage Monarch	81	Service Boat No. 2	55
Private Robertson VC	44	River Gambler	56	Salvor	66	Service Boat No. 4	55
Prosna	110	River Queen	40	Sam Laud	37	Seth Green	70
Provmar Terminal	56	Riverview	77	Sam McBride	45	Shamrock	65
Push Hog	64	Robert F. Deegan	85	Samuel de Champlain	38	Shannon	49
Put-in-Bay	68	Robert John	60	Samuel Risley	44	Sharon M I	66
		Robert Noble	86	San	110	Sharon M. Selvick	76
Q		Robert S. Pierson	61	Sandpiper	56	Shenehon	70
Qamutik	69	Robert W.	81	Sandra Mary	68	Sheri Lynn S	72
Qikiqtaaluk W.	103	Robinson Bay	79	Sandy Graham	40	Shipsands	81
Quinte Loyalist	69	Rochelle Kaye	75	Sarah Andrie	37	Shirley Irene	59
		Rocket	74	Sarah B.	50	Shoreline II	77
R		Rodopi	109	Sarah Desgagnés	54	Shoreline (The)	76
Raba	110	Roerborg	115	Sarah No. 1	48	Shoveler	109
Racine	82	Roger Blough	51	Sarah Spencer	80	Showboat	65
Radcliffe R. Latimer	35	Ronald J. Dahlke	47	Sawyer 1	59	Sichem Beijing	112
Radisson	78, 80	Rosaire A. Desgagnés	52	Sea Bear	75	Sichem Challenge	113
Radium Yellowknife	81	Rosalee D.	81	Sea Eagle II	80	Sichem Defiance	113
Ranger III	84	Rosemary	65	Sea Fox II	80	Sichem Marseille	113
Ray Durocher	48	Rossi A. Desgagnés	54	Seahound	69	Sichem Melbourne	113
Rebecca Ann	47	R.O. Sweezy	57	Sea Hunter III	50	Sichem Mumbai	113
Rebecca Lynn	37	Rosy	103	Sea Prince II	74	Sichem New York	113
Red Witch	80	RTC 108	74	Seaway Supplier	75	Silversides	120

S.S. BADGER

A NATIONAL HISTORIC LANDMARK

Big Ship, More FUN!

A truly one-of-a-kind experience that provides a fun, relaxing cruise across Lake Michigan between Ludington, MI and Manitowoc, WI.

1-800-841-4243 • www.ssbadger.com

Maritime Drawings of
ANTHONY STRUBLIC

ORIGINALS, PRINTS AND COMMISSIONS

Best In Show Winner!

(715) 923-2695
Marinette, Wisconsin

*Mention this ad for a special
promotion on commission work*

greatlakesartist@yahoo.com
Facebook.com/greatlakesartwork
strublicmaritimedrawings.com

★ **Great Lakes Ship & Lighthouse DVDs** ★

DVDs that bring the Great Lakes home!

☐ **SEE THE SHIPS** – VOL. 1–3   VOL. 4 NEW!
50 ships per DVD / U.S. & CAN. Fleets in action at various ports, rivers & locks | 76 min. each | Narration On/Off

☐ **SEE THE SALTIES** – VOL. 1
54 Salties in action | 75 min. | Narration On/Off Options

☐ **GREAT LAKES SHIPS** (SERIES) **VOL. 1–10**
15 ships per DVD | $22.95–$14.95 ea. CALL FOR PRICE

LIGHTHOUSES ★ WATERFALLS ★ STATE PARKS ★ OVERLOOKS

LAKE SUPERIOR SCENIC ADVENTURES
☐ Vol. 1 – Minnesota's North Shore
☐ Vol. 2 – MI & WI South Shore

LIGHTHOUSES OF LAKE MICHIGAN
☐ Vol. 1 – The East Shore

☐ **APOSTLE ISLANDS LIGHTHOUSES & SEA CAVES**
Each DVD 65-100 min. / Narration On/Off Options

EACH TITLE $24.95 / BUY 2 OR MORE TITLES ▶ EACH ONLY $22.95

PLUS SHIPPING: 1 TITLE $6 • 2 TITLES $8 • 3+ FREE
Wisconsin Residents add 5.5% sales tax

VISA CHECK   **PLETS EXPRESS** MONEY ORDER MasterCard
P.O. BOX 217 • ALTOONA, WI 54720 • 715-833-8899

Vessel Name	Page #
Simcoe Islander	45
Simon Cote	85
Sioux	63
Sjard	102
Skawa	110
Skyline Queen	68
Skyview	77
Sloman Helios	111
Sloman Herakles	111
Sloman Hermes	111
Solando	111
Solina	110
Songa Challenge	101
Songa Emerald	101
Songa Opal	101
Songa Peace	101
Soo Pilot	78
South Bass	68
South Carolina	52
South Channel	44
Spartan	38, 60
Spartan II	38
Spencer F. Baird	83
Spirit of Buffalo	41
Spirit of Chicago	79
Spruceglen	42
Spuds	75
Stacey Dawn	45
Stade	111
Stanford H. Smith	83
Star II	108
Star of Chicago	77
State of Michigan	52
STC 2004	41
St. Clair	37
S.T. Crapo	58
Ste. Claire V	37
Steelhead	68, 80
Stella Borealis	44, 81
Stella Polaris	112
Sten Arnold	111
Sten Baltic	111
Sten Bergen	111
Sten Hidra	111
Sten Idun	111
Sten Moster	111
Stephan M. Asher	75
Sterling Energy	80
Stewart J. Cort	58
St. Lawrence II	40
St. Marys Cement	80
St. Marys Cement II	80
St. Marys Challenger	75
St. Marys Conquest	75
Stormont	66
Straits of Mackinac II	80
Strandja	109
Sturgeon	52
Sugar Islander II	48
Sullivans (The)	120

Vessel Name	Page #
Sunda	111
Sundew	59
Superior	52
Susana S	114
Susan L	76
Susan Michelle	46
S/VM 86	66
Swan Baltic	113
Swan Biscay	113

T

Taagborg	115
Taiga Desgagnés	52
Tanner	59, 68
Tasing Swan	113
Taukamaim	61
Teclutsa	60
Tecumseh	62
Tecumseh II	74
Tenacious	64
Terry D	41
Texas	52
Thamesborg	115
Thomas Rennie	45
Thomas R. Morrish	75
Thousand Islander	50
Thousand Islander II	50
Thousand Islander III	50
Thousand Islander IV	50
Thousand Islander V	50
Three Rivers	106
Thunder Bay	43
Thunder Cape	43
Timberland	50
Tim McKeil	66
Timmy A	75
Tim S. Dool	35
Titan	64
Tobias	66
Topaz I	66
Torrent	109
Tracer	101
Tradewind Adventure	113
Trans-St-Laurent	81
Trillium	45
Trinityborg	115
Trudy	108
Tufty	109
Tundra	109
Turbulent	77
Turquois I	66

U

Umgeni	113
Umiak I	104
Umiavut	69
Uncle Sam 7	82
Undaunted	72
Utopia	58

Vessel Name	Page #	Vessel Name	Page #	Vessel Name	Page #	Vessel Name	Page #

V

Vaasaborg	115
Vac	69
Valerie B.	48
Valley Camp	123
Vancouverborg	115
Varnebank	110
Veler	82
Vermont	52
Viateur's Spirit	66
Victoriaborg	115
Victorian Princess	86
Victor L. Schlaeger	44
Victory	62
Victory I	114
Victory II	114
Vida C.	45
Vigilant I	69
Vikingbank	110
Virginia	52
Virginiaborg	115
Vista King	68
Vista Queen	86
Vista Star	86
Vitosha	109
Vlieborg	116
VM/S Hercules	79
VM/S St. Lambert	79
Volgaborg	116
Voorneborg	116
Voyageur	68, 77
Voyageur II	50

W

Walpole Islander	86
Walter J. McCarthy Jr.	37
Warner Provider	86
Washington	52, 86
Welcome (The)	76
Welland	46
Wendella LTD	86
Wendy Anne	79
Wenonah	70
Wenonah II	69
Western Pilot	70
W. G. Jackson	50
Whistler	110
Whitby	68
Whitefish Bay	43, 83
Wicko	110
Wigeon	110
Wilfred M. Cohen	74
Wilfred Sykes	44
Wilf Seymour	66
William A. Irvin	120
William C. Gaynor	76
William C. Selvick	76
William Darrell	57
William G. Mather	120
William H. Latham	70
William Hoey	49
William Inglis	45
William L. Warner	86
William Rest	49
William Thornton	81
Willmac	68
Wilson T. Cooper	45
Windmill Point	81
Windy	80
Wisconsin	52
W. I. Scott Purvis	74
W.J. Isaac Purvis	74
W. J. Ivan Purvis	74
Wm. Lyon Mackenzie	81
Wm. Market	68
W. N. Twolan	87
Wolfe Islander III	69
Wyandot	76
Wyatt M.	67
Wyn Cooper	49
Wyoming	52

Y-Z

Yankee Clipper	86
YM Jupiter	116
YM Saturn	116
Yulia	108
Zealand Beatrix	116
Zealand Delilah	116
Zélada Desgagnés	52
Zeus	46

DRE DESIGNS

GREAT LAKES MARINE PRODUCTS

CALENDARS
NOTEBOOKS
MOUSEPADS
BOOKMARKS
COASTERS
MAGNETS
MUGS
T-SHIRTS
TOTE BAGS
PILLOWS
AND MORE

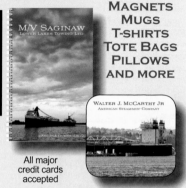

2018 Freighter
Photography
by Andrea Guerriero
(Cover: S/S Alpena)

All major
credit cards
accepted

Use promo code **KYS2018** to get 5% off. Orders over $100 get a free gift

DESIGNS WITH YOU IN MIND

705.971.4076 • andrea@dredesignsglmp.com

DREDESIGNSGLMP.com

BUILD YOUR OWN GREAT LAKES FLEET

Lake Freighter Minis, LLC invites you to build your own fleet of ship models!

Each model kit is laser printed on 100 pound paper and is fully colored,
no painting involved - just cut, fold and glue. Illustrated instructions
are included.

15 model kits available, including Edmund Fitzgerald, S.S. Badger
Paul R. Tregurtha, Walter J. McCarthy Jr., Cliffs Victory
and the Roger Blough (pictured) .

View full product line and authorized retailers at
www.lakefreighterminis.com
View our YouTube video

Lake Freighter Minis

LAKE FREIGHTER MINIS, LLC

Fleet Listings

Algoma Central
fleetmates
G3 Marquis and
Algoma Harvester
meet on the
St. Marys River.
(Roger LeLievre)

G3 MARQUIS

1CHI

ALGOMA HARVESTER

LAKES / SEAWAY FLEETS

Listed after each vessel in order are Type of Vessel, Year Built, Type of Engine, Maximum Cargo Capacity (at midsummer draft in long tons) or Gross Tonnage*, Overall Length, Breadth and Depth (from the top of the keel to the top of the upper deck beam) or Draft*. Only vessels over 30 feet long are included. The figures given are as accurate as possible and are for informational purposes only. Vessels and owners are listed alphabetically as per American Bureau of Shipping and Lloyd's Register of Shipping format. Builder yard and location, as well as other pertinent information, are listed for major vessels. Former names of vessels and years of operation under the former names appear in parentheses. A number in brackets following a vessel's name indicates how many vessels, including the one listed, have carried that name.

KEY TO TYPE OF VESSEL

2B ....Brigantine	DV ....Drilling Vessel	PV ....Patrol Vessel
2S ....2-Masted Schooner	DW ....Scow	RR................................Roll On/Roll Off
3S ....3-Masted Schooner	ES .... Excursion Ship	RT .... Refueling Tanker
4S ....4-Masted Schooner	EV .... Environmental Response	RV.........................Research Vessel
AC...Auto Carrier	FB ....Fireboat	SB ....Supply Boat
AT ....Articulated Tug	FD...................Floating Dry Dock	SC ....Sand Carrier
ATB ....Articulated Tug/Barge	GC .... General Cargo	SR .... Search & Rescue
BC...................................Bulk Carrier	GL....................................Gate Lifter	SU.................................Self-Unloader
BK...................Bulk Carrier/Tanker	GU .... Grain Self-Unloader	SV ....Survey Vessel
BT ....Buoy Tender	HL.......................Heavy Lift Vessel	TB ....Tugboat
CA ....Catamaran	IB..Ice Breaker	TF ....Train Ferry
CC .... Cement Carrier	IT .... Integrated Tug	TK ....Tanker
CF ....Car Ferry	ITB...............Integrated Tug/Barge	TS ....Tall Ship
CO ....Container Vessel	MB ....Mailboat	TT ....Tractor Tugboat
CS ....Crane Ship	MU ....Museum Vessel	TV .... Training Vessel
DB ....Deck Barge	PA .... Passenger Vessel	TW ....Towboat
DH..........................Hopper Barge	PB................................Pilot Boat	WB ....Workboat
DR ....Dredge	PF ....Passenger Ferry	
DS ....Spud Barge	PK.................Package Freighter	

KEY TO PROPULSION

B...Barge	R.............................Steam – Triple Exp. Compound Engine
D...Diesel	S............................ Steam – Skinner "Uniflow" Engine
DE...................................Diesel Electric	T.............................Steam – Turbine Engine
Q ....Steam – Quad Exp. Compound Engine	W..Sailing Vessel (Wind)

Fleet Name Vessel Name	Vessel IMO #	Vessel Type	Year Built	Engine Type	Cargo Cap. or Gross*	Overall Length	Vessel Breadth	Vessel Depth

A

ABACO MARINE TOWING LLC, CLAYTON, NY

Bowditch		TB	1954	D	76*	71' 00"	22' 00"	8' 04"

Built: Missouri Valley Steel Inc., Leavenworth, KS (ST-1991, Oriskany, Hot Dog)

ALGOMA CENTRAL CORP., ST. CATHARINES, ON *(algonet.com)*

Algoma Buffalo	7620653	SU	1978	D	24,300	634' 10"	68' 00"	40' 00"

Built: Bay Shipbuilding Co., Sturgeon Bay, WI (Buffalo {3} '78'-'18)

Algoma Compass {4}	7326245	SU	1973	D	29,200	680' 00"	78' 00"	42' 00"

Built: American Shipbuilding Co., Toledo, OH (Roger M. Kyes '73-'89, Adam E. Cornelius {4} '89-'18)

Algoma Conveyor	9619268	BC	2018	D	39,400	740' 00"	78' 00"	48' 03"

Built: Nantong Mingde Heavy Industry Co. Ltd., Nantong City, China

Algoma Discovery	8505848	BC	1987	D	34,380	729' 00"	75' 09"	48' 05"

Built: 3 Maj Brodogradiliste d.d., Rijeka, Croatia (Malinska '87-'97, Daviken '97-'08)

Algoma Enterprise	7726677	SU	1979	D	33,854	730' 00"	75' 11"	46' 07"

Built: Port Weller Dry Docks, Port Weller, ON (Canadian Enterprise '79-'11)

Algoma Equinox	9613927	BC	2013	D	39,400	740' 00"	78' 00"	48' 03"

Built: Nantong Mingde Heavy Industry Co. Ltd., Nantong City, China

Algoma Guardian	8505850	BC	1987	D	34,380	729' 00"	75' 09"	48' 05"

Built: 3 Maj Brodogradiliste d.d., Rijeka, Croatia (Omisalj '87-'97, Goviken '97-'08)

Algoma Harvester	9613939	BC	2014	D	39,400	740' 00"	78' 00"	48' 03"

Built: Nantong Mingde Heavy Industry Co. Ltd., Nantong City, China

Algoma Innovator	9773375	SU	2017	D	24,900	650' 08"	78' 00"	44' 09"

Built: 3 Maj Brodogradiliste d.d., Rijeka, Croatia

Fleet Name / Vessel Name	Vessel IMO #	Vessel Type	Year Built	Engine Type	Cargo Cap. or Gross*	Overall Length	Vessel Breadth	Vessel Depth
Algoma Integrity	9405162	SU	2009	D	33,047	646' 07"	105' 06"	58' 02"

Built: Estaleiro Ilha S.A., Rio de Janeiro, Brazil; Vessel is too large for the St. Lawrence Seaway but is a frequent visitor to the St. Lawrence River (Gypsum Integrity '09-'15)

Algoma Mariner	9587893	SU	2011	D	37,399	740' 00"	77' 11"	49' 03"

Built: Chengxi Shipyard Co. Ltd., Jiangyin City, China (Laid down as Canadian Mariner {2})

Algoma Niagara	9619270	BC	2017	D	39,400	740' 00"	78' 00"	48' 02"

Built:Yangzijiang Shipbuilding Group Limited, Jingjiang City, Jiangsu Province, China

Algoma Olympic	7432783	SU	1976	D	33,859	730' 00"	75' 00"	46' 06"

Built: Port Weller Dry Docks, Port Weller, ON (Canadian Olympic '76-'11)

Algoma Sault	9619282	BC	2017	D	39,400	740' 00"	78' 00"	48' 02"

Built:Yangzijiang Shipbuilding Group Limited, Jingjiang City, Jiangsu Province, China

Algoma Spirit	8504882	BC	1986	D	34,380	729' 00"	75' 09"	48' 05"

Built: 3 Maj Brodogradiliste d.d., Rijeka, Croatia (Petka '86-'00, Sandviken '00-'08)

Algoma Strongfield	9613953	BC	2015	D	39,400	740' 00"	78' 00"	48' 03"

Built: Nantong Mingde Heavy Industry Co., Ltd., Nantong City, China (CWB Strongfield '15-'17)

Algoma Transport	7711737	SU	1979	D	32,678	730' 00"	75' 11"	46' 07"

Built: Port Weller Dry Docks, Port Weller, ON (Canadian Transport '79-'11)

American Valor	5024738	SU	1953	T	26,200	767' 00"	70' 00"	36' 00"

Built: American Shipbuilding Co., Lorain, OH; lengthened 120' by Fraser Shipyard, Superior, WI, in '74; converted to a self-unloader in '82; entered long-term lay-up Nov. 13, 2008, at Toledo, OH; registered in Canada in 2018 as Valo but the name was not applied to the vessel (Armco '53-'06)

John B. Aird	8002432	SU	1983	D	31,000	730' 00"	75' 10"	46' 06"

Built: Collingwood Shipyards, Collingwood, ON

John D. Leitch	6714586	SU	1967	D	34,127	730' 00"	77' 11"	45' 00"

Built: Port Weller Dry Docks, Port Weller, ON; rebuilt with new mid-body, widened 3' by the builders in '02 (Canadian Century '67-'02)

Radcliffe R. Latimer	7711725	SU	1978	D	36,668	740' 00"	77' 11"	49' 03"

Built: Collingwood Shipyards, Collingwood, ON; rebuilt with a new forebody at Chengxi Shipyard Co. Ltd., Jiangyin City, China, in '09 (Algobay '78-'94, Atlantic Trader '94-'97, Algobay '97-'12)

Tim S. Dool	6800919	BC	1967	D	31,054	730' 00"	77' 11"	39' 08"

Built: Saint John Shipbuilding & Drydock Co., Saint John, NB; widened by 3' at Port Weller Dry Docks, St. Catharines, ON, in '96 (Senneville '67-'94, Algoville '94-'08)

ALGOMA TANKERS LTD., ST. CATHARINES, ON – A DIVISION OF ALGOMA CENTRAL CORP.

Algocanada	9378591	TK	2008	D	11,453	426' 01"	65' 00"	32' 08"

Built: Eregli Shipyard, Zonguldak, Turkey

Algoma Sault at the CSX # 4 Coal Dock in Toledo. OH. *(Jim Hoffman)*

Fleet Name Vessel Name	Vessel IMO #	Vessel Type	Year Built	Engine Type	Cargo Cap. or Gross*	Overall Length	Vessel Breadth	Vessel Depth
Algoma Dartmouth	9327516	RT	2007	D	3,512	296' 11"	47' 11"	24' 11"
Built: Turkter Shipyard, Tuzla, Turkey; vessel is engaged in bunkering operations at Saint John, NB (Clipper Bardolino '07-'08, Samistal Due '08-'09)								
Algoma Hansa	9127186	TK	1998	D	16,775	472' 07"	75' 06"	40' 08"
Built: Alabama Shipyard Inc., Mobile, AL (Amalienborg '98-'98)								
Algonorth	9362152	TK	2008	D	16,958	493' 06"	75' 04"	40' 06"
Built: Tuzla Shipbuilding Industry Co. Inc., Tuzla, Bosnia and Herzegovina (Ramira '08-'18)								
Algonova {2}	9378589	TK	2008	D	11,453	426' 01"	65' 00"	32' 08"
Built: Eregli Shipyard, Zonguldak, Turkey (Eregli 04 '07-'08)								
Algoscotia {2}	9273222	TK	2004	D	19,160	488' 03"	78' 00"	42' 00"
Built: Jiangnan Shipyard (Group) Co. Ltd., Shangahi, China								
Algosea {2}	9127198	TK	1998	D	17,258	472' 07"	75' 04"	40'08"
Built: Alabama Shipyard Inc., Mobile, AL (Aggersborg '98-'05)								
Algoterra	9442249	TK	2010	D	16,000	473' 00"	75' 05"	40' 08"
Built: Jiangnan Shipyard Corp,. Shanghai, China (Louise Knutsen '10-'19)								
***OPERATED BY ALGOMA CENTRAL CORP. FOR G3 CANADA LTD.** (g3.ca)*								
G3 Marquis	9613941	BC	2014	D	39,400	740' 00"	78' 00"	48' 03"
Built: Nantong Mingde Heavy Industry Co. Ltd., Nantong City, China (CWB Marquis '14-'16)								
AMERICAN STEAMSHIP CO., WILLIAMSVILLE, NY *(americansteamship.com)*								
American Century	7923196	SU	1981	D	80,900	1,000' 00"	105' 00"	56' 00"
Built: Bay Shipbuilding Co., Sturgeon Bay, WI (Columbia Star '81-'06)								
American Courage	7634226	SU	1979	D	24,300	636' 00"	68' 00"	40' 00"
Built: Bay Shipbuilding Co., Sturgeon Bay, WI; (Fred R. White Jr. '79-'06)								
American Integrity	7514696	SU	1978	D	80,900	1,000' 00"	105' 00"	56' 00"
Built: Bay Shipbuilding Co., Sturgeon Bay, WI (Lewis Wilson Foy '78-'91, Oglebay Norton '91-'06)								
American Mariner	7812567	SU	1980	D	37,300	730' 00"	78' 00"	42' 00"
Built: Bay Shipbuilding Co., Sturgeon Bay, WI (Laid down as Chicago {3})								
American Spirit	7423392	SU	1978	D	62,400	1,004' 00"	105' 00"	50' 00"
Built: American Shipbuilding Co., Lorain, OH (George A. Stinson '78-'04)								
Burns Harbor {2}	7514713	SU	1980	D	80,900	1,000' 00"	105' 00"	56' 00"
Built: Bay Shipbuilding Co., Sturgeon Bay, WI								
H. Lee White {2}	7366362	SU	1974	D	35,400	704' 00"	78' 00"	45' 00"
Built: Bay Shipbuilding Co., Sturgeon Bay, WI								
Indiana Harbor	7514701	SU	1979	D	80,900	1,000' 00"	105' 00"	56' 00"
Built: Bay Shipbuilding Co., Sturgeon Bay, WI								

(Corey Hammond)

(Jake Bourdage)

| **John J. Boland** {4} | 7318901 | SU | 1973 | D | 34,000 | 680' 00" | 78' 00" | 45' 00" |

Built: Bay Shipbuilding Co., Sturgeon Bay, WI; spent 2015 in lay-up at Huron, Ohio (Charles E. Wilson '73–'00)

| **Sam Laud** | 7390210 | SU | 1975 | D | 24,300 | 634' 10" | 68' 00" | 40' 00" |

Built: Bay Shipbuilding Co., Sturgeon Bay, WI

| **St. Clair** {3} | 7403990 | SU | 1976 | D | 44,800 | 770' 00" | 92' 00" | 52' 00" |

Built: Bay Shipbuilding Co., Sturgeon Bay, WI; heavily damaged by fire on Feb. 16, 2019, at Toledo, OH

| **Walter J. McCarthy Jr.** | 7514684 | SU | 1977 | D | 80,500 | 1,000' 00" | 105' 00" | 56' 00" |

Built: Bay Shipbuilding Co., Sturgeon Bay, WI (Belle River '77–'90)

AMHERSTBURG FERRY CO. INC, AMHERSTBURG, ON *(boblo.ca/amherstburg-ferry-company)*

| **Columbia** | | PA/CF | 1946 | D | 46* | 65' 00" | 28' 10" | 8' 06" |

Built: Champion Auto Ferries, Algonac, MI (Crystal O, St. Clair Flats)

| **Ste. Claire V** | | PA/CF | 1997 | D | 82* | 86' 06" | 32' 00" | 6' 00" |

Built: Les Ateliers Maurice Bourbonnais Ltée, Gatineau, QC (Courtney O., M. Bourbonnais)

ANDRIE INC., MUSKEGON, MI *(andrietg.com)*

| **A-390** | | TK | 1982 | B | 2,346* | 310' 00" | 60' 00" | 17' 00" |

Built: St. Louis Shipbuilding & Steel Co., St. Louis, MO (Canonie 40 '82–'92)

| **A-397** | | TK | 1962 | B | 2,928* | 270' 00" | 60' 01" | 22' 05" |

Built: Dravo Corp., Pittsburgh, PA (Auntie Mame '62–'91, Iron Mike '91–'93)

| **A-410** | | TK | 1955 | B | 3,793* | 335' 00" | 54' 00" | 17' 00" |

Built: Ingalls Shipbuilding Corp., Birmingham, AL (Methane '55–'63, B-6400 '63–'71, Kelly '71–'86, Canonie 50 '86–'93)

| **Barbara Andrie** | 5097187 | TB | 1940 | D | 298* | 122' 00" | 29' 07" | 16' 00" |

Built: Pennsylvania Shipyards Inc., Beaumont, TX (Edmond J. Moran '40–'76)

| **Endeavour** | | TK | 2009 | B | 7,232* | 360' 00" | 60' 00" | 24' 00" |

Built: Jeffboat LLC, Jeffersonville, IN

| **Karen Andrie** {2} | 6520454 | TB | 1965 | D | 516* | 120' 00" | 31' 06" | 16' 00" |

Built: Gulfport Shipbuilding, Port Arthur, TX (Sarah Hays '65–'93)

| **Rebecca Lynn** | 6511374 | TB | 1964 | D | 433* | 112' 07" | 31' 06" | 16' 00" |

Built: Gulfport Shipbuilding, Port Arthur, TX (Kathrine Clewis '64–'96)

| **Sarah Andrie** | 7114032 | TB | 1970 | D | 190* | 99' 05" | 32' 04" | 6' 07" |

Built: Main Iron Works, Houma, LA (Seminole Sun '70–'97, Declaration '97–'99, Caribe Service '99–'15)

OPERATED BY ANDRIE INC. FOR LAFARGE HOLCIM

| **G. L. Ostrander** | 7501106 | AT | 1976 | D | 198* | 140' 02" | 40' 01" | 22' 03" |

Built: Halter Marine, New Orleans, LA; paired with barge Integrity (Andrew Martin '76–'90, Robert L. Torres '90–'94, Jacklyn M '94–'04)

ST. CLAIR DEVASTATED BY FIRE

On Feb. 16, 2019, fire swept through the American Steamship Co. self-unloader *St. Clair*, laid up for the winter at Toledo, OH. The only casualty was the vessel itself, which American Steamship Co. hopes to repair. *St. Clair* was built in 1977 (see listing above).

St. Clair's last trip of the season through the Soo Locks, Dec. 29, 2018. (Logan Vasicek)

Fleet Name / Vessel Name	Vessel IMO #	Vessel Type	Year Built	Engine Type	Cargo Cap. or Gross*	Overall Length	Vessel Breadth	Vessel Depth
Innovation	9082336	CC	2006	B	7,320*	460' 00"	70' 00"	37' 00"
Built: Bay Shipbuilding Co., Sturgeon Bay, WI								
Integrity	8637213	CC	1996	B	14,000	460' 00"	70' 00"	37' 00"
Built: Bay Shipbuilding Co., Sturgeon Bay, WI								
Samuel de Champlain	7433799	AT	1975	D	299*	140' 02"	39' 02"	20' 00"
Built: Mangone Shipbuilding, Houston, TX; paired with barge Innovation (Musketeer Fury '75-'78, Tender Panther '78-'79, Margarita '79-'83, Vortice '83-'99, Norfolk '99-'06)								
OPERATED BY ANDRIE INC. FOR OCCIDENTAL CHEMICAL CORP., MUSKEGON, MI								
Spartan	7047461	AT	1969	D	190*	121' 01"	32' 01"	10' 09"
Built: Burton Shipyard, Port Arthur, TX; paired with barge Spartan II (Lead Horse '69-'73, Gulf Challenger '73-'80, Challenger {2} '80-'93, Mark Hannah '93-'10)								
Spartan II		TK	1980	B	8,050	407' 01"	60' 00"	21' 00"
Built: Sturgeon Bay Shipbuilding Co., Sturgeon Bay, WI (Hannah 6301 '80-'10)								
OPERATED BY ANDRIE INC. FOR U.S. OIL, A DIVISION OF U.S. VENTURE INC., APPLETON, WI (usoil.com)								
Albert	7517686	AT	1979	D	249*	114' 05"	35' 00"	18' 08"
Built: American Gulf Shipyard Inc., LaRose, LA (Hercules '79-'81, El Bronco Grande '81-'06, Craig Eric Reinauer '06-'18)								
Great Lakes {2}		TK	1982	B	5,024*	414' 00"	60' 00"	30' 00"
Built: Bay Shipbuilding Co., Sturgeon Bay, WI (Amoco Great Lakes '82-'85)								
Margaret	1588140	TK	2005	B	2005	391' 00"	74' 00"	27' 00"
Paired with tug Albert (RTC-101 '05-'18)								
Michigan {10}	8121795	AT	1982	D	292*	107' 08"	34' 00"	16' 00"
Built: Bay Shipbuilding Co., Sturgeon Bay, WI (Amoco Michigan '82-'85)								
APOSTLE ISLANDS CRUISES INC., BAYFIELD, WI (apostleisland.com)								
Archipelago		ES	2018	D	55*	64' 08"	28' 00"	8' 00"
Ashland Bayfield Express		PA	1995	D	13*	49' 00"	18' 05"	5' 00"
Island Princess {2}		ES	1973	D	63*	65' 07"	20' 05"	7' 03"
ARNOLD FREIGHT COMPANY, ST. IGNACE, MI								
Corsair		CF	1955	D	98*	94' 06"	33' 01"	8' 01"
Built: Blount Marine Corp., Warren, RI								
ASHTON MARINE CO., NORTH MUSKEGON, MI (ashtontugs.com)								
Candace Elise	8016380	TB	1981	D	199*	100' 00"	32' 00"	14' 08"
Built: Modern Marine Power Inc., Houma LA (Perseverance '81-'83, Mr. Bill G '83-'90, El Rhino Grande '90-'97, Stephan Dann '97-'15)								
ASI GROUP LTD., STONEY CREEK, ON (asi-group.com)								
ASI Clipper		SV	1939	D	64*	70' 00"	23' 00"	6' 06"
Built: Port Colborne Iron Works, Port Colborne, ON (Stanley Clipper '39-'94, Nadro Clipper '94-'08)								
ATLAS MARINE SERVICES LLC, FISH CREEK, WI								
Atlas		PA	1992	D	12*	30' 04"	11' 05"	5' 04"
Northern Lighter		GC	1973	D	5*	36' 00"	9' 09"	1' 06"
AZCON METALS, DULUTH, MN (azcon.net)								
J.B. Ford		CC	1904	R	8,000	440' 00"	50' 00"	28' 00
Built: American Shipbuilding Co., Lorain, OH; converted to a self-unloading cement carrier in '59; last operated Nov. 15, 1985; most recently used as a cement storage and transfer vessel at Superior, WI, and now awaiting scrapping at Duluth, MN (Edwin F. Holmes '04-'16, E. C. Collins '16-'59)								

B

Fleet Name / Vessel Name	Vessel IMO #	Vessel Type	Year Built	Engine Type	Cargo Cap. or Gross*	Overall Length	Vessel Breadth	Vessel Depth
B & L TUG SERVICE, THESSALON, ON								
C. West Pete		TB	1958	D	29*	65' 00"	17' 05"	6' 00"
Built: Erieau Shipbuilding & Drydock Co. Ltd., Erieau, ON								
BABCOCK WELDING & MARINE SERVICES, SARNIA, ON								
Lime Island		TB	1953	D	13*	42' 02"	12' 00"	5' 05"
Built: Knudson Brothers Shipbuilding, Sturgeon Bay, WI								
BAY CITY BOAT LINES LLC, BAY CITY, MI (baycityboatlines.com)								
Islander		ES	1946	D	39*	53' 04"	19' 09"	5' 04"
Princess Wenonah		ES	1954	D	96*	64' 09"	31' 00"	7' 03"
Built: Sturgeon Bay Shipbuilding Co., Sturgeon Bay, WI (William M. Miller '54-'98)								
BAY SHIPBUILDING CO., DIV. OF FINCANTIERI MARINE GROUP LLC, STURGEON BAY, WI (bayshipbuildingcompany.com)								
Bayship		TB	1943	D	19*	45' 00"	12' 04"	5' 03"
Built: Sturgeon Bay Shipbuilding Co., Sturgeon Bay, WI (Sturshipco)								

Roger Blough sported fresh paint in 2018. *(Marc Dease)*

Cement barge Integrity/tug G.L. Ostrander with fleetmate Innovation in the distance.
(Gordy Garris)

Fleet Name / Vessel Name	Vessel IMO #	Vessel Type	Year Built	Engine Type	Cargo Cap. or Gross*	Overall Length	Vessel Breadth	Vessel Depth
BAYSAIL, BAY CITY, MI (baysailbaycity.org)								
Appledore IV		2S/ES	1989	W/D	48*	85' 00"	18' 08"	8' 0
Built: Treworgy Yachts, Palm Coast, FL								
Appledore V		2S/ES	1992	W/D	34*	65' 00"	14' 00"	8' 0
Built: Treworgy Yachts, Palm Coast, FL (Westwind, Appledore)								
BEAUSOLEIL FIRST NATION TRANSPORTATION, CHRISTIAN ISLAND, ON (chimnissing.ca)								
Indian Maiden		PA/CF	1987	D	91.5*	73' 06"	23' 00"	8' 0
Built: Duraug Shipyard & Fabricating Ltd., Port Dover, ON								
Sandy Graham		PA/CF	1957	D	212*	125' 07"	39' 09"	8'
Built: Barbour Boat Works Inc., New Bern, NC								
BEAVER ISLAND BOAT CO., CHARLEVOIX, MI (bibco.com)								
Beaver Islander		PF/CF	1963	D	95*	96' 03"	27' 02"	8'
Built: Sturgeon Bay Shipbuilding, Sturgeon Bay, WI								
Emerald Isle {2}	8967840	PF/CF	1997	D	95*	130' 00"	38' 00"	12'
Built: Washburn & Doughty Associates Inc., East Boothbay, ME								
BLUE HERON CO. LTD., TOBERMORY, ON (blueheronco.com)								
Blue Heron V		ES	1983	D	24*	54' 06"	17' 05"	7'
Blue Heron 8		ES	2015	D	90*	63' 58	23' 00"	6'
Flowerpot		ES	1978	D	39*	47' 02"	15' 08"	5'
Flowerpot Express		ES	2011	D	59*	49' 07"	16' 05"	4'
Great Blue Heron		ES	1994	D	112*	79' 00"	22' 00"	6'
BLUEWATER FERRY CO., SOMBRA, ON (bluewaterferry.com)								
Daldean		CF	1951	D	145*	75' 00"	35' 00"	7'
Built: Erieau Shipbuilding & Drydock Co. Ltd., Erieau, ON								
Ontamich		CF	1939	D	55*	65' 00"	28' 10"	8'
Built: Champion Auto Ferries, Harsens Island, MI (Harsens Island '39-'73)								
BRENNAN MARINE, LACROSSE, WI (jfbrennan.com)								
Bulldog	8651879	TB	1944	D	142*	86' 00"	23' 00"	10'
Built: Equitable Equipment Co., Madisonville, LA (ST-707 '44-'60, Forney '60-'07, Edward H. '07-'17, Jean C. '17-								
BRIGANTINE INC., KINGSTON, ON. (brigantine.ca)								
St. Lawrence II		TV	1954	W/D	34*	72' 00"	15' 00"	8'
BUFFALO DEPARTMENT OF PUBLIC WORKS, BUFFALO, NY (emcotter.com)								
Edward M. Cotter		FB	1900	D	208*	118' 00"	24' 00"	11'
Built: Crescent Shipbuilding, Elizabeth, NJ (W. S. Grattan 1900-'53, Firefighter '53-'54)								
BUFFALO RIVER HISTORY TOURS, BUFFALO, NY (buffaloriverhistorytours.com)								
Harbor Queen		PA	2016	D	48*	63' 00"	24' 00"	10'
River Queen		PA	2014	D	5*	45' 00"	12' 00"	3'

CSL Assiniboine in the Rock Cut at Neebish Island, MI. (Sam Hankins

BUFFALO SAILING ADVENTURES INC., BUFFALO, NY (spiritofbuffalo.com)

Fleet Name / Vessel Name	Vessel IMO #	Vessel Type	Year Built	Engine Type	Cargo Cap. or Gross*	Overall Length	Vessel Breadth	Vessel Depth
Spirit of Buffalo		2S/ES	1992	D/W	34*	73' 00"	15' 06"	7' 02"

BUSCH MARINE INC., CARROLLTON, MI (buschmarine.com)

Fleet Name / Vessel Name	Vessel IMO #	Vessel Type	Year Built	Engine Type	Cargo Cap. or Gross*	Overall Length	Vessel Breadth	Vessel Depth
BMT 3		DB	1965	B	280*	120' 01"	36' 01"	7' 06"
Edwin C. Busch		TB	1935	D	18*	42' 06"	11' 11"	5' 00"

Built: Manitowoc Shipbuilding Co., Manitowoc, WI (Stella B '35-'79, Paul L. Luedtke '79-'98, Joanne '98-'09)

Gregory J. Busch	5156725	TB	1919	D	299*	151' 00"	27' 06"	14' 07"

Built: Whitney Bros. Co., Superior, WI (Humaconna '19-'77)

STC 2004		DB	1963	B	1,230*	250' 00"	50' 00"	12' 00"

C

CALUMET RIVER FLEETING INC., CHICAGO, IL (calumetriverfleeting.com)

Fleet Name / Vessel Name	Vessel IMO #	Vessel Type	Year Built	Engine Type	Cargo Cap. or Gross*	Overall Length	Vessel Breadth	Vessel Depth
Aiden William		TB	1954	D	120*	82' 00"	23' 06"	9' 09"

Built: Defoe Shipbuilding Co., Bay City, MI (John A. McGuire '54-'87, William Hoey {1} '87-'94, Margaret Ann '94-'08, Steven Selvick '08-'14)

Audrie S		TW	1956	D	268*	102' 00"	28' 00"	8' 00"

Built: Calumet Shipyard & Drydock Co., Chicago, IL (Cindy Jo '56-'66, Katherine L. '66-'93, Daryl C. Hannah '93-'12)

John Marshall	7223261	TB	1972	D	199*	111' 00"	30' 00"	9' 07"

Built: Main Iron Works, Houma, LA (Miss Lynn '72-'78, Newpark Sunburst '78-'83, Gulf Tempest '83-'89, Atlantic Tempest '89-'89, Catherine Turecamo '89-'14)

John M. Selvick	8993370	TB	1898	D	256*	118' 00"	24' 03"	16' 00"

Built: Chicago Shipbuilding Co., Chicago, IL (Fire tug Illinois {1}1898-'41, John Roen III '41-'74)

Kimberly Selvick		TW	1975	D	93*	57' 07"	28' 00"	10' 00"

Built: Grafton Boat Co., Grafton, IL (Scout 1 '75-'02)

Lake Trader		DB	1982	B	2,262*	250' 00"	72' 00"	17' 00"

Built: Forked Island Shipyard Inc., Abbeville, LA (TJ 2501, Primary 1)

Mary E. Hannah		D	1945	D	612*	149' 00"	33' 00"	16' 00"

Built: Marietta Manufacturing, Marietta, GA (U.S. Army LT-821 '45-'47, Brooklyn '47-'66, Lee Reuben '66-'75)

Nathan S		TB	1962	D	198*	91' 05"	28' 05"	12' 05"

Built: Main Iron Works, Houma, LA (Donald C. Hannah '62-'09, Donald C. '09-'17)

Niki S		TW	1971	D	39*	42' 00"	18' 00"	6' 00"

Built: Scully Bros. Boat Builders, Morgan City, LA (Miss Josie '71-'79, Matador VI '79-'08)

Terry D		TB	1954	D	76*	66' 00"	19' 00"	9' 00"

Built: Liberty Dry Dock Inc., Brooklyn, NY (Sanita '54-'77, Soo Chief '77-'81, Susan M. Selvick '81-'96, Nathan S. '96-'02, John M. Perry '02-'08, Zuccolo '08-'12, Carla Selvick '12-'14)

CANADA STEAMSHIP LINES INC., MONTREAL, QC – DIVISION OF THE CSL GROUP INC. (cslships.com)

Fleet Name / Vessel Name	Vessel IMO #	Vessel Type	Year Built	Engine Type	Cargo Cap. or Gross*	Overall Length	Vessel Breadth	Vessel Depth
Atlantic Huron {2}	8025680	SU	1984	D	34,860	736' 07"	77' 11"	46' 04"

Built: Collingwood Shipyards, Collingwood, ON; converted to a self-unloader in '89 and widened 3' in '03 at Port Weller Dry Docks, St. Catharines, ON (Prairie Harvest '84-'89, Atlantic Huron {2} '89-'94, Melvin H. Baker II {2} '94-'97)

Cuyahoga at full speed on Lake Ontario. (Jeff Cameron)

Fleet Name Vessel Name	Vessel IMO #	Vessel Type	Year Built	Engine Type	Cargo Cap. or Gross*	Overall Length	Vessel Breadth	Vessel Depth
Baie Comeau {3}	9639892	SU	2013	D	37,690	739' 10"	77' 11"	48' 05"

Built: Chengxi Shipyard Co. Ltd., Jiangyin City, China

Baie St. Paul {2}	9601027	SU	2012	D	37,690	739' 10"	77' 11"	48' 05"

Built: Chengxi Shipyard Co. Ltd., Jiangyin City, China

Cedarglen {2}	5103974	BC	1959	D	29,518	730' 00"	75' 09"	40' 04"

*Built: Schlieker-Werft, Hamburg, Germany; rebuilt, lengthened with a new forebody at Davie Shipbuilding Co., Lauzon, QC, in '77 ([**Stern Section**] Ems Ore '59-'76, [**Fore Section**] Montcliffe Hall '76-'88, Cartierdoc '88-'02)*

CSL Assiniboine	7413218	SU	1977	D	36,768	739' 10"	78' 00"	48' 05"

Built: Davie Shipbuilding Co., Lauzon, QC; rebuilt with a new forebody at Port Weller Dry Docks, St. Catharines, ON, in '05; repowered in '15 (Jean Parisien '77-'05)

CSL Laurentien	7423108	SU	1977	D	37,795	739' 10"	78' 00"	48' 05"

*Built: Collingwood Shipyards, Collingwood, ON; rebuilt with new forebody in '01 at Port Weller Dry Docks, St. Catharines, ON; repowered in '15 (**Stern section:** Louis R. Desmarais '77-'01)*

CSL Niagara	7128423	SU	1972	D	37,694	739' 10"	78' 00"	48' 05"

*Built: Collingwood Shipyards, Collingwood, ON; rebuilt with a new forebody in '99 at Port Weller Dry Docks, St. Catharines, ON (**Stern section:** J. W. McGiffin '72-'99)*

CSL St-Laurent	9665281	BC	2014	D	35,529	739' 10"	77' 11"	48' 05"

Built: Yangfan Shipbuilding Co. Ltd., Zhoushan City, China

CSL Tadoussac	6918716	SU	1969	D	30,051	730' 00"	77' 11"	41' 11"

Built: Collingwood Shipyards, Collingwood, ON; rebuilt with new mid-body, widened 3' at Port Weller Dry Docks, St. Catharines, ON, in '01 (Tadoussac {2} '69-'01)

CSL Welland	9665279	BC	2014	D	35,529	739' 10"	77' 11"	48' 05"

Built: Yangfan Shipbuilding Co. Ltd., Zhoushan City, China

Ferbec {2}	9259848	SU	2002	D	28,910	615' 02"	101' 08"	54' 11"

Built: COSCO KHI Ship Engineering Co. Ltd., Nantong, China; vessel is too large for the St. Lawrence Seaway but is a frequent visitor to the St. Lawrence River (Orientor 2 '02-10, CSL Melbourne '10-'17)

Frontenac {5}	6804848	SU	1968	D	26,822	729' 07"	75' 00"	39' 08"

Built: Davie Shipbuilding Co., Lauzon, QC; converted to a self-unloader by Collingwood Shipyards, Collingwood, ON, in '73

Oakglen {3}	7901148	BC	1980	D	35,067	729' 11"	75' 10"	47' 01"

Built: Boelwerf Vlaanderen Shipbuilding N.V., Temse, Belgium (Federal Danube '80-'95, Lake Ontario '95-'09)

Rt. Hon. Paul J. Martin	7324405	SU	1973	D	37,694	739' 07"	77' 11"	48' 04"

*Built: Collingwood Shipyards, Collingwood, ON; rebuilt with a new forebody in '00 at Port Weller Dry Docks, St. Catharines, ON (**Stern section:** H. M. Griffith '73-'00)*

Salarium	7902233	SU	1980	D	35,123	730' 00"	75' 11"	46' 06"

Built: Collingwood Shipyards, Collingwood, ON (Nanticoke '80-'09)

Spruceglen {2}	8119261	BC	1983	D	33,824	730' 01"	75' 09"	48' 00"

Built: Govan Shipyards, Glasgow, Scotland
(Selkirk Settler '83-'91, Federal St. Louis '91-'91, Federal Fraser {2} '91-2001, Fraser '01-'02)

Tug Wisconsin en-route to Monroe, MI, from Milwaukee in 2018. (Paul C. LaMarre III)

Fleet Name Vessel Name	Vessel IMO #	Vessel Type	Year Built	Engine Type	Cargo Cap. or Gross*	Overall Length	Vessel Breadth	Vessel Depth
Thunder Bay {2}	9601039	SU	2013	D	37,690	739' 10"	77' 11"	48' 05"
Built: Chengxi Shipyard Co. Ltd., Jiangyin City, China								
Whitefish Bay {2}	9639880	SU	2013	D	37,690	739' 10"	77' 11"	48' 05"
Built: Chengxi Shipyard Co. Ltd., Jiangyin City, China								

CANADIAN COAST GUARD (FISHERIES AND OCEANS CANADA), OTTAWA, ON *(www.ccg-gcc.gc.ca)*
CENTRAL AND ARCTIC REGION, MONTREAL, QC

Fleet Name Vessel Name	Vessel IMO #	Vessel Type	Year Built	Engine Type	Cargo Cap. or Gross*	Overall Length	Vessel Breadth	Vessel Depth
A. LeBlanc	9586095	PV	2014	D	253*	141' 07"	22' 09"	9' 09
Built: Irving Shipbuilding Inc., Halifax, NS								
Amundsen	7510846	IB	1978	D	5,910*	295' 09"	63' 09"	31' 04"
Built: Burrard Dry Dock Co., North Vancouver, BC (Sir John Franklin '78-'03)								
Cape Chaillon, Cape Commodore, Cape Discovery, Cape Dundas, Cape Hearne,								
Cape Providence, Cape Rescue		SR	2004	D	34*	47' 09"	14' 00"	4' 05"
Cape Lambton, Cape Mercy, Thunder Cape		SR	2000	D	34*	47' 09"	14' 00"	4' 05"
Cape Storm		SR	1999	D	34*	47' 09"	14' 00"	4' 05"
Caporal Kaeble V	9586045	PV	2012	D	253*	141' 07"	22' 09"	9' 09"
Built: Irving Shipbuilding Inc., Halifax, NS								
Captain Molly Kool	9199646	IB	2001	D	3,382*	274' 06"	57' 00"	27' 09"
Built: Havyard Leirvik AS, Leirvik, Norway (Vidar Viking '01-'18)								
Caribou Isle		BT	1985	D	92*	75' 06"	19' 08"	7' 04"
Built: Breton Industrial & Marine Ltd., Port Hawkesbury, NS								
Constable Carrière	9586069	PV	2012	D	253*	141' 07"	22' 09"	9' 09"
Built: Irving Shipbuilding Inc., Halifax, NS								
Corporal Teather C.V.	9586057	PV	2012	D	253*	141' 07"	22' 09"	9' 09"
Built: Irving Shipbuilding Inc., Halifax, NS								
Cove Isle		BT	1980	D	80*	65' 07"	19' 08"	7' 04"
Built: Canadian Dredge & Dock Co. Ltd., Kingston, ON								
Des Groseilliers	8006385	IB	1983	D	5,910*	322' 07"	64' 00"	35' 06"
Built: Port Weller Dry Docks, St. Catharines, ON								
F. C. G. Smith	8322686	SV	1985	D	439*	114' 02"	45' 11"	11' 02"
Built: Georgetown Shipyard, Georgetown, PEI								
Griffon	7022887	IB	1970	D	2,212*	234' 00"	49' 00"	21' 06"
Built: Davie Shipbuilding Co., Lauzon, QC								
Île Saint-Ours		BT	1986	D		75' 05"	23' 00"	4' 04"
Built: Breton Industrial & Marine Ltd., Port Hawkesbury, NS								
Kelso		RV	2009	D	63*	57' 07"	17' 01"	4' 09"
Built: ABCO Industries Ltd., Lunenburg, NS								

Nancy J behind Nels J at Fraser Shipyards in Superior, WI. *(Paul Scinocca)*

Fleet Name / Vessel Name	Vessel IMO #	Vessel Type	Year Built	Engine Type	Cargo Cap. or Gross*	Overall Length	Vessel Breadth	Vessel Depth
Limnos	6804903	RV	1968	D	489*	147' 00"	32' 00"	12' 00"
Built: Port Weller Dry Docks, St. Catharines, ON								
Martha L. Black	8320432	IB	1986	D	3,818*	272' 04"	53' 02"	25' 02"
Built: Versatile Pacific Shipyards, Victoria, BC								
Pierre Radisson	7510834	IB	1978	D	5,910*	322' 00"	62' 10"	35' 06"
Built: Burrard Dry Dock Co., North Vancouver, BC								
Private Robertson VC	9586033	PV	2012	D	253*	141' 07"	22' 09"	9' 09"
Built: Irving Shipbuilding Inc., Halifax, NS								
Samuel Risley	8322442	IB	1985	D	1,988*	228' 09"	47' 01"	21' 09"
Built: Vito Steel Boat & Barge Construction Ltd., Delta, BC								

The Canadian Coast Guard is currently rebuilding two additonal icebreakers, **Balder Viking** and **Tor VIking II**. For particulars, see **Captain Molly Kool** above. The vessels will get new names before entering service.

CANAMAC BOAT CRUISES, TORONTO, ON

Stella Borealis		ES	1989	D	356*	118' 00"	26' 00"	7' 00"
Built: Duratug Shipyard & Fabricating Ltd., Port Dover, ON								

CARGILL LIMITED, BAIE COMEAU, QC *(cargillca)*

L'Anse du Moulin	8668248	TB	2007	D	350*	90' 05"	36' 07"	13' 08"
Built: Shanghai Harbor Foxing, Shanghai, China (Hai Gang 107 '07–'14, Svitzer Wombi '14–'15, Svitzer Cartier '15–'17, Océan Cartier '17–'18)								

CARMEUSE NORTH AMERICA (ERIE SAND & GRAVEL), ERIE, PA *(carmeusena.com)*

J. S. St. John	5202524	SC	1945	D	415*	174' 00"	31' 09"	15' 00"
Built: Smith Shipyards & Engineering Corp., Pensacola, FL (USS YO-178 '45–'51, Lake Edward '51–'67)								

CAUSLEY MARINE CONTRACTING LLC, BAY CITY, MI

Jill Marie		TB	1891	D	24*	60' 00"	12' 06"	6' 00"
Built: Cleveland Shipbuilding Co., Cleveland, OH; oldest active commercial tug on the Great Lakes (Ciscoe 1891-1953, Capama-S '53–'97, Gail K '97–'07)								

CEMBA MOTOR SHIPS LTD., PELEE ISLAND, ON

Cemba		TK	1960	D	17*	50' 00"	15' 06"	7' 06"
Built: Elmer Haikala, Wheatley, ON								

CENTRAL MARINE LOGISTICS INC., GRIFFITH, IN *(centralmarinelogistics.com)*

Edward L. Ryerson	5097606	BC	1960	T	27,500	730' 00"	75' 00"	39' 00"
Built: Manitowoc Shipbuilding Co., Manitowoc, WI; in long-term lay-up at Superior, WI, since May 2009								
Joseph L. Block	7502320	SU	1976	D	37,200	728' 00"	78' 00"	45' 00"
Built: Bay Shipbuilding Co., Sturgeon Bay, WI								
Wilfred Sykes	5389554	SU	1949	T	21,500	678' 00"	70' 00"	37' 00"
Built: American Shipbuilding Co., Lorain, OH; converted to a self-unloader by Fraser Shipyards, Superior, WI, in '75								

CENTRAL MICHIGAN UNIVERSITY, COLLEGE OF SCIENCE & TECHNOLOGIES, MOUNT PLEASANT, MI

Chippewa		RV	2013	D	17*	34' 09"	12' 00"	6' 03"

CHAMPION'S AUTO FERRY, ALGONAC, MI *(hiferry.com)*

Champion		CF	1941	D	69*	65' 00"	25' 09"	5' 08"
Middle Channel		CF	1997	D	81*	79' 00"	30' 00"	6' 05"
North Channel		CF	1967	D	67*	75' 00"	30' 04"	6' 01"
South Channel		CF	1973	D	94*	79' 00"	30' 03"	6' 01"

CHARITY ISLAND TRANSPORT INC., AU GRES, MI *(charityisland.net)*

North Star		PA	1949	D	14*	50' 05"	14' 06"	3' 06"

CHICAGO DEPARTMENT OF WATER MANAGEMENT, CHICAGO, IL

James J. Versluis		TB	1957	D	126*	83' 00"	22' 00"	11' 02"
Built: Sturgeon Bay Shipbuilding Co., Sturgeon Bay, WI								

CHICAGO FIRE DEPARTMENT, CHICAGO, IL

Christopher Wheatley		FB	2011	D	300*	90' 00"	25' 00"	12' 02"
Built: Hike Metal Products Ltd., Wheatley, ON								
Victor L. Schlaeger		FB	1949	D	350*	92' 06"	24' 00"	11' 00"

CHICAGO'S FIRST LADY CRUISES, CHICAGO, IL *(cruisechicago.com)*

Chicago's Classic Lady		ES	2014	D	93*	98' 00"	32' 00"	6' 02"
Chicago's Fair Lady		ES	1979	D	82*	72' 04"	23' 01"	7' 01"
Chicago's First Lady		ES	1991	D	62*	96' 00"	22' 00"	9' 00"
Chicago's Leading Lady		ES	2011	D	92*	92' 07"	32' 00"	6' 09"
Chicago's Little Lady		ES	1999	D	70*	69' 02"	22' 08"	7' 00"

CHICAGO FROM THE LAKE LTD., CHICAGO, IL *(chicagoline.com)*

Ft. Dearborn		ES	1985	D	72*	64' 10"	22' 00"	7' 03"

Fleet Name / Vessel Name	Vessel IMO #	Vessel Type	Year Built	Engine Type	Cargo Cap. or Gross*	Overall Length	Vessel Breadth	Vessel Depth
Innisfree		ES	1980	D	35*	61'09"	15'06"	5'07"
Marquette {6}		ES	1957	D	39*	50'07"	15'00"	5'05"

CITY OF TORONTO, TORONTO, ON *(toronto.ca/parks)*

Ned Hanlan II		TB	1966	D	22*	41'06"	14'01"	5'05"
Built: Erieau Shipbuilding & Drydock Co. Ltd., Erieau, ON								
Ongiara	6410374	PA/CF	1963	D	180*	78'00"	12'04"	9'09"
Built: Russel Brothers Ltd., Owen Sound, ON								
Sam McBride		PF	1939	D	387*	129'00"	34'11"	6'00"
Built: Toronto Dry Dock Co. Ltd., Toronto, ON								
Thomas Rennie		PF	1951	D	387*	129'00"	32'11"	6'00"
Built: Toronto Dry Dock Co. Ltd., Toronto, ON								
Trillium		PF	1910	R	564*	150'00"	30'00"	8'04"
Built: Poulson Iron Works, Toronto, ON; last sidewheel-propelled vessel on the Great Lakes								
William Inglis		PF	1935	D	238*	99'00"	24'10"	6'00"
Built: John Inglis Co. Ltd., Toronto, ON (Shamrock {2} '35-'37)								

CJC CRUISES INC., GRAND LEDGE, MI *(detroitprincess.com)*

Detroit Princess		PA	1993	D	1,430*	222'00"	62'00"	11'01"
Built: Leevac Shipyards Inc., Jennings, LA (Players Riverboat Casino II '93-'04)								

CLEARWATER MARINE LLC, HOLLAND, MI *(clearwatermarinellc.com)*

G.W. Falcon		TB	1936	D	22*	49'07"	13'08"	6'02"
Built: Fred E. Alford, Waukegan, IL (Lillie B. '36-'57)								

CLEVELAND FIRE DEPARTMENT, CLEVELAND, OH

Anthony J. Celebrezze		FB	1961	D	42*	66'00"	17'00"	5'00"
Built: Paasch Marine Services Inc., Erie, PA								

CLINTON RIVER CRUISE CO., MOUNT CLEMENS, MI *(clintonrivercruisecompany.com)*

Captain Paul II		PA	1960	D	14*	44'07"	11'00"	4'00"
Clinton		PA	1949	D	10*	63'07"	15'03"	4'08"
Clinton Friendship		PA	1984	D	43*	64'08"	22'00"	4'05"

COLLINGWOOD CHARTERS INC., COLLINGWOOD, ON *(collingwoodcharters.ca)*

Huronic		PA	1999	D	60	56'03"	19'00"	6'04"

CONSTRUCTION POLARIS, L'ANCIENNE-LORETTE, QC *(constructionpolaris.com)*

Point Viking	5118840	TB	1962	D	207*	98'05"	27'10"	13'05"
Built: Davie Shipbuilding Co., Lauzon, QC (Foundation Viking '62-'75)								

COOPER MARINE LTD., SELKIRK, ON

Ella G. Cooper		PB	1972	D	21*	43'00"	14'00"	6'05"
Janice C. No. 1		TB	1980	D	33*	57'00"	20'00"	6'00"
J. W. Cooper		PB	1984	D	25*	48'00"	14'07"	5'00"
Kimberley A. Cooper		TB	1974	D	17*	40'00"	13'05"	4'05"
Mrs. C.		PB	1991	D	26*	50'00"	14'05"	4'05"
Stacey Dawn		TB	1993	D	14*	35'09"	17'04"	3'05"
Wilson T. Cooper		DB	2009	D	58*	56'08"	23'06"	5'08"

CORPORATION OF THE TOWNSHIP OF FRONTENAC ISLANDS, WOLFE ISLAND, ON *(frontenacislands.ca)*

Howe Islander		CF	1946	D	13*	53'00"	12'00"	3'00"
Built: Canadian Dredge & Dock Co. Ltd., Kingston, ON								
Simcoe Islander		PF	1964	D	24*	47'09"	18'00"	3'06"
Built: Canadian Dredge & Dock Co. Ltd., Kingston, ON								

COBBY MARINE (1985) INC., KINGSVILLE, ON

Vida C.		TB	1960	D	17*	46'03"	15'05"	3'02"

CROISIÈRES AML INC., QUÉBEC CITY, QC *(croisieresaml.com)*

AML Alize		ES	1980	D	39*	41'00"	15'01"	6'01"
Built: Julien Tremblay, Arvida, QC (Le Coudrier 2)								
AML Cavalier Maxim	5265904	ES	1962	D	752*	191'02"	42'00"	11'07"
Built: John I. Thornycroft & Co., Wollston, Southampton, England (Osborne Castle '62-'78, Le Gobelet D' Argent '78-'88, Gobelet D' Argent '88-'89, Le Maxim '89-'93)								
AML Grand Fleuve		ES	1987	D	499*	145'00"	30'00"	5'06"
Built: Kanter Yacht Co., St. Thomas, ON								
AML Levant	9056404	ES	1991	D	380*	112'07"	29'0"	10'02"
Built: Goelette Marie Clarisse Inc., LaBaleine, QC (Famille Dufour)								
AML Louis-Jolliet	5212749	ES	1938	R	2,436*	170'01"	70'00"	17'00"
Built: Davie Shipbuilding Co., Lauzon, QC								
AML Suroît		ES	2002	D	171*	82'00"	27'00"	6'00"
Built: RTM Construction, Petite Rivière-St-François, QC (Le Coudrier de l'Isle '02-'14)								

Fleet Name / Vessel Name	Vessel IMO #	Vessel Type	Year Built	Engine Type	Cargo Cap. or Gross*	Overall Length	Vessel Breadth	Vessel Depth
AML Zephyr		ES	1992	D	171*	82' 00"	27' 00"	6' 00"
Built: Katamarine International, Paspebiac, QC (Le Coudrier de l'Anse '92-'14)								

CROISIÈRES M/S JACQUES-CARTIER INC., TROIS-RIVIERES, QC (msjacquescartier.com)

Jacques-Cartier		ES	1924	D	589*	132' 05"	35' 00"	9' 08"
Built: Davie Shipbuilding Co., Lauzon, QC (Rebuilt ' 75, '18)								

CRUISE TORONTO INC., TORONTO ON (cruisetoronto.com)

Obsession III		ES	1967	D	160*	66' 00"	25' 00"	6' 01"
Built: Halter Marine, New Orleans, LA (Mystique)								

CTMA, CAP-AUX-MEULES, QC (ctma.ca)

C.T.M.A. Vacancier	7310260	PA/RR	1973	D	11,481*	388' 04"	70' 02"	43' 06"
Built: J.J. Sietas KG Schiffswerft, Hamburg, Germany (Aurella '80-'82, Saint Patrick II '82-'98, Egnatia II '98-'00, Ville de Sete '00-'01, City of Cork '01-'02)								
C.T.M.A. Voyageur	7222229	PA/RR	1972	D	4,526*	327' 09"	52' 06"	31' 07"
Built: Trosvik Versted A/S, Brevik, Norway (Anderida '72-'81, Truck Trader '81-'84, Sealink '84-'86, Mirela '86-'86)								
Madeleine	7915228	PA	1981	D	10,024*	381' 04"	60' 06"	41' 00"
Built: Verolme Cork Dockyard Ltd., Cobh, Ireland (Isle of Inishturk)								

D

DAN MINOR & SONS INC., PORT COLBORNE, ON

Andrea Marie I		WB	1986	D	87*	75' 02"	24' 07"	7' 03"
Built: Ralph Hurley, Port Burwell, ON								
Jeanette M.		WB	1981	D	31*	70' 00"	20 01"	6' 00"
Built: Hike Metal Products, Wheatley, ON								
Susan Michelle		TB	1995	D	89*	79' 10"	20' 11"	6' 02"
Built: Vic Powell Welding Ltd., Dunnville, ON								
Welland		TB	1954	D	94*	86' 00"	20' 00"	8' 00"
Built: Russel-Hipwell Engines, Owen Sound, ON								

DANN MARINE TOWING, CHESAPEAKE CITY, MD (dannmarine.com)

Calusa Coast	7942295	TB	1978	D	186*	110' 00"	30' 01"	11' 00"
Built: Bollinger Shipyards, Lockport, LA (Marc G., Katrina G.); paired with barge Delaware								
Delaware	1588255	TK	2006	B	98*	292' 00"	60' 00"	24' 00"
Vessel owned by Kirby Offshore Marine Operating LLC, Houston, TX								
Zeus	9506071	TB	1964	D	98*	104' 02"	29' 03"	13' 05"
Built: Houma Shipbuilding Co., Houma, LA; paired with barge Robert F. Deegan								

DEAN CONSTRUCTION CO. LTD., WINDSOR, ON (deanconstructioncompany.com)

Americo Dean		TB	1956	D	15*	45' 00"	15' 00"	5' 00"
Built: Erieau Shipyard, Erieau, ON								
Annie M. Dean		TB	1981	D	58*	50' 00"	19' 00"	5' 00"
Built: Dean Construction Co., LaSalle, ON								

NACC Quebec at Hamilton, ON. (Ted Wilush)

Fleet Name / Vessel Name	Vessel IMO #	Vessel Type	Year Built	Engine Type	Cargo Cap. or Gross*	Overall Length	Vessel Breadth	Vessel Depth
Bobby Bowes		TB	1944	D	11*	37' 04"	10' 02"	3' 06"
Built: Russel Brothers Ltd., Owen Sound, ON								
Canadian Jubilee		DR	1978	B	896*	149' 09"	56' 01"	11' 01"
Neptune III		TB	1939	D	23*	53' 10"	15' 06"	5' 00"
Built: Herb Colley, Port Stanley, ON								

DEAN MARINE & EXCAVATING INC., MOUNT CLEMENS, MI (deanmarineandexcavating.com)

Andrew J.		TB	1950	D	25*	47' 00"	15' 07"	8' 00"
Built: J.F. Bellinger & Sons, Jacksonville, FL								
Kimberly Anne		TB	1965	D	65*	55' 02"	18' 08"	8' 00"
Built: Main Iron Works, Houma, LA (Lady Lisa, Lucy, Miss Alma)								
Madison R.	5126615	TB	1958	D	194*	103' 00"	26' 06"	12' 00"

DETROIT CITY FIRE DEPARTMENT, DETROIT, MI

Curtis Randolph		FB	1979	D	85*	77' 10"	21' 06"	9' 03"
Built: Peterson Builders Inc., Sturgeon Bay, WI								

DEWEY MARINE LEASING LLC, ROCHESTER, NY (deweymarineleasing.com)

Ronald J. Dahlke		TB	1903	D	58*	63' 04"	17' 06"	9' 00"
Built: Johnston Bros., Ferrysburg, MI (Bonita '03-'14, Chicago Harbor No. 4 '14-'60, Eddie B. '60-'69, Seneca Queen '69-'70, Ludington '70-'96, Seneca Queen '96-'04)								

DIAMOND JACK'S RIVER TOURS, DETROIT, MI (diamondjack.com)

Diamond Belle		ES	1958	D	93*	93' 06"	25' 00"	7' 00"
Built: Hans Hansen Welding Co., Toledo, OH (Mackinac Islander {2} '58-'90, Sir Richard '90-'91)								
Diamond Jack		ES	1955	D	82*	72' 00"	25' 00"	7' 03"
Built: Christy Corp., Sturgeon Bay, WI (Emerald Isle {1} '55-'91)								
Diamond Queen		ES	1956	D	94*	92' 00"	25' 00"	7' 02"
Built: Marinette Marine Corp., Marinette, WI (Mohawk '56-'96)								

DISCOVERY WORLD AT PIER WISCONSIN, MILWAUKEE, WI (discoveryworld.org)

Denis Sullivan	1100209	TV/ES	2000	W/D	99*	138' 00"	22' 08"	10' 06"
Built: Wisconsin Lake Schooner, Milwaukee, WI								

DONJON MARINE CO. INC., HILLSIDE, NJ (donjon.com)

Rebecca Ann		TB	1994	D	52*	60' 00	18' 07"	7' 00"
Built: Empire Harbor Marine Inc., Thomson, NY; stationed at Erie, PA (Herbert P. Brake '94-'14)								

DONKERSLOOT MARINE DEVELOPMENT CORP., NEW BUFFALO, MI (donkerslootmarine.com)

Miss Jamie Lynn		DR	1989	D	254*	120' 00"	34' 00"	5' 06"

DUC D' ORLEANS CRUISE BOAT, CORUNNA, ON (ducdorleans.com)

Duc d' Orleans II		ES	1987	D	120*	71' 03"	23' 02"	7' 07"
Built: Blount Marine Corp., Warren, RI (Spirit of Newport '87-'06)								

DUNDEE ENERGY LTD., TORONTO, ON (dundee-energy.com)

Vessels are engaged in oil and gas exploration on Lake Erie. Listing begins on the next page.

***Frontenac* arrives at Toronto with a cargo of salt.** (Bill Bird)

Fleet Name / Vessel Name	Vessel IMO #	Vessel Type	Year Built	Engine Type	Cargo Cap. or Gross*	Overall Length	Vessel Breadth	Vessel Depth
Dr. Bob	8771992	DV	1973	B	1,022*	160' 01"	54' 01"	11' 01"
Built: Cenac Shipyard Co. Inc., Houma, LA (Mr. Chris '73-'03)								
J.R. Rouble	8767020	DV	1958	D	562*	123' 06"	49' 08"	16' 00"
Built: American Marine Machinery Co., Nashville, TN (Mr. Neil)								
Miss Libby		DV	1972	B	924*	160' 01"	54' 01"	11' 01"
Built: Service Machine & Shipbuilding Corp., Morgan City, LA								
Sarah No. 1		TB	1969	D	43*	72' 01"	17' 03"	6' 08"
Built: Halter Marine, New Orleans, LA (Auries)								

DUROCHER MARINE, DIV. OF KOKOSING CONSTRUCTION CO., CHEBOYGAN, MI (kokosing.biz)

Champion {3}		TB	1974	D	125*	75' 00"	23' 05"	9' 05"
Built: Service Machine & Shipbuilding Co., Amelia, LA								
General {2}		TB	1954	D	119*	71' 00"	19' 06"	10' 00"
Built: Missouri Valley Bridge & Iron Works, Leavenworth, KS (U. S. Army ST-1999 '54-'61, USCOE Au Sable '61-'84, Challenger {3} '84-'87)								
Nancy Anne		TB	1969	D	73*	60' 00"	20' 00"	8' 00"
Built: Houma Shipbuilding Co., Houma, LA								
Ray Durocher		TB	1943	D	20*	45' 06"	12' 05"	7' 06"
Valerie B.		TB	1981	D	101*	65' 00"	25' 06"	10' 00"
Built: Rayco Shipbuilders & Repairers, Bourg, LA (Mr. Joshua, Michael Van)								

E

EASTERN UPPER PENINSULA TRANSPORTATION AUTHORITY, SAULT STE. MARIE, MI (eupta.net)

Drummond Islander III		CF	1989	D	96*	108' 00"	37' 00"	7' 02"
Built: Moss Point Marine Inc., Escatawpa, MS								
Drummond Islander IV		CF	2000	D	97*	148' 00"	40' 00"	12' 00"
Built: Basic Marine Inc., Escanaba, MI								
Neebish Islander II		CF	1946	D	90*	89' 00"	25' 09"	5' 08"
Built: Lock City Machine/Marine, Sault Ste. Marie, MI (Sugar Islander '46-'95)								
Sugar Islander II		CF	1995	D	90*	114' 00"	40' 00"	10' 00"
Built: Basic Marine Inc., Escanaba, MI								

ECOMARIS, MONTREAL, QC (ecomaris.org)

Eco Maris		TV/2S	1999	W/D	28*	65' 02"	17' 07"	8' 03"
Roter Sand '99-'18								

EMPRESS OF CANADA ENTERPRISES LTD., TORONTO, ON (empressofcanada.com)

Empress of Canada		ES	1980	D	399*	116' 00"	28' 00"	6' 06"
Built: Hike Metal Products, Wheatley, ON (Island Queen V {2} '80-'89)								

Tanker Jana Desgagnés at anchor on Lake Ontario. (Jeff Cameron)

ERIE ISLANDS PETROLEUM INC., PUT-IN-BAY, OH *(putinbayfuels.com)*

Fleet Name Vessel Name	Vessel IMO #	Vessel Type	Year Built	Engine Type	Cargo Cap. or Gross*	Overall Length	Vessel Breadth	Vessel Depth
Cantankerus		TK	1955	D	43*	56' 00"	14' 00"	6' 06"

Built: Marinette Marine Corp., Marinette, WI

ESSROC CANADA INC., PICTON, ON

Metis	5233585	CC	1956	B	5,800	331' 00"	43' 09"	26' 00"

Built: Davie Shipbuilding Co., Lauzon, QC; lengthened 72', deepened 3'6" in '59 and converted to a self-unloading cement barge in '91 by Kingston Shipbuilding & Dry Dock Co., Kingston, ON

F-G

FITZ SUSTAINABLE FORESTRY MANAGEMENT LTD., MANITOWANING, ON

Wyn Cooper		TB	1973	D	25*	48' 00"	13' 00"	4' 00"

Built: Place Gas & Oil Co. Ltd., Toronto, ON

FRASER SHIPYARDS INC., SUPERIOR, WI *(frasershipyards.com)*

FSY II		TB	2013	D	32*	45' 00"	13' 00"	6' 05"

Built: Fraser Shipyards Inc., Superior, WI

FSY III		TB	1959	D	30*	47' 04"	13' 00"	6' 06"

Built: Fraser-Nelson Shipyard & Drydock Co., Superior, WI (Susan A. Fraser '59-'78, Maxine Thompson '78-'14)

FSY IV		TB	1956	D	24*	43' 00"	12' 00"	5' 06"

Built: Fraser-Nelson Shipyard & Drydock Co., Superior, WI (Wally Kendzora '56-'14)

GAELIC TUGBOAT CO., DETROIT, MI *(gaelictugboat.com)*

Patricia Hoey {2}	5285851	TB	1949	D	146*	88' 06"	25' 06"	11' 00"

Built: Alexander Shipyard Inc., New Orleans, LA (Propeller '49-'82, Bantry Bay '82-'91)

Shannon	8971669	TB	1944	D	145*	101' 00"	25' 08"	13' 00"

Built: Consolidated Shipbuilding Corp., Morris Heights, NY (USS Connewango [YT / YTB / YTM-388] '44-'77)

William Hoey	5029946	TB	1951	D	149*	88' 06"	25' 06"	11' 00"

Built: Alexander Shipyard Inc., New Orleans, LA (Atlas '51-'84, Susan Hoey {1} '84-'85, Atlas '85-'87, Carolyn Hoey '87-'13)

GALCON MARINE LTD., TORONTO, ON *(galconmarine.com)*

Barney Drake (The)		TB	1954	D	10*	31' 02"	9' 05"	3' 04"

Built: Toronto Drydock Co. Ltd., Toronto ON (T.T.&S. No. 9)

Kenteau		TB	1937	D	15*	54' 07"	16' 04"	4' 02"

Built: George Gamble, Port Dover, ON

Patricia D		TB	1958	D	12*	38' 08"	12' 00"	3' 08"

Built: Toronto Drydock Co. Ltd., Toronto, ON (Big Chief III)

William Rest		TB	1961	D	62*	65' 00"	18' 06"	10' 06"

Built: Erieau Shipbuilding & Drydock Co. Ltd., Erieau, ON

Liner Hamburg and Manitowoc on the hook near Alpena, MI. (Ben and Chanda McClain)

Fleet Name Vessel Name	Vessel IMO #	Vessel Type	Year Built	Engine Type	Cargo Cap. or Gross*	Overall Length	Vessel Breadth	Vessel Depth
GANANOQUE BOAT LINE LTD., GANANOQUE, ON *(ganboatline.com)*								
Thousand Islander	7227346	ES	1972	D	200*	96' 11"	22' 01"	5' 05"
Thousand Islander II	7329936	ES	1973	D	200*	99' 00"	22' 01"	5' 00"
Thousand Islander III	8744963	ES	1975	D	376*	118' 00"	28' 00"	6' 00"
Thousand Islander IV	7947984	ES	1976	D	347*	110' 09"	28' 04"	10' 08"
Thousand Islander V	8745187	ES	1979	D	246*	88' 00"	24' 00"	5' 00"
GANNON UNIVERSITY, ERIE, PA *(gannon.edu)*								
Environaut		RV	1950	D	18*	48' 00"	13' 00"	4' 05"
GENESIS ENERGY, HOUSTON, TX *(genesisenergy.com)*								
Genesis Victory	8973942	TB	1981	D	398*	105' 00"	34' 00"	17' 00"
Built: Halter Marine, New Orleans, LA (Eric Candies '81-'05, Huron Service '05-'15)								
GM 6506		TB	2007	B	5,778*	345' 06"	60' 00"	29' 00"
Built: Bollinger Marine Fabricators, Amelia, LA; paired with the tug Genesis Victory								
GEO. GRADEL CO., TOLEDO, OH *(geogradelco.com)*								
George Gradel		TB	1956	D	128*	84' 00"	26' 00"	9' 02"
Built: Parker Brothers & Co. Inc., Houston, TX (Harbor Queen '56-'76, St. John '76-'16)								
John Francis		TB	1965	D	99*	75' 00"	22' 00"	9' 00"
Built: Bollinger Shipbuilding Inc., Lockport, LA (Dad '65-'98, Creole Eagle '98-'03)								
Josephine		TB	1957	D		86' 09"	20' 00"	7' 06"
Built: Willemsoord Naval Yard, Den Helder, Netherlands; recreational tug								
Mighty Jake		TB	1969	D	15*	36' 00"	12' 03"	7' 03"
Built: Lone Star Marine Salvage, Houston, TX								
Mighty Jessie		TB	1954	D	57*	61' 02"	18' 00"	7' 03"
Built: John J. Mathis Co., Camden, NJ								
Mighty John III		TB	1962	D	24*	45' 00"	15' 00"	5' 10"
Built:Toronto Drydock Co., Toronto, ON (Niagara Queen '62-'99)								
Norman G		DB	2016	B	578*	141' 01"	54' 00"	10' 00"
Pioneerland		TB	1943	D	53*	58' 00"	16' 08"	8' 00"
Built: Maritime Oil Transport Co., Houston, TX								
Prairieland		TB	1955	D	35*	49' 02"	15' 02"	6' 00"
Built: Main Iron Works, Houma, LA								
Timberland		TB	1946	D	20*	41' 03"	13' 01"	7' 00"
Built:George S. VerDuin, Grand Haven, MI								
GILLEN MARINE CONSTRUCTION LLC, MEQUON, WI *(gillenmarine.com)*								
Kristin J.		TB	1963	D	60*	52' 06"	19' 01"	7' 04"
Built: St. Charles Steel Works, Thibodaux, LA (Jason A. Kadinger '63-'06)								
GOODTIME CRUISE LINE INC., CLEVELAND, OH *(goodtimeiii.com)*								
Goodtime III		ES	1990	D	95*	161' 00"	40' 00"	11' 00"
Built: Leevac Shipyards Inc., Jennings, LA								
GRAND PORTAGE / ISLE ROYALE TRANSPORTATION LINES, GRAND PORTAGE, MN *(isleroyaleboats.com)*								
Sea Hunter III		ES	1985	D	47*	65' 00"	16' 00"	7' 05"
Voyageur II		ES	1970	D	40*	63' 00"	18' 00"	5' 00"
GRAND RIVER NAVIGATION CO. – SEE LOWER LAKES TRANSPORTATION CO.								
GRAND VALLEY STATE UNIVERSITY, ROBERT B. ANNIS WATER RESOURCES, MUSKEGON, MI *(gvsu.edu/wri)*								
D. J. Angus		RV	1986	D	16*	45' 00"	14' 00"	4' 00"
W. G. Jackson		RV	1996	D	80*	64' 10"	20' 00"	5' 00"
GRAYFOX ASSOCIATION, PORT HURON, MI *(nscsgrayfox.org)*								
Grayfox [TWR-825]		TV	1985	D	213*	120' 00"	25' 00"	12' 00"
Built: Marinette Marine Corp., Marinette, WI; based at Port Huron, MI (USS TWR-825 '85-'97)								
GREAT LAKES DOCK & MATERIALS LLC, MUSKEGON, MI *(greatlakesdock.com)*								
Defiance		TW	1965	D	39*	48' 00"	18' 00"	6' 03"
Built: Harrison Bros. Drydock, Mobile, AL								
Duluth		TB	1954	D	87*	70' 01"	19' 05"	9' 08"
Built: Missouri Valley Bridge & Iron Works, Leavenworth, KS (U. S. Army ST-2015 '54-'62)								
Ethan George		TB	1940	D	27*	42' 05"	12' 08"	6' 06"
Built: Sturgeon Bay Shipbuilding, Sturgeon Bay, WI (Holland, Captain Roy)								
Fischer Hayden		TB	1967	D	64*	54' 00"	22' 01"	7' 01"
Built: Main Iron Works Inc., Houma, LA (Gloria G. Cheramie, Joyce P. Crosby)								
Meredith Ashton	8951487	TB	1981	D	127*	68' 08"	26' 01"	9' 04"
Built: Service Marine Group Inc., Amelia, LA (Alpha, Specialist, The Rock '12-'16)								
Sarah B.		TB	1953	D	23*	45' 00"	13' 00"	7' 00"
Built: Nashville Bridge Co., Nashville, TN (ST-2161 '53-'63, Tawas Bay '63-'03)								

Fleet Name / Vessel Name	Vessel IMO #	Vessel Type	Year Built	Engine Type	Cargo Cap. or Gross*	Overall Length	Vessel Breadth	Vessel Depth
GREAT LAKES FLEET INC., DULUTH, MN (KEY LAKES INC., MANAGER)								
Arthur M. Anderson {2}	5025691	SU	1952	T	25,300	767' 00"	70' 00"	36' 00"
Built: American Shipbuilding Co., Lorain, OH; lengthened 120' in '75 and converted to a self-unloader in '82 at Fraser Shipyards, Superior, WI; entered possible long-term lay-up at Duluth, MN, on 1-15-'17								
Cason J. Callaway	5065392	SU	1952	T	25,300	767' 00"	70' 00"	36' 00"
Built: Great Lakes Engineering Works, River Rouge, MI; lengthened 120' in '74 and converted to a self-unloader in '82 at Fraser Shipyards, Superior, WI								
Edgar B. Speer	7625952	SU	1980	D	73,700	1,004' 00"	105' 00"	56' 00"
Built: American Shipbuilding Co., Lorain, OH								
Edwin H. Gott	7606061	SU	1979	D	74,100	1,004' 00"	105' 00"	56' 00"
Built: Bay Shipbuilding Co., Sturgeon Bay, WI; converted from shuttle self-unloader to deck-mounted self-unloader at Bay Shipbuilding, Sturgeon Bay, WI, in '96								
Great Republic	7914236	SU	1981	D	25,600	634' 10"	68' 00"	39' 07"
Built: Bay Shipbuilding Co., Sturgeon Bay, WI (American Republic '81-'11)								
John G. Munson {2}	5173670	SU	1952	D	25,550	768' 03"	72' 00"	36' 00"
Built: Manitowoc Shipbuilding Co., Manitowoc, WI; lengthened 102' at Fraser Shipyards, Superior, WI, in '76; repowered in '16								
Philip R. Clarke	5277062	SU	1952	T	25,300	767' 00"	70' 00"	36' 00"
Built: American Shipbuilding Co., Lorain, OH; lengthened 120' in '74 and converted to a self-unloader in '82 at Fraser Shipyards, Superior, WI								
Presque Isle {2}	7303877	IT	1973	D	1,578*	153' 03"	54' 00"	31' 03"
Built: Halter Marine, New Orleans, LA; paired with the self-unloading barge Presque Isle								
Presque Isle {2}		SU	1973	B	57,500	974' 06"	104' 07"	46' 06"
Built: Erie Marine Inc., Erie, PA [ITB Presque Isle OA dimensions together]					1,000' 00"	104' 07"	46' 06"	
Roger Blough	7222138	SU	1972	D	43,900	858' 00"	105' 00"	41' 06"
Built: American Shipbuilding Co., Lorain, OH								
GREAT LAKES GROUP, CLEVELAND, OH *(thegreatlakesgroup.com)*								
THE GREAT LAKES TOWING CO., CLEVELAND, OH – DIVISION OF THE GREAT LAKES GROUP								
Arizona		TB	1931	D	98*	74' 08"	19' 09"	11' 06"
Arkansas		TB	1909	D	97*	81' 00"	20' 00"	12' 06"
Built: Great Lakes Towing Co., Cleveland, OH; oldest of the State class of tugs (Yale '09-'48)								
California *(Scrapping underway at Cleveland)*		TB	1926	DE	97*	74' 08"	19' 09"	11' 06
Cleveland		TB	2017	D	-100*	63' 05"	24' 02"	11' 00"
Built: Great Lakes Shipyard, Cleveland, OH								
Colorado		TB	1928	D	98*	78' 08"	20' 00"	12' 04"
Erie		TB	1971	D	243*	102' 03"	29' 00"	16' 03"
Built: Peterson Builders, Sturgeon Bay, WI (YTB 810 {Anoka} '71-'15)								
Favorite		FD	1983		300 ton capacity	90' 00"	50' 00"	5' 00"
Florida		TB	1926	D	99*	71' 00"	20' 02"	11' 02"
Built: Great Lakes Towing Co., Cleveland, OH (Florida '26-'83, Pinellas '83-'84)								
Idaho		TB	1931	DE	98*	78' 08"	20' 00"	12' 04"
Illinois {2}		TB	1914	D	98*	71' 00"	20' 00"	12' 05"
Indiana		TB	1911	DE	97*	74' 08"	19' 09"	11' 06"
Iowa		TB	1915	D	97*	74' 08"	19' 09"	11' 06"
Kansas		TB	1927	D	97*	74' 08"	19' 09"	11' 06"
Kentucky {2}		TB	1929	D	98*	78' 08"	20' 00"	12' 04"
Louisiana		TB	1917	D	97*	74' 08"	19' 09"	11' 06"
Maine {1} *(Scrapping underway at Cleveland)*		TB	1921	D	96*	71' 00"	20' 01"	11' 02"
Built: Great Lakes Towing Co., Cleveland, OH (Maine {1} '21-'82, Saipan '82-'83, Hillsboro '83-'84)								
Massachusetts		TB	1928	D	98*	78' 08"	20' 00"	12' 04"
Minnesota		TB	1911	D	98*	78' 08"	20' 00"	12' 04"
Mississippi		TB	1916	DE	97*	74' 08"	19' 09"	11' 06"
Missouri {2}		TB	1927	D	149*	88' 04"	24' 06"	12' 03"
Built: American Shipbuilding Co., Lorain, OH (Rogers City {1} '27-'56, Dolomite {1} '56-'81, Chippewa {7} '81-'90)								
Nebraska		TB	1929	D	98*	78' 08"	20' 00"	12' 05"
New Jersey		TB	1924	D	98*	78' 08"	20' 00"	12' 04"
Built: Great Lakes Towing Co., Cleveland, OH (New Jersey '24-'52, Petco-21 '52-'53)								
New York		TB	1913	D	98*	78' 08"	20' 00"	12' 04"
North Carolina {2}		TB	1952	DE	145*	87' 09"	24' 01"	10' 07"
Built: Great Lakes Towing Co., Cleveland, OH (Limestone '52-'83, Wicklow '83-'90)								
North Dakota		TB	1910	D	97*	74' 08"	19' 09"	11' 06"
Built: Great Lakes Towing Co., Cleveland, OH (John M. Truby '10-'38)								
Ohio {2}		TB	2018	D	-100*	63' 05"	24' 02"	11' 00"
Built: Great Lakes Shipyard, Cleveland, OH								

Fleet Name / Vessel Name	Vessel IMO #	Vessel Type	Year Built	Engine Type	Cargo Cap. or Gross*	Overall Length	Vessel Breadth	Vessel Depth
Oklahoma		TB	1913	DE	97*	74' 08"	19' 09"	11' 06"

Built: Great Lakes Towing Co., Cleveland, OH) (T. C. Lutz {2} '13-'34)

Ontario		TB	1964	D	243*	102' 03"	29' 00"	16' 03"

Built: Mobile Ship Repair, Mobile, AL (YTB 770 {Dahlonega} '64-'01, Jeffrey K. McAllister '01-'15)

Pennsylvania {3} *(Scrapping underway at Cleveland)*		TB	1911	D	98*	78' 08"	20' 00"	12' 04"
Rhode Island		TB	1930	D	98*	78' 08"	20' 00"	12' 04"
South Carolina *(Scrapping underway at Cleveland)*		TB	1925	D	102*	79' 06"	21' 01"	11' 03"

(Welcome {2} '25-'53, Joseph H. Callan '53-'72, South Carolina '72-'82, Tulagi '82-'83)

Superior {3}		TB	1912	D	147*	82' 00"	22' 00"	10' 07"

Built: Manitowoc Shipbuilding Co., Manitowoc, WI (Richard Fitzgerald '12-'46)

Texas		TB	1916	DE	97*	74' 08"	19' 09"	11' 06"
Vermont		TB	1914	D	98*	71' 00"	20' 00"	12' 05"
Virginia {2}		TB	1914	DE	97*	74' 08"	19' 09"	11' 06"
Washington		TB	1925	DE	97*	74' 08"	19' 09"	11' 06"
Wisconsin {4}		TB	1897	D	105*	83' 00"	21' 02"	9' 06"

Built: Union Dry Dock Co., Buffalo, NY; oldest active tug on the Great Lakes. (America {3}, Midway)

Wyoming		TB	1929	D	104*	78' 08"	20' 00"	12' 04"

GREAT LAKES MARITIME ACADEMY, TRAVERSE CITY, MI *(nmc.edu/maritime)*

Anchor Bay		TV	1953	D	23*	45' 00"	13' 00"	7' 00"

Built: Roamer Boat Co., Holland, MI (ST-2158 '53-'62)

State of Michigan	8835451	TV	1985	D	1,914*	224' 00"	43' 00"	20' 00"

Built: Tacoma Boatbuilding Co., Tacoma, WA (USNS Persistent '85-'98, USCG Persistent '98-'02)

GREAT LAKES OFFSHORE SERVICES INC., PORT DOVER, ON

H. H. Misner		TB	1946	D	28*	66' 09"	16' 04"	4' 05"

Built: George Gamble, Port Dover, ON

GREAT LAKES SCHOONER CO., TORONTO, ON *(greatlakesschooner.com)*

Challenge		ES	1980	W/D	76*	96' 00"	16' 06"	8' 00"
Kajama		ES	1930	W/D	263*	128' 09"	22' 09"	11' 08"

GREAT LAKES SCIENCE CENTER – U.S. GEOLOGICAL SURVEY, ANN ARBOR, MI *(glsc.usgs.gov)*

Arcticus		RV	2014	D	148*	77' 03"	26' 11"	11' 00"
Kaho		RV	2011	D	55*	70' 02"	18' 00"	5' 00"
Kiyi		RV	1999	D	290*	107' 00"	27' 00"	12' 02"
Muskie		RV	2011	D	55*	70' 02"	18' 00"	7' 09"
Sturgeon		RV	1977	D	325*	100'00"	25' 05"	10' 00"

GREAT LAKES SHIPWRECK HISTORICAL SOCIETY, SAULT STE. MARIE, MI *(shipwreckmuseum.com)*

David Boyd		RV	1982	D	26*	47' 00"	17' 00"	3' 00"*

GREAT LAKES WATER STUDIES INSTITUTE, TRAVERSE CITY, MI *(nmc.edu/resources/water-studies)*

Northwestern {2}		RV	1969	D	12*	55' 00"	15' 00"	6' 06"

Built: Paasch Marine Services Inc., Erie, PA (USCOE North Central '69-'98)

GROUPE DESGAGNÉS INC., QUÉBEC CITY, QC *(groupedesgagnes.com)*
OPERATED BY SUBSIDIARY TRANSPORT DESGAGNÉS

Acadia Desgagnés	9651541	GC	2013	D	7,875	393' 04"	59' 07"	34' 05"

Built: Shandong Baibuting Shipbuilding Co. Ltd., Shandong, China (BBT Ocean '12-'13, Sider Tis '13-'17)

Argentia Desgagnés	9409895	GC	2007	D	6,369	390' 08"	60' 03"	32' 08"

Built: Ustaoglu Shipyard, Zonguldak, Turkey (Ofmar '07-'17)

Claude A. Desgagnés	9488059	GC	2011	D	9,627	454' 05"	69' 11"	36' 01"

Built: Sanfu Ship Engineering, Taizhou Jiangsu, China (Elsborg '11-'12)

Miena Desgagnés	9700380	GC	2017	D	11,492	482' 04"	74' 10"	37' 01

Built: Jiangzhou Union Shipbuilding Co. Ltd., China

Nordika Desgagnés	9508316	GC	2010	D	12,936	469' 05"	74' 08"	43' 06"

Built: Xingang Shipbuilding Heavy Industry, Tianjin, China (BBC Oder '10-'17)

Rosaire A. Desgagnés	9363534	GC	2007	D	9,611	453' 00"	68' 11"	36' 01"

Built: Quingshan/Jiangdong/Jiangzhou Shipyards, Jiangzhou, China (Beluga Fortification '07-'07)

Sedna Desgagnés	9402093	GC	2009	D	9,611	456' 00"	68' 11"	36' 01"

Built: Quingshan/Jiangdong/Jiangzhou Shipyards, Jiangzhou, China (Beluga Festivity '09-'09)

Taiga Desgagnés	9303302	GC	2007	D	12,936	469' 07"	74' 08"	43' 06"

Built: Tianjin Xingang Shipyard, Tianjin, China (BBC Amazon '07-'17)

Zélada Desgagnés	9402081	GC	2008	D	9,611	455' 10"	68' 11"	36' 01"

Built: Quingshan/Jiangdong/Jiangzhou Shipyards, Jiangzhou, China (Beluga Freedom '09-'09)

THE FOLLOWING VESSELS CHARTERED TO PETRO-NAV INC., MONTREAL, QC, A SUBSIDIARY OF GROUPE DESGAGNÉS INC.

Damia Desgagnés	9766437	TK	2016	D	12,061	442' 11"	77' 01"	37' 01"

Built: Besiktas Gemi Insa A.S., Istanbul, Turkey

Two Harbors, MN (Paul Scinocca)

WANDERING WILFRED

The steamer *Wilfred Sykes* wandered from her usual Lake Michigan trade routes in 2018. The 1949-vintage vessel made several trips to Lake Superior ports two to Detroit and one to Nanticoke, ON. Boat photographers were thrilled to catch her.

Rouge River, Detroit, MI (Christopher Dark)

Muskegon, MI (Krystal Kauffman)

Fleet Name / Vessel Name	Vessel IMO #	Vessel Type	Year Built	Engine Type	Cargo Cap. or Gross*	Overall Length	Vessel Breadth	Vessel Depth
Dara Desgagnés	9040089	TK	1992	D	6,262	405' 10"	58' 01"	34' 09"
Built: MTW Shipyard, Wismar, Germany (Elbestern '92-'93, Diamond Star, '93-'10)								
Esta Desgagnés	9040077	TK	1992	D	6,262	405' 10"	58' 01"	34' 09"
Built: MTW Shipyard, Wismar, Germany (Emsstern '92-'92, Emerald Star '92-'10)								
Jana Desgagnés	9046564	TK	1993	D	6,262	405' 10"	58' 01"	34' 09"
Built: MTW Shipyard, Wismar, Germany (Jadestern '93-'94, Jade Star '94-'10)								
Maria Desgagnés	9163752	TK	1999	D	8,848	393' 08"	68' 11"	40' 05"
Built: Qiuxin Shipyard, Shanghai, China (Kilchem Asia '99-'99)								
Mia Desgagnés	9772278	TK	2017	D	12,061	442' 11"	77' 01"	37' 01"
Built: Besiktas Gemi Insa A.S., Istanbul, Turkey								
Paul A. Desgagnés	9804423	TK	2018	D	12,061	442' 11"	77' 01"	37' 01"
Built: Besiktas Gemi Insa A.S., Istanbul, Turkey								
Rossi A. Desgagnés	9804435	TK	2018	D	12,061	442' 11"	77' 01"	37' 01"
Built: Besiktas Shipyard, Altinova, Turkey								
Sarah Desgagnés	9352171	TK	2007	D	11,711	483'11"	73' 06"	41' 04"
Built: Gisan Shipyard, Tuzla, Turkey (Besiktas Greenland '07-'08)								

THE FOLLOWING VESSELS CHARTERED TO RELAIS NORDIK INC., RIMOUSKI, QC (relaisnordik.com) **A SUBSIDIARY OF GROUPE DESGAGNÉS INC.**

Bella Desgagnés	9511519	PF/RR	2012	D	6,655	312' 00"	63' 06"	22' 08"
Built: Brodogradil Kraljevica d.d., Kraljevica, Croatia								
Nordik Express	7391290	GC/CF	1974	D	1,749	219' 11"	44' 00"	16' 01"
Built: Todd Pacific Shipyards Corp., Seattle, WA (Theriot Offshore IV '74-'77, Scotoil 4 '77-'79, Tartan Sea '79-'87)								

TRANSPORT MARITIME ST-LAURENT INC., A SUBSIDIARY OF GROUPE DESGAGNÉS INC.

Espada Desgagnés	9334698	TK	2006	D	42,810	750' 00"	105' 08"	67' 01"
Built: Brodosplit, Split, Croatia (Stena Poseidon '06-'14)								
Laurentia Desgagnés	9334703	TK	2007	D	42,810	750' 00"	105' 08"	67' 01"
Built: Brodosplit, Split, Croatia (Laid down as Neste Polaris, Palva '07-'14)								

GROUPE OCÉAN INC., QUÉBEC CITY, QC (groupocean.com)

Basse-Cote	8644620	DB	1932	B	400	201' 00"	40' 00"	12' 00"
Built: Department of Marine and Fisheries Government Shipyard, Sorel, QC (Louis D. '32-'93)								
Duga	7530030	TB	1977	D	382*	114' 02"	32' 10"	16' 05"
Built: Langsten Slip & Båtbyggeri A/S, Lansten, Norway								
Escorte	8871027	TT	1964	D	120*	85' 00"	23' 07"	7' 05"
Built: Jakobson Shipyard, Oyster Bay, NY (USS Menasha [YTB / YTM-773, YTM-761] '64-'92, Menasha {1} '92-'95)								
Josee H.		PB	1961	D	66*	63' 50"	16' 02"	9' 50"
Built: Ferguson Industries Ltd., Pictou, NS (Le Bic '61-'98)								
Kim R.D.		TB	1954	D	36*	48' 08"	14' 01"	5' 01"
Built: Port Dalhousie Shipyard Co., Port Dalhousie, ON (Constructor '54-'86)								
La Prairie	7393585	TB	1975	D	110*	73' 09"	25' 09"	11' 08"
Built: Georgetown Shipyard, Georgetown, PEI								
Le Phil D.		TB	1961	D	38*	56' 01"	16' 00"	5' 08"
Built: Russel Brothers Ltd., Owen Sound, ON (Expanse)								
Mega	7347641	TB	1975	D	768*	125' 03"	42' 03"	22' 09"
Built: Oy Wartsila AB, Helsinki, Finland; mated with articulated barge Motti								
Motti	9072434	DB	1993	B	5,195*	403' 04"	78' 02"	7' 07"
Built: Kvaerner Masa Yards, Turku, Finland								
Océan Abys	8644644	DB	1948	B	1,000	140' 00"	40' 00"	9' 00"
Built: Marine Industries Ltd., Sorel, QC (Omni No. 1 '48-'94)								
Océan A. Gauthier	7305904	TB	1973	D	390*	98' 11"	36' 00"	12' 04"
Built: Star Shipyards Ltd., New Westminster, BC (Vachon '73-'17)								
Océan Arctique	9261607	TB	2005	D	512*	102' 08"	39' 05"	17' 00"
Built: Industries Ocean Inc., Ile-Aux-Coudres, QC (Stevns Arctic '05-'13)								
Océan A. Simard	8000056	TT	1980	D	286*	92' 00"	34' 00"	13' 07"
Built: Georgetown Shipyards Ltd., Georgetown, PEI (Alexis-Simard '80-'11)								
Océan Basques	7237212	TB	1972	D	396*	98' 04"	32' 08"	16' 04"
Built: Canadian Shipbuilding & Engineering Co., Collingwood, ON (Pointe Aux-Basques '72-'13)								
Océan Bertrand Jeansonne	9521526	TB	2008	D	402*	94' 05"	36' 05"	17' 02"
Built: East Isle Shipyard, Georgetown, PEI								
Océan Bravo	7025279	TB	1970	D	320*	110' 00"	28' 06"	17' 00"
Built: Davie Shipbuilding Co., Lauzon, QC (Takis V. '70-'80, Donald P '80-'80, Nimue '80-'83, Donald P. '83-'98)								
Océan Cape Crow		TB	1951	D	14*	37' 08"	10' 05"	5' 00"
Built: Russel-Hipwell Engines, Owen Sound, ON (Cape Crow '51-'16)								
Océan Cartier	8668248	TB	2007	D	350*	90' 05"	36' 07"	13' 08"
Built: Shanghai Harbor Foxing, Shanghai, China (Hai Gang 107 '07-'14, Svitzer Wombi '14-'15, Svitzer Cartier '15-'17)								

Fleet Name / Vessel Name	Vessel IMO #	Vessel Type	Year Built	Engine Type	Cargo Cap. or Gross*	Overall Length	Vessel Breadth	Vessel Depth
Océan Catatug 1		TW	2016	D	55*	52' 00"	30' 00"	8' 07"
Built: Industries Ocean Inc., Ile-Aux-Coudres, QC								
Océan Catatug 2		TW	2016	D	52*	52' 00"	30' 00"	8' 07"
Built: Industries Ocean Inc., Ile-Aux-Coudres, QC								
Océan Charlie	7312024	TB	1973	D	448*	123' 02"	31' 07"	16' 01"
Built: Davie Shipbuilding Co., Lauzon, QC (Leonard W. '73-'98)								
Océan Clovis T.	9533036	TB	2009	D	381*	94' 60"	36' 50"	17' 10"
Built: East Isle Shipyard, Georgetown, PEI (Svitzer Njal '09-'17)								
Océan Comeau	7520322	TB	1976	D	391*	99' 09"	36' 01"	12' 01"
Built: Marystown Shipyard Ltd., Marystown, NL (Pointe Comeau '76-'17)								
Océan Cote-Nord			2001	D	79*	75' 01"	18' 00"	10' 06"
Built: Industries Ocean Inc., Ile-Aux-Coudres, QC (Cote-Nord '01-'14)								
Océan Echo II	6913091	AT	1969	D	438*	104' 08"	34' 05"	18' 00"
Built: Port Weller Dry Docks, Port Weller, ON (Atlantic '69-'75, Laval '75-'96)								
Océan Express		PB	1999	D	29*	47' 02"	14' 00"	7' 05"
Built: Industries Ocean Inc., Charlevoix, QC (H-2000 '99-'00)								
Océan Georgie Bain	9553892	TB	2009	D	204*	75' 02"	29' 09"	12' 09"
Built: Industries Ocean Inc., Ile-Aux-Coudres, QC								
Océan Golf	5146354	TB	1959	D	159*	103' 00"	25' 10"	11' 09"
Built: P.K. Harris & Sons, Appledore, England (Launched as Stranton; Helen M. McAllister '59-'97)								
Océan Guide		PB	2001	D	29*	47' 02"	14' 00"	7' 05"
Built: Industries Ocean Inc., Charlevoix, QC								
Océan Henry Bain	9420916	TB	2006	D	402*	94' 08"	30' 01"	14' 09"
Built: East Isle Shipyard, Georgetown, PEI								
Océan Intrepide	9203423	TT	1998	D	302*	80' 00"	30' 01"	14' 09"
Built: Industries Ocean Inc., Ile-Aux-Coudres, QC								
Océan Iroquois		WB	1974	D	20*	37' 09"	10' 00"	6' 06"
Built: Sigama Ltd., Cap-de-la-Madeline, QC (SLS Iroquois '74-??, S/VM Iroquis ??-'09)								
Océan Jupiter	9220160	TT	1998	D	302*	80' 00"	30' 01"	14' 09"
Built: Industries Ocean Inc., Ile-Aux-Coudres, QC								
Océan K. Rusby	9345556	TB	2005	D	402*	94' 08"	30' 01"	14' 09"
Built: East Isle Shipyard, Georgetown, PEI								
Océan Lima		TB	1977	D	15*	34' 02"	11' 08"	4' 00"
(VM/S St. Louis III '77-'10)								
Océan Maisonneuve		SV	1974	D	56*	58' 03"	20' 03"	6' 05"
Built: Fercraft Marine, St. Catherine d'Alexandrie, QC (VM/S Maisonneuve '74-'16)								
Océan Nigiq		TB	2008	D	12*	31' 05"	13' 05"	6' 00"
Built: Industries Océan, Ile-aux-Coudres, QC								
Océan Pierre Julien	9688142	TB	2013	D	204*	75' 01"	30' 01"	12' 09"
Built: Industries Ocean Inc., Ile-Aux-Coudres, QC								
Océan Raymond Lemay	9420904	TB	2006	D	402*	94' 08"	30' 01"	14' 09"
Built: East Isle Shipyard, Georgetown, PEI								
Ocean Raynald T.	9533048	TB	2009	D	381*	94' 60"	36' 50"	17' 10"
Built: East Isle Shipyard, Georgetown, PEI (Stevns Iceflower '09-'09, Svitzer Nerthus '09-'17)								
Océan Ross Gaudreault	9542221	TB	2011	D	402*	94' 04"	36' 05"	17' 00"
Built: East Isle Shipyard, Georgetown, PEI								
Océan Sept-Iles	7901162	TB	1980	D	427*	98' 04"	36' 01"	13' 01"
Built: Canadian Shipbuilding & Engineering Co., Collingwood, ON (Pointe Sept-Iles '80-'13)								
Océan Serge Genois	9553907	TB	2010	D	204*	75' 01"	30' 01"	12' 09"
Built: Industries Ocean Inc., Ile-Aux-Coudres, QC								
Océan Traverse Nord	9666534	DR	2012	B	1,165*	210' 00"	42' 06"	14' 07"
Built: Industries Ocean Inc., Ile-Aux-Coudres, QC								
Océan Tundra	9645504	TB	2013	D	710*	118' 01"	42' 03"	22' 09"
Built: Industries Ocean Inc., Ile-Aux-Coudres, QC								
Ocean Uannaq		TB	2008	D	N/A	31' 06"	13' 06"	6' 00"
Built: Industries Ocean Inc., Ile-Aux-Coudres, QC								
Océan Yvan Desgagnés	9542207	TB	2010	D	402*	94' 04"	36' 05"	17' 00"
Built: East Isle Shipyard, Georgetown, PEI								
Omni-Atlas	8644668	CS	1913	B	479*	133' 00"	42' 00"	10' 00"
Built: Sir William Arrol & Co. Ltd., Glasgow, Scotland								
Omni-Richelieu	6923084	TB	1969	D	144*	83' 00"	24' 06"	13' 06"
Built: Pictou Industries Ltd., Pictou, NS (Port Alfred II '69-'82)								
R. F. Grant		TB	1934	D	78*	71' 00"	17' 00"	8' 00"
Service Boat No. 1		PB	1965	D	55*	57' 08"	16' 01"	7' 06"
Service Boat No. 2		TB	1934	D	78*	65' 02"	17' 00"	8' 01"
Service Boat No. 4		PB	1959	D	26*	39' 01"	14' 02"	6' 03"

GROUPE RIVERIN MARITIME INC., SAGUENAY, QC (grouperiverin.com)

Jean-Joseph	8817382	GC	1990	D	1,999*	257' 08"	41' 00"	21' 06"

    Built: Ferus Smit, Westerbroek, Netherlands (Bothniaborg '90-'04, Westerborg '04-'06, Maple '06-'08, Myras '08-'13, Hav Sund '13-'15)

H

HAMILTON PORT AUTHORITY, HAMILTON, ON (hamiltonport.ca)

Judge McCombs		TB	1948	D	10*	33' 01"	10' 03"	4' 00"

    Built: Northern Shipbuilding & Repair Co. Ltd., Bronte, ON (Bronte Sue '48-'50)

HAMILTON HARBOUR QUEEN CRUISES, HAMILTON, ON (hamiltonharbourqueen.ca)

Hamilton Harbour Queen		ES	1956	D	252*	100' 00"	40' 00"	4' 05"

    Built: Russel-Hipwell Engines, Owen Sound, ON (Johnny B. '56-'89, Garden City '89-'00, Harbour Princess '00-'05)

HARBOR LIGHT CRUISE LINES INC., TOLEDO, OH (sandpiperboat.com)

Sandpiper		ES	1984	D	37*	65' 00"	16' 00"	3' 00"

HARBOR BOAT CRUISE CO., TORONTO, ON (rivergambler.ca)

River Gambler		ES	1992	D	332*	100' 06"	16' 00"	4' 07"

    Built: Jacques Beauchamp, Windsor, ON

HARBOR COUNTY ADVENTURES, NEW BUFFALO, MI (harborcountryadventures.com)

Emita II		ES	1953	D	13*	60' 08"	21' 01"	6' 05"

HEDDLE MARINE SERVICE INC., HAMILTON, ON (heddlemarine.com)

Hamilton Energy	6517328	RT	1965	D	1,282	201' 05"	34' 01"	14' 09"

    Built: Grangemouth Dockyard Co., Grangemouth, Scotland; laid up at Hamilton, ON (Partington '65-'79, Shell Scientist '79-'81, Metro Sun '81-'85)

King Fish 1		TB	1955	D	24*	47' 09"	13' 00"	5' 03"

    Built: Russel Hipworth Engines Ltd., Owen Sound, ON (Anglo Duchess '55-'84, Duchess V '84-'??)

Lac Manitoba		TB	1944	D	51*	64' 00"	16' 07"	7' 10"

    Built: Central Bridge Co., Trenton, ON; being rebuilt at Hamilton, ON (Tanac 75 '44-'52, Manitoba '52-'57)

Provmar Terminal	5376521	TK	1959	B	7,300	403' 05"	55' 06"	28' 05"

    Built: Sarpsborg Mekaniske, Verksted, Norway; last operated in 1984; laid up at Hamilton, ON (Varangnes '59-'70, Tommy Wiborg '70-'74, Ungava Transport '74-'85)

John G. Munson unloading stone at the Reiss dock in Duluth, MN. (Chris Winters)

HERITAGE MARINE, KNIFE RIVER, MN (heritagemarinetug.com)

Edward H. {2}	8990471	TB	1970	D	196*	102' 08"	29' 00"	16' 03"

Built: Peterson Builders Inc., Sturgeon Bay, WI (YTB-809-Agawam '70-'02, Fort Point '02-'17)

Helen H.	8624670	TB	1967	D	138*	82' 03"	26' 08"	10' 05"

Built: Bludworth Shipyard, Corpus Christi, TX (W. Douglas Masterson '67-'11)

Nancy J.	6504838	TB	1964	D	186*	92' 17"	29' 05"	14' 00"

Built: Main Iron Works, Houma, La (Horace, Point Comfort-'14)

Nels J. {2}		TB	1952	D	197*	101' 00"	26' 07"	12' 06"

Built: National Steel and Shipbuilding Co., San Diego, CA (LT-2078 '52-'64, YTM-748-Yuma '64-'80, Delaware '80-'89, Mobile Point '89-'95, Delaware '95-'08, Mobile Point '08-'09, Lesli M '09-'12, Taurus '12-'17)

HORNBLOWER CANADA CO., NIAGARA FALLS, ON (niagaracruises.com)

Niagara Guardian		PA	2013	D	38*	68' 09"	15' 07"	7' 05"
Niagara Thunder		PA	2014	D	185*	83' 02"	35' 09"	8' 09"
Niagara Wonder		PA	2014	D	185*	83' 02"	35' 09"	8' 09"

HORNE TRANSPORTATION LTD., WOLFE ISLAND, ON (wolfeisland.com/ferry.php)

William Darrell		CF	1952	D	66*	66' 00"	28' 00"	6' 00"

HUFFMAN EQUIPMENT RENTAL INC., EASTLAKE, OH

Benjamin Ridgway		TW	1969	D	51*	53' 00"	18' 05"	7' 00"
Bert Huffman		TW	1979	D	34*	38' 00"	13' 06"	5' 02"
Hamp Thomas		TB	1968	D	22*	43' 00"	13' 00"	4' 00"
Paddy Miles		TB	1934	D	16*	45' 04"	12' 04"	4' 07"

HURON LADY CRUISES, PORT HURON, MI (huronlady.com)

Huron Lady II		ES	1993	D	82*	65' 00"	19' 00"	10' 00"

(Lady Lumina '93-'99)

HYDRO-QUEBEC, MONTREAL, QC

Des Chenaux		TB	1953	D	46*	51' 08"	16' 00"	7' 08"

Built: Chantiers Manseau Ltd., Sorel, QC

R.O. Sweezy		TB	1991	D	29*	41' 09"	14' 00"	5' 07"

Built: Jean Fournier, Quebec City, QC (Citadelle I '91-'92)

ILLINOIS & MICHIGAN OIL LLC, JOLIET, IL

Daniel E		TW	1967	D	70*	70' 00"	18' 06"	6' 08"

Built: River Enterprises Inc., Morris, IL (Foster M. Ford '67-'84)

Fleet Name Vessel Name	Vessel IMO #	Vessel Type	Year Built	Engine Type	Cargo Cap. or Gross*	Overall Length	Vessel Breadth	Vessel Depth
David E		TW	1952	D	236*	95' 00"	30' 00"	8' 06"

Built: Sturgeon Bay Shipbuilding & Drydock Co., Sturgeon Bay, WI (Irving Crown '52-'01)

Derek E		TB	1907	D	85*	72' 06"	20' 01"	10' 06"

Built: Benjamin T. Cowles, Buffalo, NY (John Kelderhouse '07-'13, Sachem '13-'90)

Lisa E		TB	1963	D	75*	65' 06"	20' 00"	8' 06"

Built: Main Iron Works Inc., Houma, LA (Dixie Scout '63-'90)

INFINITY AND OVATION YACHT CHARTERS LLC, ST. CLAIR SHORES, MI (infinityandovation.com)

Infinity		PA	2001	D	82*	117' 00"	22' 00"	6' 00"
Ovation		PA	2005	D	97*	138' 00"	27' 00"	7' 00"

I

INLAND LAKES MANAGEMENT INC., ALPENA, MI

Alpena {2}	5206362	CC	1942	T	13,900	519' 06"	67' 00"	35' 00"

Built: Great Lakes Engineering Works, River Rouge, MI; shortened by 120' and converted to a self-unloading cement carrier at Fraser Shipyards, Superior, WI, in '91 (Leon Fraser '42-'91)

J.A.W. Iglehart	5139179	CC	1936	T	12,500	501' 06"	68' 03"	37' 00"

Built: Sun Shipbuilding and Drydock Co., Chester, PA; converted from a saltwater tanker to a self-unloading cement carrier at American Shipbuilding Co., South Chicago, IL , in '65; last operated Oct. 29, 2006; in use as a cement storage/transfer vessel at Superior, WI (Pan Amoco '36-'55, Amoco '55-'60, H. R. Schemm '60-'65)

S.T. Crapo	5304011	CC	1927	T	8,900	402' 06"	60' 03"	29' 00"

Built: Great Lakes Engineering Works, River Rouge, MI; last operated Sept. 4, 1996; in use as a cement storage and transfer vessel at Green Bay, WI

INLAND SEAS EDUCATION ASSOCIATION, SUTTONS BAY, MI (schoolship.org)

Inland Seas		RV	1994	W	41*	61' 06"	17' 00"	7' 00"

Built: Treworgy Yachts, Palm Coast, FL

Utopia		RV	1946	W	49*	65' 0"	18' 00"	6' 08"

INLAND TUG & BARGE LTD., BROCKVILLE, ON

Katanni		TB	1991	D	19*	34' 08"	14' 05"	5' 05"

Built: Duratug Shipyard & Fabricating Ltd., Port Dover, ON

INTERLAKE STEAMSHIP CO., MIDDLEBURG HEIGHTS, OH (interlakesteamship.com)

Dorothy Ann	8955732	AT/TT	1999	D	1,090*	124' 03"	44' 00"	24' 00"

Built: Bay Shipbuilding Co., Sturgeon Bay, WI; paired with self-unloading barge Pathfinder; overall length for Dorothy Ann / Pathfinder is 700' 02"

Herbert C. Jackson	5148417	SU	1959	D	24,800	690' 00"	75' 00"	37' 06"

Built: Great Lakes Engineering Works, River Rouge, MI; converted to a self-unloader at Defoe Shipbuilding Co., Bay City, MI, in '75; repowered in '16

Hon. James L. Oberstar	5322518	SU	1959	D	31,000	806' 00"	75' 00"	37' 06"

Built: American Shipbuilding Co., Toledo, OH; lengthened 96' in '72; converted to a self-unloader in '81 at Fraser Shipyards, Superior, WI; repowered in '09 (Shenango II '59-'67, Charles M. Beeghly '67-'11)

James R. Barker	7390260	SU	1976	D	63,300	1,004' 00"	105' 00"	50' 00"

Built: American Shipbuilding Co., Lorain, OH

John Sherwin {2}	5174428	BC	1958	B	31,500	806' 00"	75' 00"	37' 06"

Built: American Shipbuilding Co., Toledo, OH; lengthened 96' at Fraser Shipyards, Superior, WI, in '73; last operated Nov. 16, 1981; in long-term lay-up at DeTour, MI

Kaye E. Barker	5097450	SU	1952	D	25,900	767' 00"	70' 00"	36' 00"

Built: American Shipbuilding Co., Toledo, OH; lengthened 120' at Fraser Shipyards, Superior, WI, in '76; converted to a self-unloader at American Shipbuilding Co., Toledo, OH, in '81; repowered in '12 (Edward B. Greene '52-'85, Benson Ford {3} '85-'89)

Lee A. Tregurtha	5385625	SU	1942	D	29,360	826' 00"	75' 00"	39' 00"

Built: Bethlehem Shipbuilding and Drydock Co., Sparrows Point, MD; converted from a saltwater tanker to a Great Lakes bulk carrier in '61; lengthened 96' in '76 and converted to a self-unloader in '78, all at American Shipbuilding Co., Lorain, OH; repowered in '06 (Laid down as Mobiloil; launched as Samoset; USS Chiwawa [AO-68] '42-'46, Chiwawa '46-'61, Walter A. Sterling '61-'85, William Clay Ford {2} '85-'89)

Mesabi Miner	7390272	SU	1977	D	63,300	1,004' 00"	105' 00"	50' 00"

Built: American Shipbuilding Co., Lorain, OH

Pathfinder {3}	5166768	SU	1953	B	10,577	606' 00"	70' 03"	36' 03"

Built: Great Lakes Engineering Works, River Rouge, MI; converted from a powered vessel to a self-unloading barge at Bay Shipbuilding Co., Sturgeon Bay, WI, in '98; paired with articulated tug Dorothy Ann (J. L. Mauthe '53-'98)

Paul R. Tregurtha	7729057	SU	1981	D	68,000	1,013' 06"	105' 00"	56' 00"

Built: American Shipbuilding Co., Lorain, OH; largest vessel on the lakes (William J. DeLancey '81-'90)

Stewart J. Cort	7105495	SU	1972	D	58,000	1,000' 00"	105' 00"	49' 00"

Built: Erie Marine Inc., Erie, PA; built for Bethlhem Steel Corp., first 1,000-footer on the Great Lakes

ISLAND FERRY SERVICES CORP., CHEBOYGAN, MI

Polaris		PF	1952	D	99*	60' 02"	36' 00"	8' 06"

ISLE ROYALE LINE INC., COPPER HARBOR, MI (isleroyale.com)

Isle Royale Queen IV		PA/PK	1980	D	93*	98' 09"	22' 01"	7' 00"

Built: Neuville Boat Works Inc., New Iberia, LA (American Freedom, John Jay, Shuttle V, Danielle G, Harbor Commuter V)

J-K

J.W. WESTCOTT CO., DETROIT, MI (jwwestcott.com)

Joseph J. Hogan		MB	1957	D	16*	40' 00"	12' 05"	5' 00"
(USCOE Ottawa '57-'95)								
J. W. Westcott II		MB	1949	D	14*	46' 01"	13' 03"	4' 05"

Built: Paasch Marine Service, Erie, PA; floating post office has its own U.S. ZIP code, 48222

JEFF FOSTER, SUPERIOR, WI

Sundew		IB	1944	DE	1,025*	180' 00"	37' 05"	17' 04"

Built: Marine Ironworks and Shipbuilding Corp., Duluth, MN; former U.S. Coast Guard cutter WLB-404 was decommissioned in 2004 and turned into a marine museum; returned to private ownership in 2009

JUBILEE QUEEN CRUISE LINES, TORONTO, ON (jubileequeencruises.ca)

Jubilee Queen		ES	1986	D	269*	122' 00"	23' 09"	5' 05"
(Pioneer Princess III '86-'89)								

KEHOE MARINE CONSTRUCTION CO., LANSDOWNE, ON (kehoemarine.com)

Halton		TB	1942	D	15*	42' 08"	14' 00"	5' 08"
Built: Muir Bros. Dry Dock Co. Ltd., Port Dalhousie, ON (Workboat No. 8)								
Houghton		TB	1944	D	15*	45' 00"	13' 00"	6' 00"
Built: Port Houston Iron Works, Houston, TX (ST-573 '44-'48)								
Sawyer 1		TB	1946	D	11*	35' 02"	10' 02"	4' 04"
Built: Russel Bros. Ltd., Owen Sound, ON (Coulonge, Compass Rose VI)								

KELLEYS ISLAND BOAT LINES, MARBLEHEAD, OH (kelleysislandferry.com)

Carlee Emily		PA/CF	1987	D	98*	101' 00"	34' 06"	10' 00"
Built: Blount Marine Corp., Warren, RI (Endeavor '87-'02)								
Juliet Alicia		PA/CF	1969	D	95*	88' 03"	33' 00"	6' 08"
Built: Blount Marine Corp., Warren, RI (Kelley Islander)								
Shirley Irene		PA/CF	1991	D	68*	160' 00"	46' 00"	9' 00"
Built: Ocean Group Shipyard, Bayou La Batre, AL								

KINDRA LAKE TOWING LP, CHICAGO, IL (kindralake.com)

Buckley		TW	1958	D	94*	95' 00"	26' 00"	11' 00"
Built: Parker Bros. Shipyard, Houston, TX (Linda Brooks '58-'67, Eddie B. {2} '67-'95)								
Ellie		TB	1970	D	29*	39' 07"	16' 00"	4' 06"
Built: Big River Shipbuilding Inc., Vicksburg, MS (Miss Bissy '09)								
Morgan		TB	1974	D	134*	90' 00"	30' 00"	10' 06"
Built: Peterson Builders Inc., Sturgeon Bay, WI (Donald O'Toole '74-'86, Bonesey B. '86-'95)								
Old Mission		TB	1945	D	94*	85' 00"	23' 00"	10' 04"
Built: Sturgeon Bay Shipbuilding, Sturgeon Bay, WI (U. S. Army ST-880 '45-'47, USCOE Avondale '47-'64, Adrienne B. '64-'95)								
Tanner		TW	1977	D	62*	56' 06"	22' 03"	6' 06"
Built: Thrift Shipbuilding Inc., Sulphur, LA; owned by Jamattca Inc., Chicago, IL (J.H. Tanner 76-'00)								

KING CO. (THE), HOLLAND, MI

Barry J		TB	1943	D	26*	46' 00"	13' 00"	7' 00"
Built: Sturgeon Bay Shipbuilding & Dry Dock Co., Sturgeon Bay, WI								
Buxton II		DR	1976	B	147*	130' 02"	28' 01"	7' 00"
Built: Barbour Boat Works Inc., Holland, MI								
Carol Ann		TB	1981	D	86*	61' 05"	24' 00"	8' 07"
Built: Rodriguez Boat Builders, Bayou La Batre, AL								
John Henry		TB	1954	D	66*	65' 04"	19' 04"	9' 06"
Built: Missouri Valley Steel, Leavenworth, KS (U. S. Army ST-2013 '54-'80)								
Julie Dee		TB	1937	D	64*	68' 08"	18' 01"	7' 06"
Built: Herbert Slade, Beaumont, TX (Dernier, Jerry O'Day, Cindy B)								
Matt Allen		TB	1961	D	146*	80' 04"	24' 00"	11' 03"
Built: Nolty Theriot Inc., Golden Meadow, LA (Gladys Bea '61-'73, American Viking '73-'83, Maribeth Andrie '83-'05)								
Miss Edna		TB	1935	D	13*	36' 08"	11' 02"	4' 08"
Built: Levingston Shipbuilding, Orange, TX								

KINGSTON 1,000 ISLANDS CRUISES, KINGSTON, ON *(1000islandscruises.on.ca)*

Island Belle I		ES	1988	D	150*	65' 00"	22' 00"	8' 00"

    Built: Kettle Creek Boat Works, Port Stanley, ON (Spirit of Brockville '88-'91)

Island Queen III		ES	1975	D	300*	96' 00"	26' 00"	11' 00"

    Built: Marlin Yacht Co., Summerstown, ON

Papoose III		ES	1968	D	110*	64' 08"	23' 03"	7' 03"

    Built: Hike Metal Products Ltd., Wheatley, ON (Peche Island II ('68'-'93)

L

LAKE ERIE ISLAND CRUISES LLC, SANDUSKY, OH *(goodtimeboat.com)*

Goodtime I		ES	1960	D	81*	111' 00"	29' 08"	9' 05"

    Built: Blount Marine Corp., Warren, RI

LAKE EXPRESS LLC, MILWAUKEE, WI *(lake-express.com)*

Lake Express	9329253	PA/CF	2004	D	96*	179' 02"	57' 07"	16' 00"

    Built: Austal USA, Mobile, AL; high-speed ferry service from Milwaukee, WI, to Muskegon, MI;
    capacity is 250 passengers, 46 autos

LAKE MICHIGAN CARFERRY, LUDINGTON, MI *(ssbadger.com)*

Badger	5033583	PA/CF	1953	S	4,244*	410' 06"	59' 06"	24' 00"

    Built: Christy Corp., Sturgeon Bay, WI; traditional ferry service from Ludington, MI, to Manitowoc, WI; capacity is
    520 passengers, 180 autos; last coal-fired steamship on the Great Lakes; listed on the National Register of
    Historic Places in 2016; last vessel in Great Lakes service powered by Skinner Unaflow engines

Spartan		PA/CF	1952	S	4,244*	410' 06"	59' 06"	24' 00"

    Built: Christy Corp., Sturgeon Bay, WI; last operated Jan. 20, 1979; in long-term lay-up at Ludington, MI

LAKEHEAD TUG BOATS INC., THUNDER BAY, ON *(lakeheadtugs.com)*

George N. Carleton		TB	1943	D	97*	82' 00"	21' 00"	11' 00"

    Built: Russel Brothers Ltd., Owen Sound, ON (HMCS Glenlea [W-25] '43-'45, Bansaga '45-'64)

Robert John		TB	1945	D	98*	82' 00"	20' 01"	11' 00"

    Built: Canadian Dredge & Dock Co., Kingston, ON (HMCS Gleneagle [W-40] '45-'46, Bansturdy '46-'65)

Teclutsa		TB	1973	D	235*	102' 85"	30' 00"	15' 00"

    Built: Marinette Marine Ltd., Marinette, WI (YTB-822 – USS Pawhuska '73-'95)

Wolf River		BC	1956	D	5,880	349' 02"	43' 07"	25' 04"

    Built: Port Weller Dry Docks, Port Weller, ON; last operated in 1998; in long-term lay-up at Thunder Bay, ON
    (Tecumseh {2} '56-'67, New York News {3} '67-'86, Stella Desgagnés '86-'93, Beam Beginner '93-'95)

LAKES PILOTS ASSOCIATION, PORT HURON, MI *(lakespilots.com)*

Huron Belle		PB	1979	D	38*	50' 00"	15' 07"	7' 09"

    Built: Gladding-Hearn Shipbuilding, Somerset, MA; pilot service at Detroit, MI

Huron Maid		PB	1977	D	26*	46' 00"	12' 05"	3' 05"

    Built: Hans Hansen Welding Co., Toledo, OH; pilot service at Port Huron, MI

The sterns of the classic lakers
Kaye E. Barker, Hon James L. Oberstar
and Cason J. Callaway. (Roger LeLievre)

Fleet Name / Vessel Name	Vessel IMO #	Vessel Type	Year Built	Engine Type	Cargo Cap. or Gross*	Overall Length	Vessel Breadth	Vessel Depth
Huron Spirit		PB	2016	D	47*	52' 05"	16' 07"	8' 01"

Built: Gladding Hearn Shipbuilding, Somerset, MA; pilot service at Port Huron, MI

LAMBTON MARINE LTD., PORT LAMBTON, ON

Mary Ellen I		TB	2008	D	18*	41' 08"	14' 02"	7' 0"

LAURENTIAN PILOTAGE AUTHORITY, MONTREAL, QC (pilotagestlaurent.gc.ca)

Grandes Eaux		PB	2008	D	63*	62' 06"	17' 02"	9' 05"
Taukamaim		PB	2012	D	82*	72' 01"	19' 05"	10' 05"

Vessels offer pilot service at Les Escoumins, QC, on the St. Lawrence River

LEGEND CRUISES LLC, STURGEON BAY, WI (ridethefireboat.com)

Fred A. Busse		ES	1937	D	99*	92' 00"	22' 04"	9' 06"

Built: Defoe Boat & Motor Works, Bay City, MI; former Chicago fireboat offers cruises at Sturgeon Bay, WI

LES BARGES DE MATANE INC., MATANE, QC (bargesmatane.com)

Point Vim	518852	TB	1962	D	207*	98' 06"	26' 18"	12' 02"

Built: Davie Shipbuilding Co., Lauzon, QC (Foundation Vim '62-'74)

LOWER LAKES TOWING LTD., PORT DOVER, ON (randlogisticsinc.com)
A SUBSIDIARY OF RAND LOGISTICS INC., NEW YORK, NY

Cuyahoga	5166392	SU	1943	D	15,675	620' 00"	60' 00"	35' 00"

Built: American Shipbuilding Co., Lorain, OH; converted to a self-unloader by Manitowoc Shipbuilding Co., Manitowoc, WI, in '74; repowered in '01 (J. Burton Ayers '43-'95)

Kaministiqua	8119285	BC	1983	D	34,500	730' 01"	75' 09"	48' 00"

Built: Govan Shipyards, Glasgow, Scotland (Saskatchewan Pioneer '83-'95, Lady Hamilton '95-'06, Voyageur Pioneer '06-'08)

Manitoulin {6}	8810918	SU	1991	D	25,000	662' 09"	77' 09"	44' 11"

Former saltwater tanker rebuilt for Great Lakes service in 2015 with a new self-unloading bow section. **Bow section** *built 2014-15 at Chengxi Shipyards, Jiangyin, China.* **Stern section** *built in 1991 at Uljanik Shipyard, Pula, Croatia. (Trelsi '91-'01, Euro Swan '01-'11, Lalandia Swan '11-'15)*

Michipicoten {2}	5102865	SU	1952	D	22,300	698' 00"	70' 00"	37' 00"

Built: Bethlehem Shipbuilding & Drydock Co., Sparrows Point, MD; lengthened 72' by American Shipbuilding Co., S. Chicago, IL, in '57; converted to a self-unloader by American Shipbuilding Co., Toledo, OH, in '80; repowered in '11 (Elton Hoyt 2nd '52-'03)

Mississagi	5128467	SU	1943	D	15,800	620' 06"	60' 00"	35' 00"

Built: Great Lakes Engineering Works, River Rouge, MI; converted to a self-unloader by Fraser Shipyards, Superior, WI, in '67; repowered in '85 (Hill Annex '43-'43, George A. Sloan '43-'01)

Ojibway	5105831	BC	1952	D	20,668	642' 03"	67' 00"	35' 00"

Built: Defoe Shipbuilding Co., Bay City, MI; repowered in '05 (Charles L. Hutchinson {3} '52-'62, Ernest R. Breech '62-'88, Kinsman Independent '88-'05, Voyageur Independent '05-'08)

Robert S. Pierson	7366403	SU	1974	D	19,650	630' 00"	68' 00"	36' 11"

Built: American Shipbuilding Co., Lorain, OH (Wolverine {2} '74-'08)

Saginaw {3}	5173876	SU	1953	D	20,200	639' 03"	72' 00"	36' 00"

Built: Manitowoc Shipbuilding Co., Manitowoc, WI, repowered in '08 (John J. Boland {3} '53-'99)

Evans Spirit discharging pyrophillite from Long Pond, NL, at Pier12N in Hamilton, ON. (Ted Wilush)

Fleet Name Vessel Name	Vessel IMO #	Vessel Type	Year Built	Engine Type	Cargo Cap. or Gross*	Overall Length	Vessel Breadth	Vessel Depth
Tecumseh {2}	7225855	BC	1973	D	29,510	641' 00"	78' 00"	45' 03"

Built: Lockheed Shipbuilding & Construction Co., Seattle, WA (Sugar Islander '73-'96, Islander '96-'96, Judy Litrico '96-'06, Tina Litrico '06-'11)

GRAND RIVER NAVIGATION CO., NEW YORK, NY, OWNER – AN AFFILIATE OF LOWER LAKES TOWING LTD.

Ashtabula	8637495	SU	1982	B	17,982	610' 01"	78' 01"	49' 08"

Built: Bay Shipbuilding Co., Sturgeon Bay, WI (Mary Turner '82-'12)

Calumet {3}	7329314	SU	1973	D	19,650	630' 00"	68' 00"	36' 11"

Built: American Shipbuilding Co., Lorain, OH (William R. Roesch '73-'95, David Z. Norton {3} '95-'07, David Z. '07-'08)

CTC No. 1		CC	1943	R	16,300	620' 06"	60' 00"	35' 00"

Built: Great Lakes Engineering Works, River Rouge, MI; last operated Nov. 12, 1981; former cement storage/transfer vessel is laid up at South Chicago, IL; (Launched as McIntyre; Frank Purnell {1} '43-'64, Steelton {3} '64-'78, Hull No. 3 '78-'79, Pioneer {4} '79-'82)

Defiance	8109761	ATB	1982	D	196*	145' 01"	44' 00"	21' 00"

Built: Marinette Marine Corp., Marinette, WI; paired with barge Ashtabula (April T. Beker '82-'87, Beverly Anderson '82-'12)

Invincible	7723819	ATB	1979	D	180*	100' 00"	35' 00"	22' 06"

Built: Atlantic Marine Inc., Fort George Island, FL; paired with barge Menominee (R. W. Sesler '79-'91)

Manistee	5294307	SU	1943	D	14,900	620' 06"	60' 03"	35' 00"

Built: Great Lakes Engineering Works, River Rouge, MI; converted to a self-unloader by Manitowoc Shipbuilding Co., Manitowoc, WI, in '64; repowered in '76; entered long-term lay-up at Toledo, Ohio, in December 2015 (launched as Adirondack. Richard J. Reiss {2} '43-'86, Richard Reiss '86-'05)

Manitowoc	7366398	SU	1973	D	19,650	630' 00"	68' 00"	36' 11"

Built: American Shipbuilding Co., Lorain, OH (Paul Thayer '73-'95, Earl W. Oglebay '95-'07, Earl W. '07-'08)

Maumee {2}	5293341	SU	1953	B	25,500	703' 08"	70' 00"	36' 00"

Built: Great Lakes Engineering Works, River Rouge, MI; lengthened 120' by Fraser Shipyards, Superior, WI, in '75; converted to a self-unloader by Bay Shipbuilding, Sturgeon Bay, WI, in '83; converted to a barge by the owners in '07 (Reserve '53-'08, James L. Kuber '08-'19)

Menominee	5336351	SU	1952	B	22,300	616' 10"	70' 00"	37' 00"

Built: Bethlehem Steel Corp., Sparrows Point, MD; lengthened 72' by American Shipbuilding, South Chicago, IL, in '58; converted to a self-unloader by Fraser Shipyards, Superior, WI, in '80; converted to a barge by Erie Shipbuilding, Erie, PA, in '06; (Sparrows Point '52-'90, Buckeye {3} '90-'06, Lewis J. Kuber '06-'17)

Olive L. Moore	8635227	AT	1928	D	524*	125' 00"	39' 02"	13' 09"

Built: Manitowoc Shipbuilding Co., Manitowoc, WI (John F. Cushing '28-'66, James E. Skelly '66-'66)

Victory	8003292	TB	1980	D	194*	140' 00"	43' 01"	18' 00"

Built: McDermott Shipyard Inc., Amelia, LA; paired with barge Maumee

Atlantic Huron in the Welland Canal. (Matt Miner)

Fleet Name Vessel Name	Vessel IMO #	Vessel Type	Year Built	Engine Type	Cargo Cap. or Gross*	Overall Length	Vessel Breadth	Vessel Depth

LUEDTKE ENGINEERING CO., FRANKFORT, MI *(luedtke-eng.com)*

Alan K. Luedtke   TB   1944   D   149*   86′ 04″   23′ 00″   10′ 03″
Built: Allen Boat Co., Harvey, LA; inactive at Ludington, MI (U. S. Army ST-527 '44-'55, USCOE Two Rivers '55-'90)

Ann Marie   TB   1954   D   81*   71′ 00″   19′ 05″   9′ 06″
Built: Smith Basin & Drydock, Pensacola, FL (ST-1449 '54- '80, Lewis Castle '80-'98, Apache '98-'01)

Chris E. Luedtke   TB   1936   D   18*   42′ 05″   11′ 09″   5′ 00″
Built: Manitowoc Shipbuilding, Manitowoc, WI (Manshipco '36-'80)

Erich R. Luedtke   TB   1939   D   18*   42′ 05″   11′ 09″   5′ 00″
Built: Manitowoc Shipbuilding, Manitowoc, WI

Gretchen B   TB   1943   D   18*   41′ 09″   12′ 05″   6′ 00″
Built: Sturgeon Bay Shipbuilding, Sturgeon Bay, WI (ST-175 '43-'46, Jane T '46-'70)

Karl E. Luedtke   TB   1928   D   32*   55′ 02″   14′ 09″   6′ 00″
Built: Leathem D. Smith Dock Co., Sturgeon Bay, WI (Betty D. '28-'32, Killarney '32-'35)

Krista S   TB   1954   D   93*   67′ 09″   20′ 01″   7′ 07″
Built: Arnold V. Walker Shipyard, Pascagoula, MS (Sea Traveler '54-'87, Sea Wolf '87-'01, Jimmy Wray '01-'08)

Paul L. Luedtke   TB   1988   D   97*   75′ 00″   26′ 00″   9′ 06″
Built: Terrebonne Fabricators Inc., Houma, LA (Edward E. Gillen III '88-'13)

M

MCM MARINE INC., SAULT STE. MARIE, MI *(mcmmarine.com)*

Drummond Islander II   TB   1961   D   97*   65′ 00″   36′ 00″   9′ 00″

Madison   TB   1975   D   17*   33′ 08″   13′ 05″   4′ 07″

Mohawk   TB   1945   D   46*   65′ 00″   19′ 00″   10′ 06″
Built: Robert Jacob Shipbuilding, City Island, NY (YTL-440 '45-'75)

No. 55   DR   1927   DE   721*   165′ 00″   42′ 08″   12′ 00″

No. 56   DS   1928   DE   1,174*   165′ 00″   42′ 04″   15′ 07″

Sioux   DS   1954   B   504*   120′ 00″   50′ 00″   10′ 00″
(The company also operates two small push boats, Kelli Anne and Tammy.)

MacDONALD MARINE LTD., GODERICH, ON *(www.mactug.com)*

Debbie Lyn   TB   1950   D   10*   45′ 00″   14′ 00″   10′ 00″
Built: Matheson Boat Works, Goderich, ON (Skipper '50-'60)

Donald Bert   TB   1953   D   11*   45′ 00″   14′ 00″   10′ 00″
Built: Matheson Boat Works, Goderich, ON

Manitowoc fights winter ice with assistance from a USCG icebreaker. (USCG)

Fleet Name / Vessel Name	Vessel IMO #	Vessel Type	Year Built	Engine Type	Cargo Cap. or Gross*	Overall Length	Vessel Breadth	Vessel Depth
Dover		TB	1931	D	70*	84' 00"	17' 00"	6' 00"
Built: Canadian Mead-Morrison Co. Ltd., Welland, ON (Earleejune, Iveyrose)								
MACKINAC ISLAND STATE PARK COMMISSION, MACKINAC ISLAND, MI								
LCM 6			1952	D	N/A	56' 00"	14' 01"	3 10"
(U.S. Army LCM 6050)								
MADELINE ISLAND FERRY LINE INC., LaPOINTE, WI (madferry.com)								
Bayfield {2}		PA/CF	1952	D	83*	120' 00"	43' 00"	10' 00"
Built: Chesapeake Marine Railway, Deltaville, VA (Charlotte '52-'99)								
Island Queen {2}		PA/CF	1966	D	90*	75' 00"	34' 09"	10' 00"
Madeline		PA/CF	1984	D	94*	90' 00"	35' 00"	8' 00"
Nichevo II		PA/CF	1962	D	89*	65' 00"	32' 00"	8' 09"
MAID OF THE MIST STEAMBOAT CO. LTD., NIAGARA FALLS, ON (maidofthemist.com)								
Maid of the Mist VI		ES	1990	D	155*	78' 09"	29' 06"	7' 00"
Maid of the Mist VII		ES	1997	D	160*	80' 00"	30' 00"	7' 00"
MALCOLM MARINE, ST. CLAIR, MI (malcolmmarine.com)								
Capt. Keith		TB	1955	D	39*	53' 03"	15' 06"	6' 04"
Built: Diamond Manufacturing, Savannah GA (Richard Merritt '55-'13)								
Debbie Lee		TB	1955	D	13*	32' 00"	11' 00"	4' 04"
Built: U.S. Coast Guard, Baltimore, MD (CG-40397, Hooligan, Shy Poke)								
Manitou {2}	8971695	TB	1942	D	199*	110' 00"	26' 02"	15' 06"
Built: U.S. Coast Guard, Curtis Bay, MD (USCGC Manitou [WYT-60] '43-'84)								
MANITOU ISLAND TRANSIT, LELAND, MI (manitoutransit.com)								
Manitou Isle		PA/PK	1946	D	39*	52' 00"	14' 00"	8' 00"
Mishe Mokwa		PA/CF	1966	D	49*	65' 00"	17' 06"	8' 00"
MARINE NAVIGATION AND TRAINING ASSOCIATION, INC. , CHICAGO, IL (manatra.org)								
Manatra [YP-671]		TV	1974	D	67*	80' 05"	17' 09"	5' 04"
Name stands for MArine NAvigation and TRaining Association (USS YP-671 '74-'89)								
MARINE RECYCLING CORP., PORT COLBORNE & PORT MAITLAND, ON (marinerecycling.ca)								
Charlie E.		TB	1943	D	32*	63' 00"	16' 06"	7' 06"
Built: W.F. Kolbe & Co. Ltd., Port Dover, ON (Kolbe '43-'86, Lois T. '86-'02)								
Retired vessels Algorail, Algoway, English River and Paul H. Townsend are awaiting scrapping at Port Colborne								
MARINE SERVICES INC., OAK PARK, MI								
Push Hog		WB	1944	D	25*	40' 00"	15' 00"	5' 00"
Tenacious	5238004	TB	1960	D	149*	79' 01"	25' 06"	12' 06"
Built: Ingalls Shipbuilding Corp., Pascagoula, MS (Mobil 8 '60-'91, Tatarrax '91-'93, Nan McKay '93-'95)								
Titan		TB	1940	D	31*	56' 03"	15' 08"	7' 00"
(Gotham '40-'10)								

James R. Barker at sunset. (Robert Prusak)

Fleet Name / Vessel Name	Vessel IMO #	Vessel Type	Year Built	Engine Type	Cargo Cap. or Gross*	Overall Length	Vessel Breadth	Vessel Depth
MARIPOSA CRUISES, TORONTO, ON *(mariposacruises.com)*								
Capt. Matthew Flinders	8883355	ES	1982	D	746*	144' 00"	40' 00"	8' 06"
Built: North Arm Slipway Pty. Ltd., Port Adelaide, Australia								
Klancy II		ES	1989	D	124*	60' 02"	20' 00"	8' 02"
Northern Spirit I	8870073	ES	1983	D	489*	136' 00"	31' 00"	9' 00"
Built: Blount Marine Corp., Warren, RI (New Spirit '83–'89, Pride of Toronto '89–'92)								
Oriole	8800054	ES	1987	D	200*	75' 00"	23' 00"	9' 00"
Rosemary		ES	1960	D	52*	68' 00"	15' 06"	6' 08"
Showboat		ES	1988	D	135*	74' 00"	21' 00"	4' 00"
MARTIN GAS & OIL INC., BEAVER ISLAND, MI								
Petroqueen		TK	2015	B	112*	70' 00"	24' 00"	8' 00"
Built: Basic Marine Inc., Escanaba, MI								
Shamrock		TB	1933	D	60*	64' 00"	18' 00"	7' 03"
Built: Pennsylvania Shipyard Inc., Beaumont, TX								
McASPHALT MARINE TRANSPORTATION LTD., TORONTO, ON *(mcasphalt.com)*								
Everlast	7527332	ATB	1976	D	1,361*	143' 04"	44' 04"	21' 04"
Built: Hakodate Dock Co., Hakodate, Japan; paired with barge Norman McLeod (Bilibino '77–'96)								
John J. Carrick	9473444	TK	2008	B	11,613	407' 06"	71' 07"	30' 00"
Built: Penglai Bohai Shipyard Co. Ltd., Penglai, China								
Leo A. McArthur	9473262	ATB	2009	D	1,299	122' 00"	44' 03"	26' 02
Built: Penglai Bohai Shipyard Co. Ltd., Penglai, China; paired with barge John J. Carrick (Victorious '09–'17)								
Norman McLeod	8636219	TK	2001	B	6,809*	379' 02"	71' 06"	30' 02"
Built: Jinling Shipyard, Nanjing, China								
McKEIL MARINE LTD., BURLINGTON, ON *(mckeil.com)*								
Alouette Spirit	8641537	DB	1969	B	10,087*	425' 01"	74' 02"	29' 05"
Built: Gulfport Shipbuilding Co., Port Arthur, TX (KTC 135 '69–'04, Lambert's Spirit '04–'05)								
Beverly M I	9084047	TB	1994	D	450*	114' 06"	34' 04"	17' 04"
Built: Imamura Shipbuilding, Kure, Japan (Shek O, Hunter, Pacific Typhoon)								
Blain M	7907099	RV	1981	D	925*	165' 05"	36' 00"	19' 09"
Built: Ferguson Industries, Picton, ON (Wilfred Templeman '81–'11)								
Dover Spirit		TB	1998	D	83*	65' 00"	22' 00"	8' 00"
Built: Dovercraft Marine, Nanticoke, ON (Kaliutik '98–'18)								
Evans McKeil	8983416	TB	1936	D	284*	110' 06"	25' 06"	14' 08"
Built: Panama Canal Co., Balboa, Panama (Alhajuela '36–'70, Barbara Ann {2} '70–'89)								
Evans Spirit	9327772	GC	2007	D	14,650	459' 02"	68' 11"	34' 09"
Built: Royal Niestern Sander, Delfzijl, Netherlands (Spavalda '07–'16)								
Florence M	5118797	TB	1961	D	236*	90' 00"	28' 08"	11' 04"
Built: P.K. Harris, Appledore, UK (Foundation Vibert '61–'73, Point Vibert '73–'06)								
Florence Spirit	9314600	BC	2004	D	13,988	477' 07"	69' 07"	37' 01"
Built: Kyokuyo Shipyard Corp., Shimonoseki, Japan (Arklow Willow '04–'16)								

Kaministiqua and Manitowoc pass at Mission Point. (Stephen Hause)

Fleet Name / Vessel Name	Vessel IMO #	Vessel Type	Year Built	Engine Type	Cargo Cap. or Gross*	Overall Length	Vessel Breadth	Vessel Depth
Huron Spirit	8646642	SU	1995	B	4,542*	328' 01"	82' 25"	23' 06"
Built: Jiangdu Shipyard, Tiangsu Province, China (Mulege '95-'14)								
Jarrett M	5030086	TB	1945	D	96*	82' 00"	20' 00"	10' 00"
Built: Russel Brothers Ltd., Owen Sound, ON (Atomic '45-'06)								
Lambert Spirit	8641525	DB	1968	B	9,645	400' 01"	70' 02"	27' 06"
Built: Avondale Shipyards Inc., Avondale, LA (KTC 115 '68-'06)								
Leonard M	8519215	TB	1986	D	457*	103' 07"	36' 01"	19' 02"
Built: McTay Marine, Bromborough, England (Point Halifax '86-'12)								
Lois M	9017616	TT	1991	D	453*	35' 09"	11' 65"	5' 07"
Built: Matsuura Tekko Zosen, Higashino, Japan (Lambert '91-'14)								
McKeil Spirit	9347023	CC	2007	D	14,650	459' 02"	68' 11"	34' 0"
Built: Royal Niestern Sander, Delfzijl, The Netherlands; converted to a self-discharging cement carrier '17 (Ardita '07-'18)								
Molly M I	5118838	TB	1962	D	207*	98' 06"	27' 10"	12' 02"
Built: Davie Shipbuilding Co., Lauzon, QC (Foundation Vigour '62-'74, Point Vigour '74-'07)								
Niagara Spirit	8736021	DB	1984	D	9,164*	340' 01"	78' 02"	19' 06"
Built: FMC Corp., Portland, OR (Alaska Trader '84-'99, Timberjack '99-'08)								
Nunavut Spirit	8636673	DB	1983	B	6,076*	400' 00"	105' 00"	20' 06"
Built: FMC Corp., Portland, OR (Barge 5001)								
Salvor	5427019	TB	1963	D	407*	120' 00"	31' 00"	18' 06"
Built: Jakobson Shipyard, Oyster Bay, NY (Esther Moran '63-'00)								
Sharon M I	9084059	TB	1993	D	450*	107' 04"	34' 04"	17' 03"
Built: Inamura Shipbuilding, Kure, Japan (Mai Po, Pacific Tempest)								
Stormont	8959893	TB	1953	D	108*	80' 00"	20' 00"	15' 00"
Built: Canadian Dredge & Dock Co., Kingston, ON								
S/VM 86		DB	1958	B	487*	168' 01"	40' 00"	10' 00"
Built: Canadian Shipbuilding & Engineering Ltd., Collingwood, ON (S.L.S. 86)								
Tim McKeil	9017604	TB	1991	D	453*	107' 07"	34' 04"	17' 03"
Built: Matsuura Tekko Zosen, Higashino, Japan (Pannawonica 1 '91-'14)								
Tobias	9642253	DB	2012	B	8,870*	393' 09"	105' 07"	26' 07"
Built: Damen Shipyards Gorinchem, Gorinchem, Netherlands								
Topaz I	9508940	TK	2009	D	13,965	448' 09"	65' 07"	35' 09"
Built: Selah Shipyard, Istanbul, Turkey (Topaz-T '09-'19); a new name is expected in 2019								
Turquoise I	9404388	TK	2009	D	13,965	448' 09"	65' 07'	35' 09"
Built: Gisan Shipbuilding & Shipping, Istanbul, Turkey (Turquoise-T '09-'19); a new name is expected in 2019								
Viateur's Spirit		DB	2004	D	253*	141' 01"	52' 03"	5' 01"
Built: Port Weller Dry Dock, Port Weller, ON (Traverse René Lavasseur '04-'06)								
Wilf Seymour	5215789	TB	1961	D	442*	122' 00"	31' 00"	17' 00"
Built: Gulfport Shipbuilding, Port Arthur, TX (M. Moran '61-'70, Port Arthur '70-'72, M. Moran '72-'00, Salvager '00-'04)								

Tug Cheyenne.
(Sam Hankinson)

Fleet Name Vessel Name	Vessel IMO #	Vessel Type	Year Built	Engine Type	Cargo Cap. or Gross*	Overall Length	Vessel Breadth	Vessel Depth
Wyatt M.	8974178	TB	1948	D	123*	85' 00"	20' 00"	10' 00"

Built: Russel Brothers Ltd., Owen Sound, ON (P. J. Murer '48-'81, Michael D. Misner '81-'93, Thomas A. Payette '93-'96, Progress '96-'06)

MAMMOET-McKEIL LTD., AYR, ON – A SUBSIDIARY OF McKEIL MARINE LTD.

Dowden Spirit		DB	2014	B	2,130*	250' 02"	72' 01"	16' 04"

Built: Glovertown Shipyards Ltd., Glovertown, NL

Glovertown Spirit	9662174	DB	2012	B	2,073*	243' 07"	77' 02"	14' 09"

Built: Damen Shipyards, Gorichem, Netherlands

MM Newfoundland		DB	2011	B	2,165*	260' 00"	72' 00"	16' 01"

Built: Signal International, Pascagoula, MS

MONTREAL BOATMEN LTD., PORT COLBORNE, ON – A SUBSIDIARY OF McKEIL MARINE LTD.

Aldo H.		PB	1979	D	37*	56' 04"	15' 04"	6' 02"
Boatman No. 3		PB	1965	D	13*	33' 08"	11' 00"	6' 00"
Boatman No. 6		PB	1979	D	39*	56' 07"	18' 07"	6' 03"
Primrose		DR	1915	B	916*	136' 06"	42' 00"	10' 02"

McMULLEN & PITZ CONSTRUCTION CO., MANITOWOC, WI (mcmullenandpitz.net)

Dauntless		TB	1937	D	25*	52' 06"	15' 06"	5' 03"

Built: Erie, PA (Allan S. '37-'57)

McNALLY INTERNATIONAL INC., HAMILTON, ON (mcnallycorp.com)
A SUBSIDIARY OF WEEKS MARINE INC., CRANFORD, NJ

Bagotville		TB	1964	D	62*	65' 00"	18' 05"	8' 03"

Built: Verreault Navigation, Les Méchins, QC

Beaver Delta II		TB	1959	D	14*	35' 08"	12' 00"	4' 04"

Built: Allied Builders Ltd., Vancouver, BC (Halcyon Bay)

Beaver Gamma		TB	1960	D	17*	37' 01"	12' 09"	6' 00"

Built: Diesel Sales & Service Ltd., Burlington, ON (Burlington Bertie)

Carl M.		TB	1957	D	21*	47' 00"	14' 06"	6' 00"
D.L. Stanyer		TB	2014	D	14*	40' 03"	11' 08"	6' 02"
Jamie L.		TB	1988	D	25*	36' 04"	14' 07"	5' 09"

(Baie Ste-Anne '88-'96, T-1 '96-'98, Baie Ste-Anne II '98-'05)

J.F. Whalen		TB	2014	D	14*	40' 03"	11' 08"	6' 02"
Lac Como		TB	1944	D	63*	65' 00"	16' 10"	7' 10"

Built: Canadian Bridge Co., Walkerville, ON (Tanac 74 '44-'64)

Lac Vancouver		TB	1943	D	65*	60' 09"	16' 10"	7' 08"

Built: Central Bridge Co., Trenton, ON (Vancouver '43-'74)

Mister Joe		TB	1964	D	70*	61' 00"	19' 00"	7' 02"

Built: Russel Brothers Ltd., Owen Sound, ON (Churchill River '64-'01)

John D. Leitch makes an early arrival at Duluth, MN. *(Glenn Blaszkiewicz)*

Fleet Name / Vessel Name	Vessel IMO #	Vessel Type	Year Built	Engine Type	Cargo Cap. or Gross*	Overall Length	Vessel Breadth	Vessel Depth
Oshawa		TB	1969	D	24*	42' 09"	13' 08"	5' 04"
Paula M.		TB	1959	D	12*	48' 02"	10' 05"	3' 01"
Sandra Mary		TB	1962	D	97*	80' 00"	21' 00"	10' 09"
Built: Russel Brothers Ltd., Owen Sound, ON (Flo Cooper '62–'00)								
Whitby		TB	1978	D	24*	42' 19"	13' 08"	6' 05"
Willmac		TB	1959	D	16*	40' 00"	13' 00"	3' 07"

MERCURY CRUISES, CHICAGO, IL *(mercurycruises.com)*

Skyline Queen		ES	1959	D	45*	61' 05"	16' 10"	6' 00"

MICHELS CORP., BROWNSVILLE, WI *(michels.us)*

Edith J.		TB	1962	D	18*	43' 02"	13' 00"	5' 04"

MICHIGAN DEPARTMENT OF NATURAL RESOURCES, LANSING, MI *(michigan.gov/dnr)*

Channel Cat		RV	1968	D	24*	46' 00"	13' 06"	4' 00"
Lake Char		RV	2006	D	26*	56' 00"	16' 00"	4' 05"
Steelhead		RV	1967	D	70*	63' 00"	16' 04"	6' 06"
Tanner		RV	2016	D	26*	57' 00"	16' 00"	4' 05"

MICHIGAN TECHNOLOGICAL UNIVERSITY, HOUGHTON, MI *(mtu.edu/greatlakes/fleet/agassiz)*

Agassiz		RV	2002	D	14*	36' 00"	13' 00"	4' 00"

MIDLAND TOURS INC., PENETANGUISHENE, ON *(midlandtours.com)*

Miss Midland	7426667	ES	1974	D	106*	68' 07"	19' 04"	6' 04"
Serendipity Princess		ES	1992	D	93*	64' 09"	23' 00"	4' 07"

MIDWEST MARITIME CORP., FRANKLIN, WI

Leona B.		TB	1972	D	99*	59' 08"	24' 01"	10' 03"
(Kings Squire '72–'89, Juanita D. '78–'89, Peggy Ann '89–'93, Mary Page Hannah {2} '93–'04)								

MILLER BOAT LINE, PUT-IN-BAY, OH *(millerferry.com)*

Islander {3}		PA/CF	1983	D	92*	90' 03"	38' 00"	8' 03"
Mary Ann Market		PA/CF	2019	D	TBA	140' 00"	38' 05"	TBA
Built: Fraser Shipyards, Superior, WI								
Put-in-Bay {3}		PA/CF	1997	D	97*	136' 00"	38' 06"	9' 06"
Built: Sturgeon Bay Shipbuilding Co., Sturgeon Bay, WI; lengthened 40' at Cleveland, OH, in '09								
South Bass		PA/CF	1989	D	95*	96' 00"	38' 06"	9' 06"
Wm. Market		PA/CF	1993	D	95*	96' 00"	38' 06"	8' 09"
Built: Peterson Builders Inc., Sturgeon Bay, WI								

MILWAUKEE BOAT LINE LLC, MILWAUKEE, WI *(mkeboat.com)*

Iroquois		PA	1922	D	91*	61' 09"	21' 00"	6' 04"
Vista King		ES	1978	D	60*	78' 00"	23' 00"	5' 02"
Voyageur		PA	1988	D	94*	67' 02"	21' 00"	7' 04"

MILWAUKEE HARBOR COMMISSION, MILWAUKEE, WI *(city.milwaukee.gov/port)*

Harbor Seagull		TB	1961	D	23*	44' 05"	16' 04"	5' 00"
Joey D.		TB	2011	D	65*	60' 00"	20' 06"	6' 06"
Built: Great Lakes Shipyard, Cleveland, OH								

MILWAUKEE METROPOLITAN SEWERAGE DISTRICT, MILWAUKEE, WI

Pelagos		RV	1989	D	32*	42' 09"	13' 08"	6' 06"

MILWAUKEE RIVER CRUISE LINE, MILWAUKEE, WI *(edelweissboats.com)*

Edelweiss II		ES	1989	D	95*	73' 08"	20' 00"	2' 08"
Harbor Lady		ES	1996	D	76*	80' 08"	20' 00"	6' 00"
Lakeside Spirit		ES	1992	D	25*	63' 00"	15' 00"	4' 00"
Miss Wisconsin		ES	1994	D	51*	72' 06"	20' 00"	5' 04"

MINISTRY OF TRANSPORTATION, DOWNSVIEW, ON *(mto.gov.on.ca)*

Frontenac Howe Islander		PF/CF	2004	D	130*	100' 00"	32' 03"	5' 05"
Built: Heddle Marine Service Inc., Hamilton, ON; 15-car cable ferry to Howe Island, east of Kingston, ON								
Frontenac II	5068875	PA/CF	1962	D	666*	181' 00"	45' 00"	10' 00"
Built: Chantier Maritime de St-Laurent, St-Laurent, QC (Charlevoix {2} '62–'92); ferry from Millhaven, ON, to Amherst Island								
Glenora	5358074	PA/CF	1952	D	189*	127' 00"	33' 00"	9' 00"
Built: Port Arthur Shipbuilding Co., Port Arthur, ON (St. Joseph Islander '52–'74); ferry from Adolphustown to Glenora, ON								
Jiimaan	9034298	PA/CF	1992	D	2,807*	176' 09"	42' 03"	13' 06"
Built: Port Weller Dry Docks, Port Weller, ON; ferry from Leamington/Kingsville, ON, to Pelee Island								
Pelee Islander	5273274	PA/CF	1960	D	334*	145' 00"	32' 00"	10' 00"
Built: Erieau Shipbuilding & Drydock Co. Ltd., Erieau, ON; ferry from Leamington/Kingsville, ON, to Pelee Island								
Pelee Islander II		PA/CF	2018	D	3,147*	222' 00"	48' 50"	15' 09
Built: Asenav, Santiago, Chile; new ferry from Leamington/Kingsville, ON								

Fleet Name Vessel Name	Vessel IMO #	Vessel Type	Year Built	Engine Type	Cargo Cap. or Gross*	Overall Length	Vessel Breadth	Vessel Depth
Quinte Loyalist	5358062	PA/CF	1954	D	204*	127' 00"	32' 00"	8' 00"

Built: Erieau Shipbuilding & Drydock Co. Ltd., Erieau, ON; service to Wolfe Island/Kingston and Glenora/Adolphustown, ON

Wolfe Islander III	7423079	PA/CF	1975	D	985*	205' 00"	68' 00"	6' 00"

Built: Port Arthur Shipbuilding Co., Port Arthur, ON; ferry from Kingston, ON, to Wolfe Island, ON

MJO CONTRACTING INC., HANCOCK, MI (mjocontracting.com)

Lily North		TB	1986	D	85*	60' 00"	16' 00"	10' 02"

MONTREAL PORT AUTHORITY, MONTREAL, QC (port-montreal.com)

Denis M		TB	1942	D	21*	46' 07"	12' 08"	4' 01"

Built: Russel Brothers Ltd., Owen Sound, ON (Marcel D.)

Maisonneuve	7397749	PA	1972	D	84*	63' 10"	20' 07"	9' 03"

Built: Fercraft Marine Inc., Ste. Catherine D'Alexandrie, QC

MUNISING BAY SHIPWRECK TOURS INC., MUNISING, MI (shipwrecktours.com)

Miss Munising		ES	1967	D	50*	60' 00"	14' 00"	4' 04"

MUNISING PIRATE CRUISES, MUNISING, MI (munisingpiratecruises.com)

Good Fortune		PA	2015	D	57*	64' 80"	19' 00"	7' 00"

MUSIQUE AQUATIQUE CRUISE LINES INC., TORONTO, ON (citysightseeingtoronto.com)

Harbour Star		ES	1978	D	45*	63' 06"	15' 09"	3' 09"

MUSKOKA STEAMSHIPS & DISCOVERY CENTRE, GRAVENHURST, ON (realmuskoka.com)

Segwun		PA	1887	R	308*	128' 00"	24' 00"	7' 06"

Built: Melancthon Simpson, Toronto, ON (Nipissing {2} 1887-'25)

Wenonah II	8972003	PA	2001	D	447*	127' 00"	28' 00"	6' 00"

Built: McNally Construction Inc., Belleville, ON

MYSTIC BLUE CRUISES INC., CHICAGO, IL (mysticbluecruises.com)

Mystic Blue		PA	1998	D	97*	138' 09"	36' 00"	10' 05"

Built: Chesapeake Shipbuilding Corp., Salisbury, MD

N

NADRO MARINE SERVICES LTD., PORT DOVER, ON (nadromarine.com)

Ecosse	8624682	TB	1979	D	142*	91' 00"	26' 00"	8' 06"

Built: Hike Metal Products Ltd., Wheatley, ON (R & L No. 1 '79-'96)

Intrepid III		TB	1976	D	39*	66' 00"	17' 00"	7' 06"

Built: Halter Marine Ltd., Chalmette, LA

Seahound		TB	1941	D	57*	65' 00"	18' 00"	8' 00"

Built: Equitable Equipment Co., New Orleans, LA ([Unnamed] '41-'56, Sea Hound '56-'80, Carolyn Jo '80-'00)

Vac		TB	1942	D	36*	65' 00"	20' 04"	4' 03"

Built: George Gamble, Port Dover, ON

Vigilant I	8994178	TB	1944	D	111*	79' 06"	20' 11"	10' 02"

Built: Russell Brothers Ltd., Owen Sound, ON (HMCS Glenlivet [W-43] '44-'75, Glenlivet II '75-'77, Canadian Franko '77-'82, Glenlivet II '82-'00)

NAUTICA QUEEN CRUISE DINING, CLEVELAND, OH (nauticaqueen.com)

Nautica Queen		ES	1981	D	95*	124' 00"	31' 02"	8' 09"

Built: Blount Marine Corp., Warren, RI (Bay Queen '81-'85, Arawanna Queen '85-'88, Star of Nautica '88-'92)

NAUTICAL ADVENTURES, TORONTO, ON (nauticaladventure.com)

Empire Sandy	5071561	ES/3S	1943	D/W	338*	140' 00"	32' 08"	14' 00"

Built: Clellands Ltd., Wellington Quay-on-Tyne, England (Empire Sandy '43-'48, Ashford '48-'52, Chris M. '52-'79)

NEAS (NUNAVUT EASTERN ARCTIC SHIPPING), MONTREAL, QC (neas.ca)

Vessels offer service between St. Lawrence River ports and the Canadian Arctic between July and November

Avataq	8801618	GC	1989	D	9,653	370' 07"	62' 00"	37' 00"

Built: Miho Shipbuilding Co. Ltd., Shimizu Shizuoka Prefecture, Japan; operated by Spliethoff's, Amsterdam, Netherlands (Poleca, Mekhanik Volkosh, Tiger Speed, Lootsgracht)

Mitiq	9081306	GC	1995	D	12,754	447' 04"	62' 00"	38' 03"

Built: Frisian Shipbuilding Welgelegen B.V., Harlingen, Netherlands; operated by Spliethoff's, Amsterdam, Netherlands (Emmagracht '95-'13)

Nunalik	9466996	HL	2009	D	12,837	453' 00"	68' 11"	36' 01"

Built: Jiandong Shipyard, Jianfong, China; operated by Spliethoff's, Amsterdam, Netherlands (Beluga Fairy '09-'11, HHL Amazon '11-'16, Hemgracht '16-'17)

Qamutik	9081289	GC	1995	D	12,760	446' 00"	62' 00"	38' 02"

Built: Frisian Shipbuilding Welgelegen B.V., Harlingen, Netherlands; operated by Spliethoff's, Amsterdam, Netherlands (Edisongracht)

Umiavut	8801591	GC	1988	D	9,653	370' 07"	63' 01"	37' 00"

Built: Miho Shipbuilding Co. Ltd., Shimizu Shizuoka Prefecture, Japan; operated by Spliethoff's, Amsterdam, Netherlands (Completed as Newca; Kapitan Silin '88-'92, Lindengracht '92-'00)

Fleet Name Vessel Name	Vessel IMO #	Vessel Type	Year Built	Engine Type	Cargo Cap. or Gross*	Overall Length	Vessel Breadth	Vessel Depth
NEW YORK POWER AUTHORITY, LEWISTON, NY								
Breaker		IB/TB	1962	D	29*	43' 03"	14' 03"	5' 00"
Daniel Joncaire		IB/TB	1979	D	25*	43' 03"	15' 00"	5' 00"
Joncaire II		IB/TB	2015	D	47*	45' 00"	19' 07"	6' 01"
William H. Latham		IB/TB	1987	D	77*	61' 00"		
NEW YORK DEPARTMENT OF ENVIRONMENTAL CONSERVATION, LAKE ONTARIO UNIT, ALBANY, NY								
Seth Green		RV	1984	D	50*	47' 00"	17' 00"	8' 00"
NEW YORK STATE MARINE HIGHWAY TRANSPORTATION CO., TROY, NY (nysmarinehighway.com)								
Benjamin Elliot		TB	1960	D	27*	47' 07"	15' 02"	7' 02"
Built: Gladding-Hearn Shipbuilding, Somerset, MA (El-Jean '60-'62)								
Frances	5119246	TB	1957	D	146*	84' 08"	24' 00"	9' 06"
Built: Jakobson Shipyard, Oyster Bay, NY (Frances Turecamo '57-'12)								
Margot	5222043	TB	1958	D	141*	90' 00"	25' 00"	10' 00"
Built: Jakobson Shipyard, Oyster Bay, NY (Hustler II '58-'62, Margot Moran '62-'90, Jolene Rose '90-'93)								
NOAA GREAT LAKES ENVIRONMENTAL RESEARCH LABORATORY, ANN ARBOR, MI (glerl.noaa.gov)								
Huron Explorer		RV	1979	D	15*	41' 00"	14' 08"	4' 08"
Laurentian		RV	1974	D	129*	80' 00"	21' 06"	11' 00"
Shenehon		SV	1953	D	90*	65' 00"	17' 00"	6' 00"
NORTH CHANNEL TRANSPORT LLC, ALGONAC, MI								
Islander {2}		PA/CF	1967	D	38*	41' 00"	15' 00"	3' 06"
NORTH SHORE SCENIC CRUISES, SILVER BAY, MN (scenicsuperior.com)								
Wenonah		ES	1960	D	91*	70' 07"	19' 04"	9' 07"
NORTH SHORE MARINE TERMINAL & LOGISTICS, ESCANABA, MI (basicmarine.com)								
Erika Kobasic	8654235	TB	1939	DE	226*	110' 00"	25' 01"	14' 03"
Built: Gulfport Shipbuilding, Port Arthur, TX (USCGC Arundel [WYT / WYTM-90] '39-'84, Karen Andrie '84-'90)								
Escort		TB	1969	D	26*	50' 00"	14' 00"	6' 03"
Built: Jakobson Shipyard, Oyster Bay, NY								
Krystal		TB	1954	D	23*	45' 02"	12' 08"	6' 00"
Built: Roamer Boat Co., Holland, MI (ST-2168 '54-'62, Thunder Bay '62-'02)								
Nickelena	8654247	TB	1973	D	240*	109' 00"	30' 07"	15' 08"
Built: Marinette Marine Corp., Marinette, WI (USS Chetek [YTB-827] '73-'96, Chetek '96-'00, Koziol '00-'08)								
NORTHERN MARINE TRANSPORTATION INC., SAULT STE. MARIE, MI								
Linda Jean		PB	1950	D	17*	38' 00"	10' 00"	5' 00"
Pilot boat based at DeTour, MI								
Western Pilot		PB	1979	D	21*	40' 70"	13' 05"	5' 09"
Pilot boat based at DeTour, MI								

Robert S. Pierson waiting to unload at Clarkson, ON. Algoma Sault is opposite. (Ted Wilush)

NOVAALGOMA CEMENT CARRIERS LTD., ST. CATHARINES, ON *(www.novaalgomacc.com)*
A PARTNERSHIP BETWEEN ALGOMA CENTRAL CORP. AND NOVA MARINE HOLDINGS SA

Fleet Name / Vessel Name	IMO #	Type	Year	Engine	Cargo/Gross	Length	Breadth	Depth
NACC Alicudi	9586435	CC	2011	D	5,566	393' 03"	55' 01"	26' 11"

Built: Karis Shipping Limited, Valletta, Malta; vessel registered in Malta but serves customers on Lake Ontario seasonally

NACC Argonaut	9287302	CC	2003	D	9,255	447' 07"	69' 07"	37' 01

Built: Kyokuyo Shipyard Corp., Shimonoseki, Japan; converted to a cement carrier in '18 (Arklow Wave '03-'16, NACC Toronto '16-'18)

THE FOLLOWING VESSEL UNDER CHARTER TO McINNIS CEMENT, MONTREAL, QC

NACC Quebec	9546057	CC	2011	D	10,246	359' 02"	68' 11"	34' 09

Built: Tuzla Gemi Endustrisi A.S., Tuzla, Turkey; converted to a cement carrier in '16 (Tenace '11-'16)

O-P

OAK GROVE & MARINE TRANSPORTATION INC., CLAYTON, NY

Maple Grove		PK	1954	D	55*	73' 07"	20' 00"	9' 00"
(LCM 8168)								

ODYSSEY CRUISES, CHICAGO, IL *(odysseycruises.com/chicago)*

Odyssey II		ES	1993	D	88*	162' 05"	40' 00"	13' 05"

OFFSHORE DREDGING & CONSTRUCTION INC., MUSKEGON, MI

Andrew J.		TB	1972	D	31*	43' 08"	14' 03"	7' 05"

OHIO DEPARTMENT OF NATURAL RESOURCES, COLUMBUS, OH *(dnr.state.oh.us)*

Explorer II		RV	1999	D		53' 00"	15' 05"	4' 05"
Grandon		RV	1990	D	47*	47' 00"	16' 00"	5' 05"

OLSON DREDGE & DOCK CO., ALGONAC, MI

John Michael		TB	1913	D	41*	55' 04"	15' 01"	7' 06"

Built: Cowles Shipyard Co., Buffalo, NY (Colonel Ward '13-'23, Ross Coddington '24-'65, Joseph J. Olivieri '65-'80)

OLYMPIA CRUISE LINE INC., THORNHILL, ON *(torontocruises.com)*

Enterprise 2000		ES	1998	D	370*	121' 06"	35' 00"	6' 00"

ONTARIO MINISTRY OF NATURAL RESOURCES, PETERBOROUGH, ON *(mnr.gov.on.ca)*

Erie Explorer		RV	1981	D	72*	53' 05"	20' 01"	4' 08"

Built: Hopper Fisheries Ltd., Port Stanley, ON (Janice H.X. '81-'97)

Huron Explorer I		RV	2010	D	112*	62' 00"	21' 03"	6' 00"

Built: Hike Metal Products Ltd., Wheatley, ON

Keenosay		RV	1957	D	68*	51' 04"	20' 07"	2' 07"

Built: S.G. Powell Shipyard Ltd., Dunnville, ON

USCG Morro Bay hoisted ashore at Cleveland for inspection. *(Great Lakes Group)*

Fleet Name Vessel Name	Vessel IMO #	Vessel Type	Year Built	Engine Type	Cargo Cap. or Gross*	Overall Length	Vessel Breadth	Vessel Depth
Nipigon Osprey		RV	1990	D	33*	42' 04"	14' 09"	6' 08"
Built: Kanter Yachts Corp., St. Thomas, ON								
Ontario Explorer		RV	2009	D	84*	64' 09"	21' 03"	6' 00"
Built: Hike Metal Products Ltd., Wheatley, ON								

ONTARIO POWER GENERATION INC., TORONTO, ON

Fleet Name Vessel Name	Vessel IMO #	Vessel Type	Year Built	Engine Type	Cargo Cap. or Gross*	Overall Length	Vessel Breadth	Vessel Depth
Niagara Queen II		IB	1992	D	58*	56' 01"	18' 00"	6' 08"
Built: Hike Metal Products Ltd., Wheatley, ON								

OPEN LAKE GROUP LLC, DETROIT, MI (openlakegroup.com)

Cheyenne	6515851	TB	1965	D	146*	84' 05"	25' 03"	12' 06"
Built: Ira S. Bushey and Sons Inc., Brooklyn, NY (Glenwood '65-'70)								

OWEN SOUND TRANSPORTATION CO., OWEN SOUND, ON (ontarioferries.com)

Chi-Cheemaun	7343607	PA/CF	1974	D	6,991*	365' 05"	61' 00"	21' 00"
Built: Canadian Shipbuilding and Engineering Ltd., Collingwood, ON								

PERE MARQUETTE SHIPPING CO., LUDINGTON, MI (pmship.com)

Pere Marquette 41	5073894	SU	1941	B	3,413*	403' 00"	58' 00"	23' 05"
Built: Manitowoc Shipbuilding Co., Manitowoc, WI; converted from powered train/car ferry to a self-unloading barge in '97 (City of Midland 41 '41-'97)								
Undaunted	8963210	AT	1943	DE	569*	143' 00"	38' 00"	18' 00"
Built: Gulfport Boiler/Welding, Port Arthur, TX; paired with barge Pere Marquette 41 (USS Undaunted [ATR-126, ATA-199] '44-'63, USMA Kings Pointer '63-'93, Krystal K. '93-'97)								

PICTON TERMINALS, PICTON, ON (pictonterminals.ca)

Sheri Lynn S		TB	2017	D	55*	52' 03"	18' 02"	9' 05"
Built: Damen Shipyards, Gorinchem, Netherlands								

PICTURED ROCKS CRUISES INC., MUNISING, MI (picturedrocks.com)

Grand Island {2}		ES	1989	D	52*	68' 00"	16' 01"	7' 01"
Grand Portal		ES	2004	D	76*	64' 08"	20' 00"	8' 04"
Miners Castle		ES	1974	D	82*	68' 00"	16' 06"	6' 04"
Miss Superior		ES	1984	D	83*	68' 00"	16' 09"	10' 04"
Pictured Rocks		ES	1972	D	53*	55' 07"	13' 07"	4' 04"
Pictured Rocks Express		ES	1988	D	90*	82' 07"	28' 06"	4' 04"

PIONEER CRUISES, TORONTO, ON (pioneercruises.com)

Pioneer Princess		ES	1984	D	96*	56' 00"	17' 01"	3' 09"
Pioneer Queen		ES	1968	D	110*	85' 00"	30' 06"	7' 03"
(Peche Island III '68-'71, Papoose IV '71-'96)								

PLAUNT TRANSPORTATION CO. INC., CHEBOYGAN, MI (bbiferry.com)

Kristen D		CF	1987	D	83*	94' 11"	36' 00"	4' 06"

PORT CITY CRUISE LINES LLC, MUSKEGON, MI (aquastarcruises.com)

Aquastar		ES	1966	D	79*	64' 09"	27' 00"	5' 06"
Built: Blount Marine Corp., Warren, RI (Island Queen {1} '66-'87, Port City Princess '87-'18)								

PORTOFINO ON THE RIVER, WYANDOTTE, MI (portofinoontheriver.com)

Portofino		ES	1997	D	76*	80' 08"	20' 00"	6' 00"
Built: Skipper Liner, LaCrosse, WI (Island Girl X, Naples Royal Princess, Romantics, Infinity, The Jude Thaddeus, Infinity, Jacksonville Princess II, Miami Magic)								

PRESQUE ISLE BOAT TOURS, ERIE, PA (piboattours.com)

Lady Kate {2}		ES	1952	D	11*	59' 03"	15' 00"	3' 09"
(G.A. Boeckling II, Cedar Point III, Island Trader '89-'97)								

PURE MICHIGAN BOAT CRUISES LLC, MUNISING, MI (puremichiganboatcruises.com)

Isle Royale Queen III		PA	1959	D	88*	74' 03"	18' 04"	6' 05"
Built: T.D. Vinette Co., Escanaba, MI (Isle Royale Queen II)								

PURVIS MARINE LTD., SAULT STE. MARIE, ON (purvismarine.com)

Adanac III		TB	1913	D	108*	80' 03"	19' 03"	9' 10"
Built: Western Drydock & Shipbuilding Co., Port Arthur, ON (Edward C. Whalen '13-'66, John McLean '66-'95)								
Anglian Lady	5141483	TB	1953	D	398*	132' 00"	31' 00"	14' 00"
Built: John I. Thornecroft & Co., Southampton, England (Hamtun '53-'72, Nathalie Letzer '72-'88)								
Avenger IV	5401297	TB	1962	D	291*	120' 00"	30' 00"	19' 00"
Built: Cochrane & Sons Ltd., Selby, Yorkshire, England (Avenger '62-'85)								
G.L.B. No. 2		DB	1953	B	3,215	240' 00"	50' 00"	12' 00"
Built: Ingalls Shipbuilding Corp., Birmingham, AL (Jane Newfield '53-'66, ORG 6502 '66-'75)								
Malden		DB	1946	B	1,075	150' 00"	41' 09"	10' 03"
Built: Russel Brothers Ltd., Owen Sound, ON								

USCG icebreaker Mackinaw working above the Soo Locks as deer supervise. *(Graham Grattan)*

Right: Tug Missouri working at the Soo. *(Garryn Ordiway)*

Edwin H. Gott heads out of Duluth, MN, eastbound on Lake Superior. *(Paul Scinocca)*

Fleet Name / Vessel Name	Vessel IMO #	Vessel Type	Year Built	Engine Type	Cargo Cap. or Gross*	Overall Length	Vessel Breadth	Vessel Depth
Martin E. Johnson		TB	1959	D	26*	47' 00"	16' 00"	7' 00"
Built: Russel Hipworth Engines Ltd, Owen Sound, ON								
Osprey		TB	1944	D	36*	45' 00"	13' 06"	7' 00"
Built: Kewaunee Shipbuilding and Engineering Corp., Kewaunee, WI (ST-606 '43-'46)								
PML 2501		TK	1980	B	1,954*	302' 00"	52' 00"	17' 00"
Built: Cenac Shipyard, Houma, LA (CTCO 2505 '80-'96)								
PML 9000		DB	1968	B	4,285*	400' 00"	76' 00"	20' 00"
Built: Bethlehem Steel – Shipbuilding Division, San Francisco, CA (Palmer '68-'00)								
PML Alton		DB	1933		150	93' 00"	30' 00"	8' 00"
Built: McClintic- Marshall, Sturgeon Bay, WI								
PML Ironmaster		DB	1962	B	7,437*	360' 00"	75' 00"	25' 00"
Built: Yarrows Ltd., Esquimalt, BC (G.T. Steelmaster, Ceres, American Gulf VII, Seaspan 241, G.T. Ironmaster)								
PML Tucci		CS	1958	B	601*	150' 00"	52' 00"	10' 00"
Built: Calumet Shipyard & Drydock Co., Chicago, IL (MCD '58-'73, Minnesota '73-'88, Candace Andrie '88-'08)								
PML Tucker		DS	1971		477*	140' 00"	50' 00"	9' 00"
Built: Twin City Shipyard, St. Paul, MN (Illinois '71-'02, Meredith Andrie '02-'08)								
Reliance	7393808	TB	1974	D	708*	148' 03"	35' 07"	21' 07"
Built: Ulstein Hatlo A/S, Ulsteinvik, Norway (Sinni '74-'81, Irving Cedar '81-'96, Atlantic Cedar '96-'02)								
Rocket		TB	1901	D	40*	73' 00"	16' 00"	7' 00"
Built: Buffalo Shipbuilding Co., Buffalo, NY								
Tecumseh II		DB	1976	B	2,500	180' 00"	54' 00"	12' 00"
Built: Bergeron Machine Shop Inc., New Orleans, LA								
Wilfred M. Cohen	7629271	TB	1947	D	284*	102' 06"	28' 00"	15' 00"
Built: Newport News Shipbuilding and Drydock Co., Newport News, VA (A. T. Lowmaster '48-'75)								
W. I. Scott Purvis	5264819	TB	1938	D	203*	96' 00"	26' 00"	10' 00"
Built: Marine Industries, Sorel, QC (Orient Bay '38-'75, Guy M. No. 1 '75-'90)								
W.J. Isaac Purvis	318726	TB	1962	D	71*	72' 00"	19' 00"	12' 00"
Built: McNamara Marine Ltd., Toronto, ON (Angus M. '62-'92, Omni Sorel '92-'02, Joyce B. Gardiner '02-'09)								
W. J. Ivan Purvis	5217218	TB	1938	D	190*	100' 00"	26' 00"	10' 00"
Built: Marine Industries, Sorel, QC (Magpie '38-'66, Dana T. Bowen '66-'75)								

PUT-IN-BAY BOAT LINE CO., PORT CLINTON, OH *(jet-express.com)*

Fleet Name / Vessel Name	Vessel IMO #	Vessel Type	Year Built	Engine Type	Cargo Cap. or Gross*	Overall Length	Vessel Breadth	Vessel Depth
Jet Express		PF/CA	1989	D	93*	92' 08"	28' 06"	8' 04"
Jet Express II		PF/CA	1992	D	85*	92' 06"	28' 06"	8' 04"
Jet Express III		PF/CA	2001	D	70*	78' 02"	27' 06"	8' 02"
Jet Express IV		PF/CA	1995	D	71*	77' 02"	28' 05"	7' 07"

Q-R

QUEBEC PORT AUTHORITY, QUÉBEC, QC *(portquebec.ca)*

Fleet Name / Vessel Name	Vessel IMO #	Vessel Type	Year Built	Engine Type	Cargo Cap. or Gross*	Overall Length	Vessel Breadth	Vessel Depth
Le Cageux		TB	2011	D	24*	42' 06"	16' 01"	7' 07"
Built: Meridien Maritime Reparation Inc., Matane, QC								

QUYON FERRY, QUYON, QC *(quyonferry.com)*

Fleet Name / Vessel Name	Vessel IMO #	Vessel Type	Year Built	Engine Type	Cargo Cap. or Gross*	Overall Length	Vessel Breadth	Vessel Depth
Grant Beattie (The)		PF	2013		235*	115' 00"	46' 00"	7' 05"

RIO TINTO-ALCAN INC., LA BAIE, QC *(riotintoalcan.com)*

Fleet Name / Vessel Name	Vessel IMO #	Vessel Type	Year Built	Engine Type	Cargo Cap. or Gross*	Overall Length	Vessel Breadth	Vessel Depth
Fjord Éternité	9364348	TT	2006	D	381*	94' 00"	36' 05"	16' 04"
Built: East Isle Shipyard, Georgetown, PEI (Stevns Icecap '06-'07, Svitzer Nanna '07-'11, Stevns Icecap '10-'11)								
Fjord Saguenay	9351012	TT	2006	D	381*	94' 00"	36' 05"	16' 04"
Built: East Isle Shipyard, Georgetown, PEI (Stevns Iceflower '06-'07, Svitzer Njord '07-'09, Stevns Iceflower '09-'09)								

ROCKPORT BOAT LINE LTD., ROCKPORT, ON *(rockportcruises.com)*

Fleet Name / Vessel Name	Vessel IMO #	Vessel Type	Year Built	Engine Type	Cargo Cap. or Gross*	Overall Length	Vessel Breadth	Vessel Depth
Canada Spirit		ES	1976	D	325*	92' 00"	26' 00"	10' 00"
Built: Marlin Yacht Co., Summerstown, ON (Cayuga II '76-'82, Wayward Princess '82-'17)								
Chief Shingwauk		ES	1965	D	109*	70' 00"	24' 00"	4' 06"
Built: Hike Metal Products, Wheatley, ON								
Ida M.		ES	1970	D	29*	55' 00"	14' 00"	3' 00"
Ida M. II		ES	1973	D	121*	63' 02"	22' 02"	5' 00"
Sea Prince II		ES	1978	D	172*	83' 00"	24' 02"	6' 08"

REINAUER TRANSPORTATION COS., STATEN ISLAND, NY *(reinauer.com)*

Fleet Name / Vessel Name	Vessel IMO #	Vessel Type	Year Built	Engine Type	Cargo Cap. or Gross*	Overall Length	Vessel Breadth	Vessel Depth
Dylan Cooper	9769934	TB	2015	D	199*	113' 00"	35' 99"	18' 01"
Built: SENESCO Marine, North Kingston, RI; paired with barge RTC 108								
RTC 108		TK	2015	B	206*	413' 02"	74' 00"	26' 05

ROEN SALVAGE CO., STURGEON BAY, WI *(roensalvage.com)*

Fleet Name / Vessel Name	Vessel IMO #	Vessel Type	Year Built	Engine Type	Cargo Cap. or Gross*	Overall Length	Vessel Breadth	Vessel Depth
Chas. Asher		TB	1967	D	39*	49' 02"	17' 06"	6' 10"
Built: Sturgeon Bay Shipbuilding Co., Sturgeon Bay, WI								

John R. Asher		TB	1943	D	93*	68' 09"	20' 00"	8' 00"
Built: Platzer Boat Works, Houston, TX (U. S. Army ST-71 '43-'46, Russell 8 '46-'64, Reid McAllister '64-'67, Donegal '67-'85)								
Louie S.		TB	1956	D	10*	37' 00"	12' 00"	4' 05"
Spuds		TB	1944	D	19*	42' 00"	12' 05"	5' 04"
Built: Roen Salvage Co., Sturgeon Bay, WI								
Stephan M. Asher		TB	1954	D	60*	65' 00"	19' 01"	5' 04"
Built: Burton Shipyard Inc., Port Arthur, TX (Captain Bennie '54-'82, Dumar Scout '82-'87)								
Timmy A.		TB	1953	D	12*	33' 06"	10' 08"	5' 02"
Built: M.D. Moody & Sons, Jacksonville, FL (Calhoun '53-'64)								

RYBA MARINE CONSTRUCTION CO., CHEBOYGAN, MI (rybamarine.com)

Amber Mae		TB	1922	D	67*	65' 00"	14' 01"	10' 00"
Built: Glove Shipyard Inc., Buffalo, NY (E. W. Sutton '22-'52, Venture '52- '00)								
Kathy Lynn	8034887	TB	1944	D	140*	85' 00"	24' 00"	9' 06"
Built: Decatur Iron & Steel Co., Decatur, AL (U. S. Army ST-693 '44-'79, Sea Islander '79-'91)								
Kristin Joelle	6604016	TB	1965	D	148*	75' 05"	24' 00"	8' 06"
(Vincent J. Robin IV, Betty Smith, Seacor Enterprise '91-'97, Leo '97-'98, Ybor '98-'99, Capt. Sweet '99-'01, Susan McAllister '01-'15, Michigan '15-'17)								
Rochelle Kaye		TB	1963	D	52*	51' 06"	19' 04"	7' 00"
Built: St. Charles Steel Works Inc., Thibodeaux, LA (Jaye Anne '63-?, Katanni ?-'97)								
Thomas R. Morrish		TB	1980	D	88*	64' 00"	14' 05"	8' 06"
Built: Houma Shipbuilding Co., Houma, LA (Lady Ora '80-'99, Island Eagle '99-'04, Captain Zeke '01-'14)								

S

SAIL DOOR COUNTY, SISTER BAY, WI (saildoorcounty.com)

Edith M. Becker		PA	1984	D/W	22*	62' 00"	24' 00"	8' 06"

SAND PRODUCTS CORP., MUSKEGON, MI

LAKE SERVICE SHIPPING, MUSKEGON, MI

McKee Sons	5216458	SU	1945	B	19,900	579' 02"	71' 06"	38' 06"
Built: Sun Shipbuilding and Drydock Co., Chester, PA; converted from a saltwater vessel to a self-unloading Great Lakes bulk carrier by Maryland Drydock, Baltimore, MD, in '52; completed as a self-unloader by Manitowoc Shipbuilding Co., Manitowoc, WI, in '53; converted to a self-unloading barge by Upper Lakes Towing, Escanaba, MI, in '91; laid up at Erie, PA, 2012-14 and Muskegon, MI, since Dec. 20, 2014 (USNS Marine Angel '45-'52)								

MICHIGAN-OHIO BARGE LLC, MUSKEGON, MI

Commander		CC	1957	B	TBA	390' 00"	71' 00"	27' 00"
Built: Todd Shipyards Corp., Houston, TX; converted to a cement carrier '17-'18 at Bay Shipbuilding Co., Sturgeon Bay, WI (M-211 '57-'81, Virginia '81-'88, C-11 '88-'93, Kellstone 1 '93-'04, Cleveland Rocks '04-'18)								

PORT CITY MARINE SERVICES, MUSKEGON, MI (portcitymarine.com)

Bradshaw McKee	7644312	ATB	1977	D	174*	121' 06"	34' 06"	18' 02"
Built: Toche Enterprises Inc., Ocean Springs, MS; paired with barge St. Marys Conquest (Lady Elda '77-'78, Kings Challenger '78-'78, ITM No. 1 '78-'81, Kings Challenger '81-'86, Susan W. Hannah '86-'11)								
Colleen McAllister	7338872	TB	1967	D	194*	124' 00"	31' 06"	13' 08"
Built: Gulfport Shipbuilding Corp., Port Arthur, TX; laid up at Muskegon, MI (Ellena Hicks '67-'03)								
Katie G. McAllister	7046089	TB	1966	D	194*	124' 00"	31' 06"	13' 08"
Built: Gulfport Shipbuilding Corp., Port Arthur, TX; laid up at Muskegon, MI (Libby Black '67-'03)								
Prentiss Brown	7035547	TB	1967	D	197*	123' 05"	31' 06"	19' 00"
Built: Gulfport Shipbuilding, Port Arthur, TX; paired with barge St. Marys Challenger (Betty Culbreath '67-'03, Micheala McAllister '03-'09)								
St. Marys Challenger	5009984	CC	1906	B	N/A	N/A	56' 00"	31' 00"
Built: Great Lakes Engineering Works, Ecorse, MI; repowered in '50; converted to a self-unloading cement carrier by Manitowoc Shipbuilding Co., Manitowoc, WI, in '67; converted to a barge by Bay Shipbuilding Co., Sturgeon Bay, WI, over the winter of 2013-'14 (William P. Snyder '06-'26, Elton Hoyt II {1} '26-'52, Alex D. Chisholm '52-'66, Medusa Challenger '66-'99, Southdown Challenger '99-'04)								
St. Marys Conquest	5015012	CC	1937	B	8,500	437' 06"	55' 00"	28' 00"
Built: Manitowoc Shipbuilding Co., Manitowoc, WI; converted from a powered tanker to a self-unloading cement barge by Bay Shipbuilding, Sturgeon Bay, WI, in '87 (Red Crown '37-'62, Amoco Indiana '62-'87, Medusa Conquest '87-'99, Southdown Conquest '99-'04)								

SEA SERVICE LLC, SUPERIOR, WI (seaservicellc.com)

Sea Bear		PB	1959	D	28*	45' 08"	13' 08"	7' 00"
Provides pilot service at Duluth, MN								

SEAWAY MARINE GROUP LLC, CLAYTON, NY (seawaymarinegroup.com)

Seaway Supplier		GC	1952	D	97*	73' 06"	21' 00"	9' 04"
(LCM-8010)								

SELVICK MARINE TOWING CORP., STURGEON BAY, WI (selvickmarinetowing.com)

Fleet Name Vessel Name	Vessel IMO #	Vessel Type	Year Built	Engine Type	Cargo Cap. or Gross*	Overall Length	Vessel Breadth	Vessel Depth
Cameron O		TB	1955	D	26*	50' 00"	15' 00"	7' 03"
Built: Peterson Builders Inc., Sturgeon Bay, WI (Escort II '55-'06)								
Donny S	7436234	TB	1950	DE	461*	143' 00"	33' 01"	14' 06"
Built: Levingston Shipbuilding, Orange, TX (U. S. Army ATA-230 '49-'72, G. W. Codrington '72-'52, William P. Feeley {2} '52-'72, William W. Stender '72-'76, Mary Page Hannah '76-'14)								
Jacquelyn Yvonne		TB	1943	D	29*	45' 02"	12' 10"	7' 08"
Built: Sturgeon Bay Shipbuilding, Sturgeon Bay, WI (ST-173 '43-'55, Manistee '55-'87, Robert W. Purcell '87-'17)								
Jimmy L		TB	1939	D	148*	110' 00"	25' 00"	13' 00"
Built: Defoe Shipbuilding Co., Bay City, MI (USCGC Naugatuck [WYT / WYTM-92] '39-'80, Timmy B. '80-'84)								
Sharon M. Selvick		TB	1943	D	28*	45' 05"	12' 10"	7' 01"
Built: Kewaunee Shipbuilding & Engineering, Kewaunee, WI (U. S. Army ST-585 '43-'49, USCOE Judson '49-'94)								
Susan L		TB	1944	D	133*	86' 00"	23' 00"	10' 04"
Built: Equitable Equipment Co., New Orleans, LA (U. S. Army ST-709 '44-'47, USCOE Stanley '47-'99)								
William C. Gaynor	8423818	TB	1956	D	187*	94' 00"	27' 00"	11' 09"
Built: Defoe Shipbuilding Co., Bay City, MI (William C. Gaynor '56-'88, Captain Barnaby '88-'02)								
William C. Selvick	5322623	TB	1944	D	142*	85' 00"	23' 00"	9' 07"
Built: Platzer Boat Works, Houston, TX (U. S. Army ST-500 '44-'49, Sherman H. Serre '49-'77)								

SHELL CANADA LTD., CALGARY, AB

Juno Marie	9301641	RT	2004	D	2,191	262' 05"	45' 04"	22' 00"
Built: Miura Shipbuilding, Saiki, Japan; stationed at Montreal, QC (Alios Apollo '04-'10, Elin Apollo '10-'12, Milo '12-'16)								

SHEPLER'S MACKINAC ISLAND FERRY, MACKINAW CITY, MI (sheplersferry.com)

Capt. Shepler		PF	1986	D	71*	84' 00"	21' 00"	7' 10"
Felicity		PF	1972	D	65*	65' 00"	18' 01"	8' 03"
Hope (The)		PF	1975	D	87*	77' 00"	20' 00"	8' 03"
Miss Margy		PF	2015	D	70*	85' 00"	22' 00"	
Sacré Bleu		PK	1959	D	98*	94' 10"	31' 00"	9' 09"
The Welcome		PF	1969	D	66*	60' 06"	16' 08"	8' 02"
Wyandot		PF	1979	D	83*	77' 00"	20' 00"	8' 00"

SHORELINE CHARTERS, GILLS ROCK, WI (shorelinecharters.net)

The Shoreline		ES	1973	D	12*	33' 00"	11' 4"	3' 00"

SHORELINE CONTRACTORS INC., WELLINGTON, OH (shorelinecontractors.com)

Eagle		TB	1943	D	31*	57' 07"	35' 09"	6' 08"
Built: Defoe Shipbuilding Co., Bay City, MI (Jack Boyce '43-'78, Jan B. '78-'79, Sea Search II '79-'86)								
General		TB	1964	D	125*	63' 08"	15' 04"	6' 05"

Passenger ship Victory I at Mackinac Island, MI. (Brian Jaeshke)

Fleet Name / Vessel Name	Vessel IMO #	Vessel Type	Year Built	Engine Type	Cargo Cap. or Gross*	Overall Length	Vessel Breadth	Vessel Depth
SHORELINE SIGHTSEEING CO., CHICAGO, IL *(shorelinesightseeing.com)*								
Blue Dog		ES	1981	D	31*	47' 07"	18' 00"	5' 05"
Bright Star		ES	2003	D	93*	79' 03"	23' 00"	7' 01"
Cap Streeter		ES	1987	D	28*	63' 06"	24' 04"	7' 07"
Cityview		ES	2014	D	76*	75' 06"	34' 06"	5' 04"
Evening Star	(Tug/barge)	ES	2001	D	93*	83' 00"	23' 00"	7' 00"
Marlyn		ES	1961	D	70*	65' 00"	25' 00"	7' 00"
Riverview		ES	2013	D	76*	75' 06"	34' 06"	5' 04"
Shoreline II		ES	1987	D	89*	75' 00"	26' 00"	7' 01"
Skyview	(Tug/barge)	ES	2016	D	90*	94' 05"	35' 00"	7' 05"
Star of Chicago {2}		ES	1999	D	73*	64' 10"	22' 08"	7' 05"
Voyageur		ES	1983	D	98*	65' 00"	35' 00"	7' 00"
SNC-LAVALIN, MONTREAL, QC *(snclavalin.com)*								
Fervent		WB	2014	D	47*	56' 01"	26' 16"	6' 08"
Built: Boats Ltd., Wallasea Island, UK								
Intense		TB	2016	D	21*	41' 00"	14' 04"	7' 08"
Built: Besiktas Tersane A.S., Istanbul, Turkey								
Turbulent		TB	2016	D	38*	48' 06"	19' 00"	9' 02"
Built: Besiktas Tersane A.S., Istanbul, Turkey								
SOCIÉTÉ DES TRAVERSIERS DU QUÉBEC CITY, QUÉBEC, QC *(traversiers.gouv.qc.ca)*								
Alphonse-Desjardins	7109233	PA/CF	1971	D	1,741*	214' 00"	71' 06"	20' 00"
Built: Davie Shipbuilding Co., Lauzon, QC								
Armand-Imbeau	7902269	PA/CF	1980	D	1,285*	203' 07"	72' 00"	18' 04"
Built: Marine Industries Ltd., Sorel, QC								
Armand-Imbeau II	9703215	PA/CF	2018	D	5,000*	301' 08"		
Built: Davie Shipbuilding Co., Lauzon, QC								
Catherine-Legardeur	8409355	PA/CF	1985	D	1,348*	205' 09"	71' 10"	18' 10"
Built: Davie Shipbuilding Co., Lauzon, QC								
F.-A.-Gauthier	9669861	PA/CF	2015	DE	15,901*	436' 03"	73' 05"	26' 02"
Built: Fincantieri Castellammare di Stabia, Naples, Italy								
Felix-Antoine-Savard	9144706	PA/CF	1997	D	2,489*	272' 00"	70' 00"	21' 09"
Built: Davie Shipbuilding Co., Lauzon, QC (Fueled by liquid natural gas)								
Grue-des-Iles	8011732	PA/CF	1981	D	447*	155' 10"	41' 01"	12' 06"
Built: Bateaux Tur-Bec Ltd., Ste-Catherine, QC								
Ivan-Quinn	9554028	PA/CF	2008	D	241*	83' 07"	26' 09"	11' 03"
Built: Meridien Maritime Reparation Inc., Matane, QC								

Canadian Coast Guard icebreaker Terry Fox on Lake Ontario. She was on the Great Lakes for a refit in 2018. (Jeff Cameron)

Fleet Name Vessel Name	Vessel IMO #	Vessel Type	Year Built	Engine Type	Cargo Cap. or Gross*	Overall Length	Vessel Breadth	Vessel Depth
Jos-Deschenes	391571	PA/CF	1980	D	1,287*	203' 07"	72' 00"	18' 04"
Built: Marine Industries Ltd., Sorel, QC								
Jos-Deschenes II	9703227	PA/CF	2018	D	2.903*	286' 04"	85' 03"	22' 09""
Built: Davie Shipbuilding Co., Lauzon, QC								
Joseph-Savard	8409343	PA/CF	1985	D	1,445*	206' 00"	71' 10"	18' 10"
Built: Davie Shipbuilding Co., Lauzon, QC								
Lomer-Gouin	7109221	PA/CF	1971	D	1,741*	214' 00"	71' 06"	20' 00"
Built: Davie Shipbuilding Co., Lauzon, QC								
Lucien-L.	6721981	PA/CF	1967	D	867*	220' 10"	61' 06"	15' 05"
Built: Marine Industries Ltd., Sorel, QC								
Peter-Fraser		PA/CF	2012	DE	292*	110' 02"	39' 03"	7' 03"
Built: Chantier Naval Forillon, Gaspé, QC								
Radisson {1}		PA/CF	1954	D	1,037*	164' 03"	72' 00"	10' 06"
Built: Davie Shipbuilding Co., Lauzon, QC								
SOO LOCKS BOAT TOURS, SAULT STE. MARIE, MI *(soolocks.com)*								
Bide-A-Wee {3}		ES	1955	D	99*	64' 07"	23' 00"	7' 11"
Built: Blount Marine Corp., Warren, RI								
Hiawatha {2}		ES	1959	D	99*	64' 07"	23' 00"	7' 11"
Built: Blount Marine Corp., Warren, RI								
Holiday		ES	1957	D	99*	64' 07"	23' 00"	7' 11"
Built: Blount Marine Corp., Warren, RI								
Le Voyageur		ES	1959	D	70*	65' 00"	25' 00"	7' 00"
Built: Sturgeon Bay Shipbuilding & Dry Dock Co., Sturgeon Bay, WI								
Nokomis		ES	1959	D	70*	65' 00"	25' 00"	7' 00"
Built: Sturgeon Bay Shipbuilding & Dry Dock Co., Sturgeon Bay, WI								
SOO MARINE SUPPLY INC., SAULT STE. MARIE, MI *(soomarine.com)*								
Ojibway		SB	1945	D	53*	53' 00"	28' 00"	7' 00"
Built: Great Lakes Engineering Works, Ashtabula, OH								
SOO PILOT LLC, SAULT STE. MARIE, MI								
Soo Pilot		PB	1976	D	22*	41' 03"	13' 06"	5' 09"
Provides pilot service at Sault Ste. Marie, MI								

Fleet Name / Vessel Name	Vessel IMO #	Vessel Type	Year Built	Engine Type	Cargo Cap. or Gross*	Overall Length	Vessel Breadth	Vessel Depth
SOUTH SHORE DREDGE & DOCK INC., LORAIN, OHIO								
Cojak		TB	1954	D	11*	31' 04"	10' 09"	5' 06"
SOUTH STREET SEAPORT MUSEUM, NEW YORK, NY *(southstreetseaportmuseum.org)*								
Lettie G. Howard		2S	1893	W	58*	125' 00"	21' 00"	10' 06"
Built: Arthur D. Story, Essex, MA (Mystic C, Caviare)								
Seagoing museum ship was to sail out of Erie, PA, in 2019 as part of a collaboration with the Flagship Niagara League.								
SPIRIT CRUISES LLC, CHICAGO, IL *(spiritcruises.com/chicago)*								
Spirit of Chicago		ES	1988	D	92*	156' 00"	35' 00"	7' 01"
SPIRIT OF THE SOUND SCHOONER CO. LTD., PARRY SOUND, ON *(spiritofthesound.ca)*								
Chippewa III		PA	1954	D	47*	65' 00"	16' 00"	6' 06"
Built: Russel-Hipwell Engines Ltd., Owen Sound, ON (Maid of the Mist III '54-'56, Maid of the Mist '56-'92)								
ST. JAMES MARINE CO. & FOGG TOWING & MARINE, BEAVER ISLAND, MI *(stjamesmarine.com)*								
American Girl		TB	1922	D	63*	62' 00"	14' 00"	6' 05"
Built: Defoe Shipbuilding Co., Bay City, MI								
Wendy Anne		TB	1955	D	89*	71' 00"	20' 00"	8' 05"
Built: Smith Basin Drydock, Port Everglades, FL (ST-2199)								
ST. LAWRENCE CRUISE LINES INC., KINGSTON, ON *(stlawrencecruiselines.com)*								
Canadian Empress		PA	1981	D	463*	108' 00"	30' 00"	8' 00"
Built: Algan Shipyards Ltd., Gananoque, ON								
ST. LAWRENCE SEAWAY DEVELOPMENT CORP., MASSENA, NY *(www.seaway.dot.gov)*								
Grasse River		GL	1958	GL		150' 00"	65' 08"	5' 06"
Performance		TB	1997	D		50' 00"	16' 06"	7' 05"
Robinson Bay		TB	1958	DE	213*	103' 00"	26' 10"	14' 06"
Built: Christy Corp., Sturgeon Bay, WI								
Unnamed new construction		TB	2019	D		118' 11"	45' 00"	16' 01"
ST. LAWRENCE SEAWAY MANAGEMENT CORP., CORNWALL, ON *(greatlakes-seaway.com)*								
VM/S Hercules		GL	1962	D	2,107*	200' 00"	75' 00"	18' 08"
VM/S St. Lambert		TB	1974	D	20*	30' 08"	13' 01"	6' 05"

Stewart J. Cort on Lake Michigan, headed for Burns Harbor, IN. (Roger LeLievre)

Fleet Name / Vessel Name	Vessel IMO #	Vessel Type	Year Built	Engine Type	Cargo Cap. or Gross*	Overall Length	Vessel Breadth	Vessel Depth
ST. MARYS CEMENT INC., TORONTO, ON *(stmaryscement.com)*								
THE FOLLOWING VESSELS OPERATED BY FETTES SHIPPING, BURLINGTON, ON								
Sea Eagle II	7631860	ATB	1979	D	560*	132′00″	35′00″	19′00″
Built: Modern Marine Power Co., Houma, LA; paired with barge St. Marys Cement II (Sea Eagle '79-'81, Canmar Sea Eagle '81-'91)								
St. Marys Cement	8972077	CC	1986	B	9,400	360′00″	60′00″	23′03″
Built: Merce Industries East, Cleveland, OH								
St. Marys Cement II	8879914	CC	1978	B	19,513	496′06″	76′00″	35′00″
Built: Galveston Shipbuilding Co., Galveston, TX (Velasco '78-'81, Canmar Shuttle '81-'90)								
THE FOLLOWING VESSEL CHARTERED BY ST. MARYS CEMENT GROUP FROM GREAT LAKES & INTERNATIONAL TOWING & SALVAGE CO., BURLINGTON, ON								
Petite Forte	6826119	TB	1969	D	368*	127′00″	32′00″	14′06″
Built: Cochrane and Sons Ltd., Selby, Yorkshire, England; paired with barge St. Marys Cement								
STAR LINE MACKINAC ISLAND FERRY, ST. IGNACE, MI *(mackinacferry.com)*								
Algomah		PF/PK	1961	D	81*	93′00″	29′08″	5′02″
Built: Paasch Marine Services Inc., Erie, PA								
Anna May		ES	1947	D	94*	64′10″	30′00″	7′03″
(West Shore '47-'12)								
Cadillac {5}		PF	1990	D	73*	64′07″	20′00″	7′07″
Chippewa {6}		PF/PK	1962	D	81*	93′00″	29′08″	5′02″
Built: Paasch Marine Services Inc., Erie, PA								
Good Fortune		PA	2015	D	57*	65′00″	19′00″	7′00″
Huron {5}		PF/PK	1955	D	99*	91′06″	25′00″	7′00″
Joliet {3}		PF	1993	D	83*	64′08″	22′00″	8′03″
LaSalle {4}		PF	1983	D	55*	65′00″	20′00″	7′05″
Mackinac Islander		CF	1947	D	99*	84′00″	30′00″	8′02″
Built: Sturgeon Bay Shipbuilding, Sturgeon Bay, WI (Drummond Islander '47-'02)								
Marquette II {2}		PF	2005	D	65*	74′00″	23′06″	8′00″
Ottawa {2}		PF/PK	1959	D	81*	93′00″	29′08″	5′02″
Built: Paasch Marine Services Inc., Erie, PA								
Radisson {2}		PF	1988	D	97*	80′00″	23′06″	7′00″
Straits of Mackinac II		PF/PK	1969	D	89*	90′00″	27′06″	8′08″
Built: Blount Marine Corp., Warren, RI								
STERLING FUELS LTD., HAMILTON, ON *(sterlingfuels.ca)*								
Sterling Energy	9277058	RT	2002	D	749*	226′03″	32′10″	14′09″
Built: Selahattin Alsan Shipyard, Istanbul Turkey; refueling tanker serves vessels in the vicinity of Hamilton and Toronto, ON, and the Welland Canal (Melisa D '02-'13)								

T

Fleet Name / Vessel Name	Vessel IMO #	Vessel Type	Year Built	Engine Type	Cargo Cap. or Gross*	Overall Length	Vessel Breadth	Vessel Depth
TALL SHIP WINDY, CHICAGO, IL *(tallshipwindy.com)*								
Windy		ES/4S	1996	W	75*	148′00″	25′00″	8′00″
Built: Detyens Shipyards Inc., North Charleston, SC								
TALL SHIP RED WITCH LLC, KENOSHA, WI *(redwitch.com)*								
Red Witch		ES/2S	1986	W	41*	77′00″	17′06″	6′05″
Built: Nathaniel Zirlott, Bayou La Batre, AL								
TGL MARINE HOLDINGS ULC, TORONTO, ON								
Sarah Spencer	5002223	SU	1959	B	21,844	693′10″	72′00″	40′00″
Built: Manitowoc Shipbuilding Co., Manitowoc, WI; engine removed, converted to a self-unloading barge by Halifax Dartmouth Industries, Halifax, NS, in '89; in long-term lay-up at Toledo, OH (Adam E. Cornelius {3} '59-'89, Capt. Edward V. Smith '89-'91, Sea Barge One '91-'96)								
THOUSAND ISLAND MARINE CONSTRUCTION LTD., GANANOQUE, ON *(timarineconstruction.com)*								
Steelhead		TB	1944	D	36*	56′00″	20′00″	5′03″
Built: W.F. Kolbe & Co. Ltd., Port Dover, ON								
THOUSAND ISLANDS & SEAWAY CRUISES, BROCKVILLE, ON *(1000islandscruises.com)*								
General Brock III		ES	1977	D	56*	56′05″	15′04″	5′02″
Lady of the Isles		ES	1986	D	105*	65′00″	20′00″	6′08″
Sea Fox II		ES	1988	D	55*	39′08″	20′00″	2′00″
THUNDER BAY TUG SERVICES LTD., THUNDER BAY, ON								
Glenada		TB	1943	D	107*	80′06″	25′00″	10′01″
Built: Russel Brothers Ltd., Owen Sound, ON (HMCS Glenada [W-30] '43-'45)								
Miseford		TB	1915	D	116*	85′00″	20′00″	9′06″
Built: M. Beatty & Sons Ltd., Welland, ON								

Fleet Name Vessel Name	Vessel IMO #	Vessel Type	Year Built	Engine Type	Cargo Cap. or Gross*	Overall Length	Vessel Breadth	Vessel Depth
Point Valour		TB	1958	D	246*	97′ 08″	28′ 02″	13′ 10″
Built: Davie Shipbuilding Co., Lauzon, QC (Foundation Valour '58-'83)								
Robert W.		TB	1949	D	48*	60′ 00″	16′ 00″	8′ 06″
Built: Russel Brothers Ltd., Owen Sound, ON								
Rosalee D.		TB	1943	D	22*	55′ 00″	12′ 07″	4′ 11″
Built: Northern Shipbuilding & Repair Co., Bronte, ON								

TORONTO BOAT CRUISES, TORONTO, ON *(torontoboatcruises.com)*

Stella Borealis		ES	1989	D	277*	117′ 07″	26′ 00″	12′ 70″

TORONTO BRIGANTINE INC., TORONTO, ON *(torontobrigantine.org)*

Pathfinder		TV	1963	D/W	32*	59′ 08″	15′ 00″	8′ 00″
Built: Canadian Shipbuilding & Engineering Co., Collingwood, ON								
Playfair		TV	1973	D/W	33*	59′ 08″	15′ 00″	8′ 00″
Built: Canadian Dredge & Co., Kingston, ON								

TORONTO DRYDOCK LTD., TORONTO, ON *(torontodrydock.com)*

Coastal Titan	7700477	HL	1978	B	3,000*	300′ 00″	55′ 00″	27′ 00″
Built: Peterson Builders, Sturgeon Bay, WI; converted to a barge in '09 at Port Colborne, ON (John Henry, Marinelink Explorer, Chaulk Lifter 15)								
Menier Consol		FD	1962					
Built: Davie Shipbuilding Co., Lauzon, QC; former pulpwood carrier was converted to a floating drydock in 1984								
M.R. Kane		TB	1945	D	51*	60′ 06″	16′ 05″	6′ 07″
Built: Central Bridge Co. Ltd., Trenton, ON (Tanac V-276 '45-'47)								
Radium Yellowknife	5288956	TB	1948	D	235*	120′ 00″	28′ 00″	6′ 06″
Built: Yarrows Ltd., Esquimalt, BC								
Salvage Monarch	5308275	TB	1959	D	219*	97′ 09″	29′ 00″	13′ 06″
Built: P.K. Harris Ltd., Appledore, England								

TORONTO FIRE SERVICES, TORONTO, ON *(toronto.ca/fire)*

William Thornton		FB	1982	D	55*	70′ 10″	18′ 00″	8′ 09″
Built: Breton Industrial & Marine Ltd., Port Hawkesbury, NS (Cape Hurd '82-'14)								
Wm. Lyon Mackenzie	6400575	FB	1964	D	102*	81′ 01″	20′ 00″	10′ 00″
Built: Russel Brothers Ltd., Owen Sound, ON								

TORONTO ISLANDS TRANSIT SERVICES INC., TORONTO ON

Dartmouth III	7801776	PA	1978	D	255*	78′ 08″	31′ 00″	8′ 04″
Built: Ferguson Industries, Pictou, NS								

TORONTO PORT AUTHORITY, TORONTO, ON *(torontoport.com)*

Brutus I		TB	1992	D	10*	36′ 01″	11′ 09″	4′ 04″
Built: Mariner Jack Inc., Michigan City, IN								
David Hornell VC		PA/CF	2006	D	219*	95′ 10″	37′ 07″	7′ 05″
Built: Hike Metal Products, Wheatley, ON (TCCA 2 '09-'10)								
Iron Guppy		TB	2016	D	65*	66′ 96″	21′ 00″	10′ 24″
Built: Hike Metal Products, Wheatley, ON								
Maple City		PA/CF	1951	D	135*	70′ 06″	36′ 04″	5′ 11″
Built: Muir Brothers Dry Dock Co. Ltd., Port Dalhousie, ON; in long-term lay-up								
Marilyn Bell I		PA/CF	2009	D	270*	95′ 10″	37′ 07″	7′ 05″
Built: Hike Metal Products, Wheatley, ON (TCCA 2 '09-'10)								
Windmill Point		PA/CF	1954	D	118*	65′ 00″	36′ 00″	10′ 00″
Built: Kingston Shipyards Ltd., Kingston, ON; in long-term lay-up								

TORONTO HARBOUR TOURS INC., TORONTO, ON *(harbourtourstoronto.ca)*

Miss Kim Simpson		ES	1960	D	33*	90′ 02″	13′ 04″	3′ 09″
New Beginnings		ES	1961	D	28*	41′ 09″	13′ 01″	4′ 09″
Shipsands		ES	1972	D	23*	58′ 03″	12′ 01″	4′ 07″

TRAVERSE RIVIERE-DU-LOUP SAINT-SIMEON LTD., RIVIERE-DU-LOUP, QC *(traverserdl.com)*

Trans-St-Laurent	5409586	PA/CF	1963	D	2,173*	249′ 06″	60′ 01″	15′ 04″
Built: Geo. T. Davie & Sons Ltd., Lauzon, QC								

TRAVERSE TALL SHIP CO., TRAVERSE CITY, MI *(tallshipsailing.com)*

Manitou {1}		ES/2S	1983	W	78*	114′ 00″	21′ 00″	9′ 00″
Built: Steel Ship Corp., Portsmouth, NH								

30,000 ISLANDS CRUISE LINES INC., PARRY SOUND, ON *(islandqueencruise.com)*

Island Queen V		ES	1990	D	526*	130′ 00″	35′ 00″	6′ 06″
Built: Herb Fraser & Associates, Port Colborne, ON								

TRIDENT MARINE CORP., CLEVELAND, OH *(holidaycleveland.com)*

Holiday		PA	1964	D	25*	60′ 00″	16′ 01″	5′ 06″

U

UNCLE SAM BOAT TOURS, ALEXANDRIA BAY, NY *(usboattours.com)*

Alexandria Belle		ES	1988	D	92*	82' 00"	32' 00"	8' 00"
Island Duchess		ES	1988	D	73*	90' 03"	27' 08"	9' 00"
Island Wanderer		ES	1971	D	57*	62' 05"	22' 00"	7' 02"
Uncle Sam 7		ES	1976	D	55*	60' 04"	22' 00"	7' 01"

U.S. ARMY CORPS OF ENGINEERS – GREAT LAKES AND OHIO RIVER DIV., CINCINNATI, OH *(www.lre.usace.army.mil)*

U.S. ARMY CORPS OF ENGINEERS – BUFFALO DISTRICT

Cheraw		TB	1970	D	356*	109' 00"	30' 06"	16' 03"

Built: Southern Shipbuilding Corp., Slidell, LA (USS Cheraw [YTB-802] '70-'96)

Mike Donlon		TB	1999	TB	64*	53' 00"	19' 02"	7' 07"

Built: Marine Builders Inc., Utica, Ind.

U.S. ARMY CORPS OF ENGINEERS – DETROIT DISTRICT, LAKE MICHIGAN AREA OFFICE, KEWAUNEE SUB-OFFICE

Kenosha		TB	1954	D	82*	70' 00"	20' 00"	9' 08"

Built: Missouri Valley Bridge & Iron Works, Leavenworth, KS (U. S. Army ST-2011 '54-'65)

Manitowoc		CS	1976	B		132' 00"	44' 00"	8' 00"
Racine		TB	1931	D	61*	66' 03"	18' 05"	7' 08"

Built: Marine Iron & Shipbuilding Co., Duluth MN

U.S. ARMY CORPS OF ENGINEERS – DETROIT DISTRICT, DETROIT AREA OFFICE

Demolen		TB	1974	D	356*	109' 00"	30' 06"	16' 03"

Built: Marinette Marine Corp., Marinette, WI (USS Metacom [YTB-829] '74-'01, Metacom '01-'02)

Veler		CS	1991	B	613*	150' 00"	46' 00"	10' 06"

U.S. ARMY CORPS OF ENGINEERS – DETROIT DISTRICT, DULUTH AREA OFFICE

D. L. Billmaier		TB	1968	D	356*	109' 00"	30' 06"	16' 03"

Built: Southern Shipbuilding Corp., Slidell, LA (USS Natchitoches [YTB-799] '68-'95)

Hammond Bay		TB	1953	D	23*	45' 00"	13' 00"	7' 00"

Built: Roamer Boat Co., Holland, MI

H. J. Schwartz		DB	1995	B		150' 00"	48' 00"	11' 00"

U.S. ARMY CORPS OF ENGINEERS – DETROIT DISTRICT, SOO AREA OFFICE

Harvey		DB	1961	B		120' 00"	40' 00"	8' 00"
Nicolet		DB	1971	B		120' 00"	40' 00"	8' 00"
Owen M. Frederick		TB	1942	D	56*	65' 00"	17' 00"	7' 06"

Built: Sturgeon Bay Shipbuilding Co., Sturgeon Bay, WI

American Century downbound at Sault Ste. Marie, MI, in December 2018. (Logan Vasicek)

Fleet Name Vessel Name	Vessel IMO #	Vessel Type	Year Built	Engine Type	Cargo Cap. or Gross*	Overall Length	Vessel Breadth	Vessel Depth
Paul Bunyan		GL	1945	B		150' 00"	65' 00"	12' 06"
Built: Wiley Equipment Co., Port Deposit, MD								
Whitefish Bay		TB	1953	D	23*	45' 00"	13' 00"	7' 00"
Built: National Steel & Shipbuilding Co., San Diego, CA								

U.S. COAST GUARD 9TH COAST GUARD DISTRICT, CLEVELAND, OH *(uscg.mil/d9)*

Alder [WLB-216]	9271145	BT	2004	D	2,000*	225' 09"	46' 00"	19' 08"
Built: Marinette Marine Corp., Marinette, WI; stationed at Duluth, MN								
Biscayne Bay [WTGB-104]	8635148	IB	1979	D	662*	140' 00"	37' 06"	12' 00"
Built: Tacoma Boatbuilding Co., Tacoma, WA; stationed at St. Ignace, MI								
Bristol Bay [WTGB-102]	8635150	IB	1979	D	662*	140' 00"	37' 06"	12' 00"
Built: Tacoma Boatbuilding Co., Tacoma, WA; stationed at Detroit, MI								
Buckthorn [WLI-642]		BT	1963	D	200*	100' 00"	24' 00"	4' 08"
Built: Mobile Ship Repair Inc., Mobile, AL; stationed at Sault Ste. Marie, MI								
CGB-12001		BT	1991	B	700*	120' 00"	50' 00"	6' 00"
CGB-12002		BT	1992	B	700*	120' 00"	50' 00"	6' 00"
Hollyhock [WLB-214]	9271133	BT	2003	D	2,000*	225' 09"	46' 00"	19' 08"
Built: Marinette Marine Corp., Marinette, WI; stationed at Port Huron, MI								
Katmai Bay [WTGB-101]		IB	1978	D	662*	140' 00"	37' 06"	12' 00"
Built: Tacoma Boatbuilding Co., Tacoma, WA; stationed at Sault Ste. Marie, MI								
Mackinaw [WLBB-30]	9271054	IB	2005	D	3,407*	240' 00"	58' 00"	15' 05"
Built: Marinette Marine Corp., Marinette, WI; stationed at Cheboygan, MI								
Mobile Bay [WTGB-103]	8635162	IB	1979	D	662*	140' 00"	37' 06"	12' 00"
Built: Tacoma Boatbuilding Co., Tacoma, WA; stationed at Sturgeon Bay, WI								
Morro Bay [WTGB-106]	8635215	IB	1979	D	662*	140' 00"	37' 06"	12' 00"
Built: Tacoma Boatbuilding Co., Tacoma, WA; stationed at Cleveland, OH								
Neah Bay [WTGB-105]	8635174	IB	1980	D	662*	140' 00"	37' 06"	12' 00"
Built: Tacoma Boatbuilding Co., Tacoma, WA; stationed at Cleveland, OH								

U.S. ENVIRONMENTAL PROTECTION AGENCY, CHICAGO, IL *(epa.gov)*

Lake Explorer II		RV	1966	D	150*	86' 09"	22' 00"	7' 02"
Built: Jackobson Shipyard, Oyster Bay, NY (NOAA Rude '66-'08)								
Lake Guardian	8030609	RV	1981	D	959*	180' 00"	40' 00"	14' 00"
Built: Halter Marine Inc., Moss Point MS (Marsea Fourteen '81-'90)								

U.S. FISH & WILDLIFE SERVICE, ALPENA, MI

Spencer F. Baird	9404326	RV	2006	D	256*	95' 00"	30' 00"	9' 05"
Built: Conrad Industries Inc., Morgan City, LA								
Stanford H. Smith		RV	2018	D	37*	57' 00"	16' 00"	N/A
Built: Moran Ironworks, Onaway, MI								

Fleetmates Clyde S. VanEnkevort and Joyce L. VanEnkevort meet on the St. Marys River. (Roger LeLievre)

Fleet Name Vessel Name	Vessel IMO #	Vessel Type	Year Built	Engine Type	Cargo Cap. or Gross*	Overall Length	Vessel Breadth	Vessel Depth

U.S. NATIONAL PARK SERVICE - ISLE ROYALE NATIONAL PARK, HOUGHTON, MI *(nps.gov)*

Greenstone II		TK	2003	B	114*	70' 01"	24' 01"	8' 00"
Built: Fraser Shipyards, Superior, WI								
Ranger III	7618234	PK	1958	D	648*	152' 08"	34' 00"	13' 00"
Built: Christy Corp., Sturgeon Bay, WI								

U.S. NAVAL SEA CADET CORPS, GREAT LAKES DIVISION, MOUNT CLEMENS, MI *(prideofmichigan.org)*

Pride of Michigan [YP-673]		TV	1977	D	70*	80' 06"	17' 08"	5' 03"
Built: Peterson Builders Inc., Sturgeon Bay, WI; based at Mount Clemens, MI (USS YP-673 '77-'89)								

UNIVERSITY OF MINNESOTA LARGE LAKES OBSERVATORY, DULUTH, MN *(scse.d.umn.edu/blue-heron)*

Blue Heron		RV	1985	D	175*	87' 00"	23' 00"	11' 00"
Built: Goudy and Stevens, East Boothbay, ME (Fairtry '85-'97)								

UNIVERSITY OF WISCONSIN SCHOOL OF FRESHWATER SCIENCES, MILWAUKEE, WI *(glwi.uwm.edu)*

Neeskay		RV	1952	D	75*	71' 00"	17' 06"	7' 06"
Built: Higgins Industries, New Orleans, LA (T-494)								

TRAINING ON THE TREGURTHA

In 2018, the Interlake Steamship Co. collaborated with the U.S. Coast Guard on training exercises. Here, USCG Air Station Traverse City, MI, practices dropping crew to the deck of Lee A. Tregurtha on Lake Michigan. (Peter Groh)

LEE A. TREGURTHA

Fleet Name / Vessel Name	Vessel IMO #	Vessel Type	Year Built	Engine Type	Cargo Cap. or Gross*	Overall Length	Vessel Breadth	Vessel Depth
URGENCE MARINE INC., MONTREAL, QC (urgencemarine.com)								
Simon Cote		TB	1953	D	14*	38' 02"	11' 05"	4' 00"
USS GREAT LAKES LLC, NEW YORK, NY								
Robert F. Deegan		TK	1968	B	2,424*	225' 08"	60' 00"	18' 00"
Built: Wyatt Industries, Houston, TX; paired with tug Zeus								

V-W

VANENKEVORT TUG & BARGE INC., ESCANABA MI (vtbarge.com)								
Clyde S. VanEnkevort		ATB	2011	D	1,179*	135' 04"	50' 00"	26' 00"
Built: Donjon Shipbuilding & Repair, Erie, PA; paired with the barge Erie Trader (Ken Boothe Sr. '11-'17)								
Erie Trader		SU	2012	B	37,600	740' 04"	78' 00"	30' 00"
Built: Donjon Shipbuilding & Repair, Erie, PA (Lakes Contender '12-'17)								
Great Lakes Trader	8635966	SU	2000	B	39,600	740' 00"	78' 00"	45' 00"
Built: Halter Marine, Pearlington, MS; paired with tug Joyce L. VanEnkevort								

Fleet Name Vessel Name	Vessel IMO #	Vessel Type	Year Built	Engine Type	Cargo Cap. or Gross*	Overall Length	Vessel Breadth	Vessel Depth
Joseph H. Thompson		SU	1944	B	21,200	706' 06"	71' 06"	38' 06"
Built: Sun Shipbuilding & Drydock Co., Chester, PA; converted from a saltwater vessel to a Great Lakes bulk carrier by Maryland Dry Dock, Baltimore, MD, and American Shipbuilding Co., South Chicago, IL, in '52; converted to a self-unloading barge by the owners in '91 (USNS Marine Robin '44-'52)								
Joseph H. Thompson Jr.	5175745	ATB	1990	D	841*	146' 06"	38' 00"	30' 00"
Built at Marinette, WI, from steel left over from the conversion of Joseph H. Thompson (above)								
Joyce L. VanEnkevort	8973033	AT	1998	D	1,179*	135' 04"	50' 00"	26' 00"
Built: Bay Shipbuilding Co., Sturgeon Bay, WI; paired with barge Great Lakes Trader								
Laura L. VanEnkevort	8875310	AT	1994	D	189*	118' 08"	37' 00"	`8' 00"
Built: Halter Marine, Lockport, LA (Sidney Candies '94-'98, Nadia Ramil '98-'19)								
Michigan Trader	N/A	SU	2020	B	37,512	740' 00"	78' 00"	45' 00"
Built: Bay Shipbuilding Co., Sturgeon Bay, WI								

VERREAULT NAVIGATION INC., LES MÉCHINS, QC (verreaultnavigation.com)

Epinette II		TB	1965	D	75*	61' 03"	20' 01"	8' 05"
Built: Russel Brothers Ltd., Owen Sound, ON								
Grande Baie		TT	1972	D	194*	86' 06"	30' 00"	12' 00"
Built: Prince Edward Island Lending Authority, Charlottetown, PEI								

VICTORIAN PRINCESS CRUISE LINES, ERIE, PA (victorianprincess.com)

Victorian Princess		ES	1985	D	46*	67' 00"	24' 00"	4' 05"

VISTA FLEET, DULUTH, MN (vistafleet.com)

Vista Queen		ES	1987	D	97*	64' 00"	16' 00"	6' 02"
Built: Mid-City Steel Fabricating Inc., La Crosse, WI (Queen of Excelsior)								
Vista Star		ES	1987	D	95*	91' 00"	24' 09"	5' 02"
Built: Freeport Shipbuilding Inc., Freeport, FL (Island Empress '87-'88)								

VOIGHT'S MARINE SERVICES LTD., ELLISON BAY & GILLS ROCK, WI (islandclipper.com)

Island Clipper {2}		ES	1987	D	71*	65' 00"	20' 00"	8' 00"
Yankee Clipper		ES	1971	D	41*	46' 06"	17' 00"	6' 00"

WALPOLE-ALGONAC FERRY LINE, PORT LAMBTON, ON (walpoleislandferry.ca)

City of Algonac		CF	1990	D	82*	62' 06"	27' 09"	5' 09"
Built: Duratug Shipyard & Fabricating Ltd., Port Dover, ON								
Walpole Islander		CF	1986	D	72*	54' 05"	27' 09"	6' 03"
Built: Hike Metal Products, Wheatley, ON								

WALSTROM MARINE, HARBOR SPRINGS, MI (walstrom.com)

Elizabeth		TB	1945	D	21*	42' 02"	12' 01"	5' 05"
Built: Burger Boat Co., Manitowoc, WI (ST-912 '45-'48, Ashland '48-'72, Charles F. Liscomb '72-'94 and '94-'01, Lydie Rae '01-'03)								

WARNER PETROLEUM CORP., CLARE, MI (warnerpetroleum.com)

Coloma L. Warner	7337892	TB	1955	D	134*	86' 00"	24' 00"	10' 00"
Built: Sturgeon Bay Shipbuilding, Sturgeon Bay, WI; paired with the barge Warner Provider (Harbor Ace '55-'61, Gopher State '61-'71, Betty Gale '71-'93, Hannah D. Hannah '93-'10)								
Marysville		TK	1973	B	1,136*	200' 00"	50' 00"	12' 06"
Built: St. Louis Shipbuilding, St. Louis, MO (N.M.S. No. 102 '73-'81)								
Warner Provider	8641185	RT	1962	B	1,698*	264' 00"	52' 05"	12' 00"
Built: Port Houston Iron Works, Houston, TX (Hannah 2903); in use as a fueling barge at south Lake Michigan ports								
William L. Warner	7322055	RT	1973	D	492*	120' 00"	40' 00"	14' 00"
Built: Halter Marine, New Orleans, LA; (Jos. F. Bigane '73-'04); in use as a vessel fueling barge at Detroit, MI								

WASHINGTON ISLAND FERRY LINE, WASHINGTON ISLAND, WI (wisferry.com)

Arni J. Richter		PA/CF	2003	D	92*	104' 00"	38' 06"	10' 11"
Built: Bay Shipbuilding Co., Sturgeon Bay, WI								
Eyrarbakki		PA/CF	1970	D	95*	87' 00"	36' 00"	7' 06"
Built: Bay Shipbuilding Co., Sturgeon Bay, WI								
Karfi		PA/CF	1967	D	23*	36' 00"	16' 00"	4' 08"
Built: T.D. Vinette Co., Escanaba, MI								
Robert Noble		PA/CF	1979	D	97*	90' 04"	36' 00"	8' 03"
Built: Peterson Builders Inc., Sturgeon Bay, WI								
Washington {2}		PA/CF	1989	D	97*	100' 00"	37' 00"	9' 00"
Built: Peterson Builders Inc., Sturgeon Bay, WI								

WENDELLA SIGHTSEEING CO. INC., CHICAGO, IL (wendellaboats.com)

Linnea		ES	2010	D	77*	85' 05"	30' 00"	7' 01"
Lucia		ES	2015	D	80*	85' 05"	30' 00"	7' 01"
Ouilmette		ES	2001	D	43*	65' 00"	22' 04"	4' 05"
Wendella		ES	2007	D	77*	85' 05"	30' 00"	7' 01"
Wendella LTD		ES	1992	D	66*	68' 00"	20' 00"	4' 09"

Fleet Name / Vessel Name	Vessel IMO #	Type	Year Built	Engine Type	Cargo Cap. or Gross*	Overall Length	Breadth	Depth
WHITE LAKE DOCK & DREDGE INC., MONTAGUE, MI *(wlddi.com)*								
Captain George		TB	1929	D	61*	60' 09"	16' 07"	7' 07"
Built: Charles Ward Engine Works, Charleston, WV (Captain George '29-'73, Kurt R. Luedtke '73-'91)								
J-Krab		TW	2010	D	14*	25' 05"	14' 00"	5' 07"
Built: Mid-America Shipyards LLC, Fort Smith, AR								
Lauren A		TB	1980	D	68*	51' 05"	21' 00"	6' 00"
Built: Melancon Fabricators Inc., Lockport, LA (Janine Alicia '80-'89)								
WILLY'S CONTRACTING CO., SOUTHAMPTON, ON *(willyscontracting.com)*								
Howard W. Fitzpatrick		WB	1971	D	97*	78' 00"	20' 05"	4' 09"
Built: Grafton Boat Co. Inc., Grafton, IL (Fireboat No. 1)								
Misty Jean		TB	1947	D	34*	54' 00"	22' 00"	4' 11"
Built: Erieau Shipbuilding & Dry Dock Co., Erieau, ON (W.D. Candice)								
Pride		TB	1957	D	47*	52' 06"	29' 08"	5' 01"
Built: Strege Fisheries Inc., Racine, WI								
WINDSOR RIVER CRUISES LTD., WINDSOR, ON *(windsorrivercruises.com)*								
Macassa Bay	8624709	ES	1986	D	210*	93' 07"	29' 07"	10' 04"
Built: Boiler Pump & Marine Works Ltd., Hamilton, ON								
WOHLLEB-SOCIE CO., TOLEDO, OH								
Bessie B		TB	1947	D	30*	52' 03"	13' 09"	5' 05"
Built: Fred Socie, Toledo, OH								
WISCONSIN DEPARTMENT OF NATURAL RESOURCES, BAYFIELD & STURGEON BAY, WI *(dnr.wi.gov)*								
Coregonus		RV	2011	D	37*	60' 00"	16' 00"	5' 09"
Gaylord Nelson		RV	1992	D	12*	45' 09"	16' 00"	5' 05"
Hack Noyes		RV	1947	D	50*	56' 00"	14' 05"	4' 00"
1089856 ONTARIO LTD., THUNDER BAY, ON								
W. N. Twolan	5384360	TB	1962	D	299*	106' 00"	29' 05"	15' 00"
Built: George T. Davie & Sons, Lauzon, Q								

Side-by-side stacks at the Soo Locks: Ojibway and Paul R. Tregurtha. *(Roger LeLievre)*

We have a variety of Great Lakes Freighters Photos & Gifts. Custom & Wholesale available. (906)440-1043

YooperGifts.Com

PORTHURONCAM.COM

View the Blue Water Bridge from the Convention Center's LIVE CAM

Our Beautiful Waterfront Location!

When the Meeting Breaks Blue Water Awaits!

Amazing View of the Paul R. Tregurtha as She Passes the Blue Water Convention Center!

BLUEWATERCONVENTIONCENTER.COM
810-201-5513 • PORT HURON, MICHIGAN

Sip n' Sail Cruises

aboard Isle Royale Queen III

Sunset Cruises
Bridge Excursions
Craft Beer Cruises
Bourbon Cruises

Open Viewing Areas • Heated Cabins
Full Cash Bar & Restrooms
Private Charters Available

RATED #2
OUTDOOR ACTIVITY

tripadvisor
ON MACKINAC ISLAND

Follow us:
f o

Live Entertainment!

Departures from Mackinac Island Coal Dock
Purchase tickets at PureMichiganBoatCruises.com

Delivering More

Rand Logistics, Inc. is a leading provider of marine bulk freight shipping, ship repair and logistics services throughout the Great Lakes region. Through our fleet of fourteen U.S. and Canadian flagged vessels and our team of dedicated professionals, we provide unique and comprehensive supply chain solutions to the marketplace. We take pride in our world class safety record, exemplary maritime and technical expertise, and the unmatched efficiency and flexibility of our operations. We are the only carrier that offers significant domestic port-to-port services in both Canada and the U.S. on the Great Lakes, and due to the versatile and diverse makeup of our fleet, the only carrier that can access every commercial port in the region. Contact us for more information about how Rand Logistics and our subsidiary companies can help you with your supply chain needs.

RAND
LOGISTICS, INC.

Lower Lakes Towing, Ltd.
517 Main Street
Port Dover, Ontario, CA N0A 1NO
Phone: 519-583-0982

Rand Logistics, Inc.
333 Washington Street, Suite 201
Jersey City, New Jersey 07302
Phone: 212-863-9403
www.randlogisticsinc.com

Grand River Navigation Company
1026 Hannah Avenue, Suite D
Traverse City, Michigan, USA 49686
Phone: 231-642-4622

Conneaut Creek Ship Repair
4200 Benefit Avenue
Ashtabula, Ohio, USA 44004
Phone: 440-990-3051

Tugs Arkansas and Kentucky help Burns Harbor leave her lay-up berth. *(Chris Mazzella))*

Kaye E. Barker under a full moon. (Chris Mazzella)

Great Republic from the north pier at St. Joseph, MI. (Molly Pate)

LAKER LONGEVITY / *1906-2019*

1906: St. Marys Challenger (r'67, '14) **1936**: J.A.W. Iglehart (r'65)* **1937**: St. Marys Conquest (r:'87)

1941: Pere Marquette 41 (r'97) **1942**: Alpena (r'91), Lee A. Tregurtha (r'61) **1943**: Cuyahoga (r'74), Mississagi (r'67) **1944**: Joseph H. Thompson (r'52, '91), McKee Sons (r'53, '91**) **1949**: Wilfred Sykes

1952: Arthur M. Anderson (r'75, '82), Kaye E. Barker (r'76, '81), Cason J. Callaway (r'74, '82), Philip R. Clarke (re'74, '82), Menominee (r'06), Michipicoten (r'57, '80), Ojibway, John G. Munson **1953**: Badger, Maumee (r'07), Pathfinder (r'98), Saginaw **1957**: Commander (r'18) **1958**: John Sherwin (r'73)** **1959**: Cedarglen (r'77), Hon. James L. Oberstar (r'72, '81), Herbert C. Jackson (r'75), Sarah Spencer (r'89)**

1960: Edward L. Ryerson** **1967**: Tim S. Dool (r'96), John D. Leitch (r'02) **1968**: Frontenac (r'73) **1969**: CSL Tadoussac (r'01)

1972: Roger Blough, CSL Niagara (r'99), Stewart J. Cort **1973**: Algoma Compass, Calumet, Manitowoc, John J. Boland, Rt. Hon. Paul J. Martin (r'00), Presque Isle, Tecumseh **1974**: H. Lee White, Robert S. Pierson **1975**: Sam Laud **1976**: James R. Barker, Joseph L. Block, Algoma Olympic, St. Clair **1977**: CSL Assiniboine (r'05), CSL Laurentien (r'01), Walter J. McCarthy Jr., Mesabi Miner **1978**: Radcliffe R. Latimer (r'09), American Integrity, American Spirit, Algoma Buffalo **1979**: American Courage, Algoma Enterprise, Algoma Transport, Edwin H. Gott, Indiana Harbor

1980: American Mariner, Burns Harbor, Salarium, Edgar B. Speer, Oakglen **1981**: American Century, Great Republic, Paul R. Tregurtha **1982**: Michigan, Ashtabula **1983**: Spruceglen, Kaministiqua **1984**: Atlantic Huron (r'89, '03) **1986**: Algoma Spirit **1987**: Algoma Discovery, Algoma Guardian

1991: Manitoulin (r'15) **1992**: Dara Desgagnés, Esta Desgagnés **1993**: Jana Desgagnés **1996**: Integrity **1998**: Algosea **1999**: Maria Desgagnés

2000: Great Lakes Trader **2001**: Norman McLeod **2003**: NACC Argonaut **2004**: Algoscotia, Lake Express **2006**: Innovation **2007**: Rosaire A. Desgagnés, Argentia Desgagnés, Taiga Desgagnés, Evans Spirit, McKeil Spirit **2008**: Algocanada, Algonova, Algonorth, John J. Carrick, Zélada Desgagnés **2009**: Sedna Desgagnés **2011**: Algoma Mariner, Claude A. Desgagnés, NACC Quebec **2012**: Erie Trader, Bella Desgagnés, Baie St. Paul **2013**: Algoma Equinox, Thunder Bay, Whitefish Bay, Baie Comeau, Acadia Desgagnés **2014**: Algoma Harvester, G3 Marquis, CSL Welland, CSL St-Laurent **2016**: Mia Desgagnés, Damia Desgagnés **2017**: Algoma Strongfield, Algoma Niagara, Miena Desgagnés **2018**: Paul A. Desgagnés, Algoma Innovator, Algoma Sault **2019**: Algoma Conveyor, Rossi A. Desgagnés

(r = major rebuild; * storage barge; ** in long-term lay-up)

Cedarglen turns 60 in 2019. CSL Tadoussac has attained 50 years. Wilfred Sykes turns 70.

Seventy Seasons for the Sykes

Built by the American Shipbuilding Co., Lorain, OH, in 1949 for Inland Steel Co., the streamlined *Wilfred Sykes* was the first new American laker constructed after World War II and served as a prototype for many others that followed. When launched, the 678-foot-long by 70-foot-wide *Sykes* was the largest vessel on the Great Lakes and the first built to burn oil instead of coal. She was the first to have a cargo capacity of more than 20,000 gross tons and was also the fastest on the lakes at 16.5 mph loaded. Her design included an enclosed passage below deck so the crew could go from bow to stern without having to go outside. She was also first to have an enclosed stern, with crew rooms accessed via internal hallways rather than from the outside. Her galley was all-electric, and the cabins were air-conditioned, two more firsts. When converted to a self-unloader in 1975, the *Sykes* was also the first vessel to have the boom mounted on the stern. Here's to many more seasons for the *Mighty Wilfred!*

Wilfred Sykes above the Soo Locks, Jan. 10, 2019. *(Joy Fett)*

INNOVATION

Interlake Steamship's reputation is built on its proud history of growth and innovation. Interlake keeps on top of customers' requirements and ahead of regulatory changes by investing in its fleet. Capital improvements emphasize technology, safety, and efficiency. Re-powering and the installation of exhaust gas scrubbing systems allow Interlake to meet all North American EPA air emission standards. Improvements like these assure Interlake's customers of flexible service and reliable cargo delivery. Interlake's nine-vessel self-unloading fleet, with capacities ranging from 24,800 to 68,000 gross tons, permits targeted solutions for customers' needs.

Great Lakes transportation is our business, our only business. Let us deliver for you.

INTERLAKE STEAMSHIP
On the Great Lakes since 1913

The Interlake Steamship Company
7300 Engle Road
Middleburg Heights, Ohio 44130

Phone: 440-260-6900 • 800-327-3855
FAX: 440-260-6945

Email: boconnor@interlake-steamship.com
Website: www.interlakesteamship.com

Vessel Name	Engine Manufacturer & Model #	Engine Type	Total Engines	Total Cylinders	Rated HP	Total Props	Speed MPH
Acadia Desgagnés	MaK - 8M32C	Diesel	1	8	5,362 bhp	1	13.8
Albert *	Alpha -14V23L-VO	Diesel	2	14	2,030 bhp	2	13.8
Alder (USCG)	Caterpillar - 3608TA	Diesel	2	6	3,100 bhp	1 cpp	
Algocanada	MaK - 9M32C	Diesel	1	9	6,118 bhp	1 cpp	16.1
Algoma Buffalo	GM EMD - 20-645-E7	Diesel	2	20	7,200 bhp	1 cpp	16.1
Algoma Compass	GM EMD - 20-645-E7B	Diesel	2	20	7,200 bhp	1 cpp	16.1
Algoma Conveyor	Sulzer - 7RTA48T-B	Diesel	1	7	11,140 bhp	1	16.1
Algoma Dartmouth	MAN-B&W - 6L23/30A	Diesel	2	6	2,310 bhp	2 cpp	13.3
Algoma Discovery	Sulzer - 6RTA62	Diesel	1	6	15,499 bhp	1 cpp	16.4
Algoma Endurance	Wartsila 5RT-flex50-D	Diesel	1	5	11,863 bhp	1 cpp	16.1
Algoma Enterprise	MAN - 7L40/45	Diesel	2	7	8,804 bhp	1 cpp	13.8
Algoma Equinox	Wartsila 5RT-flex50-D	Diesel	1	5	11,863 bhp	1 cpp	16.1
Algoma Guardian	Sulzer - 6RTA62	Diesel	1	6	15,499 bhp	1 cpp	16.4
Algoma Hansa	Wartsila - 6L46A	Diesel	1	6	6,525 bhp	1 cpp	15.8
Algoma Harvester	Wartsila 5RT-flex50-D	Diesel	1	5	11,863 bhp	1 cpp	16.1
Algoma Innovator	Complete détails unavailable	Diesel			6,320 bhp		
Algoma Mariner	MAN-B&W - 6L48/60CR	Diesel	1	6	9,792 bhp	1 cpp	
Algoma Niagara	Sulzer - 7RTA48T-B	Diesel	1	7	11,140 bhp	1	16.1
Algoma Olympic	MAN - 8L40/54A	Diesel	2	8	10,000 bhp	1 cpp	15.0
Algoma Sault	Sulzer - 7RTA48T-B	Diesel	1	7	11,140 bhp	1	16.1
Algoma Spirit	Sulzer - 6RTA62	Diesel	1	6	11,284 bhp	1 cpp	16.4
Algoma Strongfield	Sulzer - 7RTA48T-B	Diesel	1	7	11,140 bhp	1	16.1
Algoma Transport	MAN - 8L40/45	Diesel	2	8	10,000 bhp	1 cpp	13.8
Algonorth	MAN (détails unavailable)	Diesel	1		8,445 bhp	1	
Algonova	MaK - 9M32C	Diesel	1	9	6,118 bhp	1 cpp	16.1
Algoscotia	Wartsila - 6L46C	Diesel	1	6	8,445 bhp	1 cpp	16.0
Algosea	Wartsila - 6L46A	Diesel	1	6	6,434 bhp	1 cpp	15.0
Alpena	De Laval Steam Turbine Co.	Turbine	1	**	4,400 shp	1	14.1
American Century	GM - EMD - 20-645-E7B	Diesel	4	20	14,400 bhp	2 cpp	17.3
American Courage	GM - EMD - 20-645-E7	Diesel	2	20	7,200 bhp	1 cpp	16.1
American Integrity	GM EMD - 20-645-E7	Diesel	4	20	14,400 bhp	2 cpp	18.4
American Mariner	GM EMD - 20-645-E7	Diesel	2	20	7,200 bhp	1 cpp	15.0
American Spirit	Pielstick - 16PC2-2V-400	Diesel	2	16	16,000 bhp	2 cpp	17.3
American Valor	Westinghouse Elec. Corp.	Turbine	1	**	7,700 shp	1	16.1
Anglian Lady *	Deutz - SBA12M528	Diesel	2	12	3,480 bhp	2 cpp	15.5
Arctic	MAN - 14V52/55A	Diesel	1	14	14,770 bhp	1	17.8
Argentia Desgagnés	Wartsila C - W6L32B3	Diesel	1	6	5,362 bhp	1	15.6
Arthur M. Anderson	Westinghouse Elec. Corp.	Turbine	1	**	7,700 shp	1	16.1
Atlantic Huron	Sulzer - 6RLB66	Diesel	1	6	11,094 bhp	1 cpp	17.3
Avataq	Hanshin - 6LF58	Diesel	1	6	5,997 bhp	1 cpp	17.3
Avenger IV *	British Polar	Diesel	1	9	2,700 bhp	1 cpp	12.0
Badger **	Skinner Steeple Compound Uniflow	Steam	2	8	3,500 ihp	2	18.4
Baie Comeau	MAN B&W - 6S50ME-B9	Diesel	1	6	11,897 bhp	1	15.5
Baie St. Paul	MAN B&W - 6S50ME-B9	Diesel	1	6	11,897 bhp	1	15.5
Barbara Andrie *	GM EMD 16-645-EF	Diesel	1	16	2,000 bhp	1	
Bella Desgagnés	Wartsila - 9L20CR	Diesel	4	9	8,320 bhp	2 azimuth	17.3
Beverly M I *	Niigata - 6L28HX	Diesel	2	6	1,971 bhp	2	16.0
Biscayne Bay (USCG)	Fairbanks Morse - 10-38D8-1/8	Diesel	2	10	2,500 bhp	1	13.8
Bradshaw McKee *	GM EMD - 12-645-E5	Diesel	2	12	4,320 bhp	2	11.5
Bristol Bay (USCG)	Fairbanks Morse - 10-38D8-1/8	Diesel	2	10	2,500 bhp	1	13.8
Burns Harbor	GM EMD - 20-645-E7	Diesel	4	20	14,400 bhp	2 cpp	18.4
Calumet	Alco - 16V251E	Diesel	2	16	5,600 bhp	1	16.1
Cason J. Callaway	Westinghouse Elec. Corp.	Turbine	1	**	7,700 shp	1	16.1

* = tug   ** = ferry

bhp: brake horsepower, a measure of diesel engine output measured at the crankshaft before entering gearbox or any other power take-out device

ihp: indicated horsepower, based on an internal measurement of mean cylinder pressure, piston area, piston stroke and engine speed; used for reciprocating engines

shp: shaft horsepower, a measure of engine output at the propeller shaft at the output of the reduction gearbox; used for steam and diesel-electric engines

cpp: controllable pitch propeller

Vessel Name	Engine Manufacturer & Model #	Engine Type	Total Engines	Total Cylinders	Rated HP	Total Props	Speed MPH
Cedarglen	B&W - 7-74VTBF-160	Diesel	1	7	8,750 bhp	1 cpp	15.5
Chi-Cheemaun **	Caterpillar - C280-6	Diesel	4	6	9,280 bhp	2	
Claude A. Desgagnés	MaK/Caterpillar - 6M43C	Diesel	1	6	7,342 bhp	1 cpp	17.8
Clyde S. VanEnkevort *	Cat-MaK - 8M32C	Diesel	2	8	10,876 bhp	2 cpp	18.4
CSL Assiniboine	MaK/Caterpillar - 6M32C	Diesel	2	6	8,060 bhp	1 cpp	
CSL Laurentien	MaK/Caterpillar - 6M32C	Diesel	2	6	8,060 bhp	1 cpp	
CSL Niagara	MaK/Caterpillar - 6M32C	Diesel	2	6	8,060 bhp	1 cpp	
CSL St-Laurent	MAN B&W 6S50ME-B	Diesel	1	6	11,897 bhp	1 cpp	15.5
CSL Tadoussac	Sulzer - 6RND76	Diesel	1	6	9,600 bhp	1	17.0
CSL Welland	MAN B&W 6S50ME-B	Diesel	1	6	11,897 bhp	1 cpp	15.5
Cuyahoga	Caterpillar - 3608	Diesel	1	8	3,000 bhp	1 cpp	12.6
Damia Desgagnés	Wärtsilä 5RT-flex 50DF	Diesel/LNG	1	5	7,305 bhp	1 cpp	15
Dara Desgagnés	B&W - 6L35MC	Diesel	1	6	5,030 bhp	1 cpp	14.4
Defiance *	GM EMD - 20-645-E7	Diesel	2	20	7,200 bhp	2	15.0
Des Groseilliers (CCG)	Alco - 16V251F	Diesel	6	16	17,700 bhp	2	18.6
Dorothy Ann *	GM EMD - 20-645-E7B	Diesel	2	20	7,200 bhp	2 Z-drive cpp	16.1
Dylan Cooper *	Complete détails unavailable	Diesel	2		2,909 bhp	2	
Edgar B. Speer	Pielstick - 18PC2-3V-400	Diesel	2	18	19,260 bhp	2 cpp	17.0
Edward L. Ryerson	General Electric Co.	Turbine	1	**	9,900 shp	1	19.0
Edwin H. Gott	MaK - 8M43C	Diesel	2	8	19,578 bhp	2 ccp	16.7
Espada Desgagnés	B&W - 6S60MC-C	Diesel	1	5	18,605 bhp	1 cpp	18.4
Esta Desgagnés	B&W - 6L35MC	Diesel	1	6	5,030 bhp	1 cpp	14.4
Evans McKeil *	GM EMD - 16-645C	Diesel	1	16	2,150 bhp	1	11.5
Evans Spirit	Wartsila - 6L38B	Diesel	1	6	5,831 bhp	1 cpp	16.1
Everlast *	Daihatsu - 8DSM-32	Diesel	2	8	6,000 bhp	2	16.5
Federal Asahi	B&W - 6S46MC-C	Diesel	1	6	10,710 bhp	1	16.1
Federal Baltic	B&W - 6S46MC-C	Diesel	1	5	10,710 bhp	1	16.1
Federal Barents	B&W - 6S46MC-C	Diesel	1	6	10,710 bhp	1	16.1
Federal Beaufort	B&W - 6S46MC-C	Diesel	1	6	10,710 bhp	1	16.1
Federal Bering	B&W - 6S46MC-C	Diesel	1	6	10,710 bhp	1	16.1
Federal Biscay	B&W - 6S46MC-C	Diesel	1	6	10,710 bhp	1	16.1
Federal Bristol	B&W - 6S46MC-C	Diesel	1	6	10,710 bhp	1	16.1
Federal Caribou	B&W - 6S46MC-C	Diesel	1	6	10,710 bhp	1	16.1
Federal Cedar	B&W - 6S46MC-C	Diesel	1	6	10,710 bhp	1	16.1
Federal Champlain	B&W - 6S46MC-C	Diesel	1	6	10,710 bhp	1	16.1
Federal Churchill	B&W - 6S46MC-C	Diesel	1	6	10,710 bhp	1	16.1
Federal Clyde	B&W - 6S46MC-C	Diesel	1	6	10,710 bhp	1	16.1
Federal Columbia	B&W - 6S46MC-C	Diesel	1	6	10,710 bhp	1	16.1
Federal Danube	B&W - 6S46MC-C	Diesel	1	6	10,686 bhp	1	16.1
Federal Dart	B&W - 5S50ME-B9	Diesel	1	5	10,731 bhp	1	16.1
Federal Dee	B&W - 5S50ME-B9	Diesel	1	5	10,731 bhp	1	16.1
Federal Delta	B&W - 5S50ME-B9	Diesel	1	5	10,731 bhp	1	16.1
Federal Elbe	B&W - 6S46MC-C	Diesel	1	6	10,686 bhp	1	16.1
Federal Ems	B&W - 6S46MC-C	Diesel	1	6	10,686 bhp	1	16.1
Federal Hudson	B&W - 6S46MC-C	Diesel	1	6	10,710 bhp	1	15.5
Federal Hunter	B&W - 6S46MC-C	Diesel	1	6	10,710 bhp	1	15.5
Federal Katsura	Mitsubishi (Tokyo) - 6UEC52LA	Diesel	1	6	9,490 bhp	1	19.2
Federal Kivalina	B&W - 6S46MC-C	Diesel	1	6	10,710 bhp	1	16.1
Federal Kumano	B&W - 6S46MC-C	Diesel	1	6	10,710 bhp	1	16.1
Federal Kushiro	Mitsubishi - 6UEC52LA	Diesel	1	6	9,626 bhp	1	16.6
Federal Leda	B&W - 6S46MC-C	Diesel	1	6	10,686 bhp	1	16.1
Federal Mackinac	B&W - 6S46MC-C	Diesel	1	6	10,540 bhp	1	16.1
Federal Margaree	B&W - 6S46MC-C	Diesel	1	6	10,686 bhp	1	16.1
Federal Mayumi	MAN B&W - 6S46MC-C	Diesel	1	6	10,686 bhp	1	16.1
Federal Mosel	Complete details unavailable	Diesel	1		11,716 bhp	1	16.7
Federal Nagara	B&W - 5S50ME-B9	Diesel	1	5	10,731 bhp	1	16.1
Federal Nakagawa	B&W - 6S46MC-C	Diesel	1	6	10,710 bhp	1	16.1
Federal Oshima	B&W - 6S46MC-C	Diesel	1	6	10,710 bhp	1	16.1
Federal Rhine	B&W - 6S50MC	Diesel	1	6	11,640 bhp	1	16.1
Federal Rideau	B&W - 6S46MC-C	Diesel	1	6	10,710 bhp	1	16.1
Federal Saguenay	B&W - 6S50MC	Diesel	1	6	11,665 bhp	1	16.1
Federal Sakura	Mitsubishi / Kobe - 6UEC52LA`	Diesel	1	5	9,490 bhp	1	19.3
Federal Satsuki	B&W - 6S46MC-C	Diesel	1	6	9,235 bhp	1	16.1

Vessel Name	Engine Manufacturer & Model #	Engine Type	Total Engines	Total Cylinders	Rated HP	Total Props	Speed MPH
Federal Schelde	B&W - 6S50MC	Diesel	1	6	11,640 bhp	1	16.1
Federal Seto	MAN B&W - 6S46MC-C	Diesel	1	6	10,711 bhp	1	16.7
Federal Shimanto	Mitsubishi - 6UEC52LA	Diesel	1	6	9,600 bhp	1	16.6
Federal Welland	B&W - 6S46MC-C	Diesel	1	6	10,710 bhp	1	16.1
Federal Weser	B&W - 6S46MC-C	Diesel	1	6	10,686 bhp	1	18.0
Federal Yukina	B&W - 6S46MC-C	Diesel	1	6	8,833 bhp	1	16.1
Federal Yoshino	Mitsubishi - 6UEC52LA	Diesel	1	6	9,600 bhp	1	16.6
Federal Yukon	B&W - 6S46MC-C	Diesel	1	6	10,710 bhp	1	15.5
Ferbec	MAN B&W - 6S50MC	Diesel	1	6	9,222 bhp	1	16.7
Florence M. *	Fairbanks Morse - 8-28D8-1/4	Diesel	2	8	1,450 bhp	2	
Florence Spirit	Wartsila C - 6L38B	Diesel	1	6	5,831 bhp	1	15.5
Frontenac	Sulzer - 6RND76	Diesel	1	6	9,600 bhp	1 cpp	17.0
G3 Marquis	Wartsila 5RT-flex50-D	Diesel	1	5	11,863 bhp	1 cpp	16.1
G.L. Ostrander *	Caterpillar - 3608-DITA	Diesel	2	8	6,008 bhp	2	17.3
Great Republic	GM EMD - 20-645-E7	Diesel	2	20	7,200 bhp	2 cpp	15.0
Griffon (CCG)	Fairbanks Morse - 8-38D8-1/8	Diesel	4	8	5,332 bhp	2	13.0
H. Lee White	GM EMD - 20-645-E7B	Diesel	2	20	7,200 bhp	1 cpp	15.0
Herbert C. Jackson	MaK - 6M32E	Diesel	2	6	6,250 bhp	1 cpp	
Hollyhock (USCG)	Caterpillar - 3608TA	Diesel	2	6	3,100 bhp	1 cpp	
Hon. James L. Oberstar	Rolls-Royce Bergen - B32:40L6P	Diesel	2	6	8,160 shp	1 ccp	17.0
Indiana Harbor	GM EMD - 20-645-E7	Diesel	4	20	14,400 bhp	2 cpp	16.1
Invincible *	GM EMD - 16-645-E7B	Diesel	2	16	5,750 bhp	2	13.8
James R. Barker	Pielstick - 16PC2-2V-400	Diesel	2	16	16,000 bhp	2 cpp	15.5
Jana Desgagnés	B&W - 6L35MC	Diesel	1	6	5,030 bhp	1 cpp	14.4
Jiimaan **	Ruston Paxman Diesels Ltd. - 6RK215	Diesel	2	6	2,839 bhp	2 cpp	15.0
John D. Leitch	B&W - 5-74VT2BF-160	Diesel	1	5	7,500 bhp	1 cpp	16.1
John G. Munson	MaK - 6M46C	Diesel	1	6	7,000 bhp	1 cpp	16.1
John J. Boland	GM EMD - 20-645-E7B	Diesel	2	20	7,200 bhp	1 cpp	15.0
Joseph H. Thompson Jr.	GE / GM Diesel - 7FDM16	Diesel	3	16	3,000 bhp	1	
Joseph L. Block	GM EMD - 20-645-E7	Diesel	2	20	7,200 bhp	1 cpp	17.3
Joyce L. VanEnkevort *	Caterpillar - 3612	Diesel	2	12	10,200 bhp	2 cpp	
Kaministiqua	Sulzer - 4RLB76	Diesel	4	4	10,880 bhp	1cpp	15.5
Karen Andrie *	GM EMD - 8-710G7C	Diesel	2	8	4,000 bhp	2	19.0
Katmai Bay (USCG)	Fairbanks Morse - 10-38D8-1/8	Diesel	2	10	2,500 bhp	1	13.8
Kaye E. Barker	Rolls-Royce Bergen - B32:40L6P	Diesel	2	6	8,160 shp	1 ccp	17.0
Lake Express **	MTU 16V4000M70	Diesel	4	16	12,616 bhp	4 water jet	40.0
Laurentia Desgagnés	B&W - 6S60MC-C	Diesel	1	5	18,605 bhp	1 cpp	18.4
Lee A. Tregurtha	Rolls-Royce Bergen B32:40L6P	Diesel	2	6	8,160 shp	1 ccp	17.0
Leo A. McArthur *	MaK - 6M25	Diesel	2	6	5,384 bhp	2 cpp	12.1
Leonard M *	Ruston P - 6RK270M	Diesel	2	6	2,097 bhp	2	13.8
Mackinaw (USCG)	Caterpillar - 3612	Diesel	3	12	9,119 bhp	2 Azipod	17.3
Manitoulin	B&W - 5L50MC	Diesel	1	5	8,113 bhp	1 cpp	16.5
Manitowoc	Alco - 16V251E	Diesel	2	16	5,600 bhp	1	16.1
Maria Desgagnés	B&W - 6S42MC	Diesel	1	6	8,361 bhp	1 cpp	16.1
Martha L. Black (CCG)	Alco - 16V251F	Diesel	3	16	8,973 bhp	2	13.8
Mary E. Hannah *	GM EMD - 16-567C	Diesel	2	16	3,200 bhp	2	15.0
McKeil Spirit	Wartsila-C	Diesel	1	6	5,831 bhp	1 cpp	16.1
Mesabi Miner	Pielstick - 16PC2-2V-400	Diesel	2	16	16,000 bhp	2 cpp	15.5
Mia Desgagnés	Wärtsilä 5RT-flex 50DF	Diesel/LNG	1	5	7,305 bhp	1 cpp	15.0
Michigan *	GM EMD - 20-645-E6	Diesel	2	16	3,900 bhp	2	13.2
Michipicoten	MaK - 6M32C	Diesel	2	6	8,160 bhp	1 cpp	14.0
Miena Desgagnés	MAN - 5G45ME-C9.5	Diesel	1	5	6,433 bhp	1	17.4
Mississagi	Caterpillar - 3612-TA	Diesel	1	12	4,500 bhp	1 cpp	13.8
Mobile Bay (USCG)	Fairbanks Morse - 10-38D8-1/8	Diesel	2	10	2,500 bhp	1	13.8
Morro Bay (USCG)	Fairbanks Morse - 10-38D8-1/8	Diesel	2	10	2,500 bhp	1	13.8
NACC Alicudi	Daihatsu Diesel - 8DKM-28	Diesel	1	8	2,848 bhp	1	13.2
NACC Argonaut	Wartsila - 6L38B	Diesel	1	6	5,912 bhp	1 cpp	15.3
NACC Quebec	Wartsila - 6L38B	Diesel	1	6	5,831 bhp	1 cpp	15
Neah Bay (USCG)	Fairbanks Morse - 10-38D8-1/8	Diesel	2	10	2,500 bhp	1	13.8
Nordik Express	GM EMD - 20-645-E7	Diesel	2	20	7,200 bhp	2 ccp	16.0
Nunalik	Caterpillar MaK - 6M43C	Diesel	1	6	7,238 bhp	1 cpp	17.3
Nunavik	MAN-B&W 7S70ME-C	Diesel	1	7	29,623 bhp	1 cpp	15.5

Vessel Name	Engine Manufacturer & Model #	Engine Type	Total Engines	Total Cylinders	Rated HP	Total Props	Speed MPH
Nordika Desgagnés	B&W - 6S46MC-C	Diesel/LNG	1	6	8,955 bhp	1	17.3
Oakglen	B&W - 6K67GF	Diesel	1	6	11,600 bhp	1	15.5
Ojibway	GE - 7FDM EFI	Diesel	1	16	4,100 bhp	1 cpp	
Paul A. Desgagnés	Sulzer - 5RT-fles 50 DF	LNG	1	5	7,305 bhp	1	15
Paul R. Tregurtha	MaK - 6M43C	Diesel	2	6	17,120 bhp	2 cpp	15.5
Pearl Mist	Caterpillar - 3516C-DITA	Diesel	2	16	3,386 bhp	2	
Petite Forte *	Ruston - 8ATC	Diesel	2	8	4,200 bhp	2	15.5
Philip R. Clarke	Westinghouse Elec. Corp.	Turbine	1	**	7,700 shp	1	16.1
Pierre Radisson (CCG)	Alco - 16V251F	Diesel	6	16	17,700 bhp	2	18.4
Prentiss Brown *	GM EMD - 12-645-E2	Diesel	2	12	3,900 bhp	1	
Presque Isle *	Mirrlees Blackstone Ltd. - KVMR-16	Diesel	2	16	14,840 bhp	2 cpp	
Quinte Loyalist **	Caterpillar - 3196	Diesel	2	6	770 bhp		
Radcliffe R. Latimer	MaK - 8M32C	Diesel	2	8	10,442 bhp	1 cpp	
Rebecca Lynn *	GM EMD - 16-567-BC	Diesel	2	16	3,600 bhp	2	
Reliance *	A.B. Nohab - SVI 16VS-F	Diesel	2	16	5,600 bhp	1 cpp	17.6
Robert S. Pierson	Alco - 16V251E	Diesel	2	16	5,600 bhp	1	17.8
Roger Blough	Pielstick - 16PC2V-400	Diesel	2	16	14,200 bhp	1 cpp	16.7
Rosaire A. Desgagnés	MaK/Caterpillar - 6M43	Diesel	1	6	7,344 bhp	1 cpp	17.8
Rt. Hon. Paul J. Martin	MaK/Caterpillar - 6M32**C**	Diesel	2	6	8,060 bhp (est)	1 cpp	
Saginaw	MaK - 6M43C	Diesel	1	6	8,160 bhp	1 cpp	16.1
Salarium	Pielstick - 10PC2-2V-400	Diesel	2	10	10,700 bhp	1 cpp	13.8
Sam Laud	GM EMD - 20-645-E7	Diesel	2	20	7,200 bhp	1 cpp	16.1
Samuel de Champlain *	GM EMD - 20-645-E5	Diesel	2	20	7,200 bhp	2 cpp	17.3
Samuel Risley (CCG)	Wartsila - VASA 12V22HF	Diesel	4	12	8,836 bhp	2 cpp	17.3
Sarah Desgagnés	MaK - 7M43	Diesel	1	7	9,517 bhp	1 cpp	15.0
Sea Eagle II *	GM EMD - 20-645-E7	Diesel	2	20	7,200 bhp	2	13.8
Sedna Desgagnés	MaK/Caterpillar - 6M43	Diesel	1	6	7,344 bhp	1 cpp	17.8
Sharon M I *	Niigata - 6L38HX	Diesel	2	6	1,934 bhp	2	16.0
Spruceglen	Sulzer - 4RLB76	Diesel	1	4	10,880 bhp	1	13.8
St. Clair	GM EMD - 20-645-E7	Diesel	3	20	10,800 bhp	1 cpp	16.7
Stewart J. Cort	GM EMD - 20-645-E7	Diesel	4	20	14,400 bhp	2 cpp	18.4
Tecumseh	Pielstick - 12PC-2V-400	Diesel	2	12	12,000 bhp	1 cpp	16.1
Taiga Desgagnés	B&W - 6S46MC-C	Diesel	1	6	9,482 bhp	1	17.3
Thunder Bay	MAN-B&W - 6S50ME-B9	Diesel	1	6	11,897 bhp	1	15.5
Tim McKeil*	Niigata 6L38HX	Diesel	2	6	2,400 bhp	2	15.3
Tim S. Dool	MaK - 8M43C	Diesel	1	8	10,750 bhp	1 cpp	17.3
Umiak I	M.A.N.-B&W - 7S70ME-C	Diesel	1	7	29,598 bhp	1 cpp	16.5
Umiavut	Hanshin - 6LF58	Diesel	1	6	6,000 bhp	1 cpp	16.2
Undaunted *	Cummins K38-M	Diesel	2	12	2,000 bhp	2	
Victory *	MaK - 6MU551AK	Diesel	2	6	7,880 bhp	2	16.1
Victory I	Caterpillar 3516TA-B	Diesel	2	16	4,000 bhp	2	11.5
Victory II	Caterpillar 3516TA-B	Diesel	2	16	4,000 bhp	2	11.5
Walter J. McCarthy Jr.	GM EMD - 20-645-E7B	Diesel	4	20	14,400 bhp	2 cpp	18.4
Whitefish Bay	MAN-B&W - 6S50ME-B9	Diesel	1	6	11,897 bhp	1	15.5
Wilfred Sykes	Westinghouse Elec. Corp.	Turbine	1	**	7,700 shp	1	16.1
Zélada Desgagnés	MaK/Caterpillar - 6M43	Diesel	1	6	7,344 bhp	1 cpp	17.8
Zeus *	Caterpillar - D399	Diesel	2	8	2,250 bhp	2	

Ed Labernik's
Marine & Wildlife Art
of the Great Lakes Region

Prints & Originals
Commissions Accepted

1717 E. 8th St., Duluth, MN 55812
(218) 724-3606 ~ elgreatlakesart@charter.net

GreatLakesArt.org

Tanker Iver Bright spent the winter of 2018-19 working on the Great Lakes. *(Paul C. LaMarre III)*

Federal Danube heaves anchor. *(Roger LeLievre)*

Saltwater Fleets

Floretgracht on the Detroit River. *(Neil Schultheiss)*

A

ABC MARITIME, NYON, SWITZERLAND *(abcmaritime.ch)*

Adfines Sea	9580962	TK	2011	D	13,239	530' 05"	75' 06"	40' 08"
(Osttank Norway '11-'12)								
Adfines Sky	9580986	TK	2011	D	13,239	530' 05"	75' 06"	40' 08"
(Osttank Italy '11-'11, Osttank Finland '11-'11)								
Adfines Star	9580974	TK	2011	D	13,239	530' 05"	75' 06"	40' 08"
(Osttank Denmark '11-'11, Osttank Sweden '11-'11)								
Adfines Sun	9580998	TK	2011	D	13,239	530' 05"	75' 06"	40' 08"
(Osttank Denmark '11-'11, Osttank Sweden '11-'11)								

ACE TANKERS CV, AMSTERDAM, NETHERLANDS *(ace-tankers.com)*

Chem Hydra	9486180	TK	2009	D	11,939	475' 01"	75' 06"	40' 08"
Chem Norma	9486192	TK	2009	D	11,939	475' 11"	75' 06"	40' 08"
Chem Polaris	9416044	TK	2008	D	11,930	481' 00"	77' 09"	42' 08"
*(Braken '08-'10, **Maemi** '10-'15)*								

AHRENKIEL STEAMSHIP GMBH & CO., HAMBURG, GERMANY *(ahrenkiel-steamship.com)*

Cape Dawson	9449429	TK	2009	D	8,278	393' 08"	66' 11"	39' 00"
(Rio Dawson '09-'09)								

ALLIANCE TANKERS, HAMILTON, BERMUDA *(alliancemaritime.com)*

Askholmen	9436381	TK	2009	D	11,551	472' 05"	74' 02"	42' 00"
*(**Hellespont Charger** '09-'14)*								
Furuholmen	9553397	TK	2010	D	11,908	473' 02"	75' 06"	40' 08"
(CF Zachary '11-'11)								
Golden Oak	9445655	TK	2008	D	8,505	419' 07"	67' 00"	37' 09"
(Sichem Berlin '08-'08, Marida Marguerite '08-'14)								
Kirkeholmen	9553402	TK	2010	D	11,908	473' 02"	75' 06"	40' 08"
(CF Sophia '10-'12)								
Larsholmen	9436410	TK	2009	D	11,551	472' 05"	74' 02"	42' 00"
*(**Hellespont Centurion** '10-'14)*								
Lokholmen	9433303	TK	2010	D	11,551	472' 05"	74' 02"	42' 00"
*(**Hellespont Crusader** '10-'14)*								

ARA GROUP, WERKENDAM, NETHERLANDS *(aragroup.nl)*

ARA Rotterdam	9240471	BC	2002	D	7,406	468' 02"	59' 10"	33' 04"
*(Sabrina '02-'02, MSC Rades '02-'04, Sabrina '04-'04, SCM Olympic '04-'05, **Sabrina** '05-'14)*								

ARMADOR GEMI ISLETMECILIGI TICARET LTD., ISTANBUL, TURKEY *(armadorshipping.com)*

Cornelia	9216597	BC	2001	D	16,807	574' 02"	75' 09"	44' 09"
(Pine '01-'04)								
Pochard S	9262534	BC	2003	D	22,655	655' 10"	77' 09"	50' 02"
*(**Pochard** '03-'14)*								

ATLANTIK DENIZCILIK TICARET VE SANAYI A.S., ISTANBUL, TURKEY *(atlantikdnz.com)*

Atlantik Miracle	9477490	TK	2008	D	7,315	424' 10"	65' 00"	34' 01"

AUERBACH SCHIFFFAHRT GMBH & CO. KG, HAMBURG, GERMANY *(auerbach-schifffahrt.de)*

Leanne Auerbach	9388912	HL	2008	D	9,611	453' 00"	70' 01"	36' 01"
*(Beluga Foresight '08-'11, **Foresight** '11-'18)*								
Maple Lea	9358034	HL	2007	D	9,611	453' 00"	68' 11"	36' 01"
*(**Beluga Flirtation** '07-'11, Thorco Horizon '11-'12, Maple Lea '12-'12, BBC Maple Lea '12-'18)*								

B

BD-SHIPSNAVO GMBH & CO., HAREN-EMS, GERMANY *(shipsnavo.de)*

Active	9343821	BC	2008	D	7,341	378' 03"	64' 04"	37' 05"
(Antilles VII '08-'14)								

BERNHARD SCHULTE GROUP OF COMPANIES, HAMBURG, GERMANY *(schultegroup.com)*

Edzard Schulte	9439852	TK	2011	D	11,246	476' 02"	75' 06"	41' 01"
Elisabeth Schulte	9439840	TK	2010	D	11,246	476' 02"	75' 06"	41' 01"
Erin Schulte	9439814	TK	2009	D	11,246	476' 02"	75' 06"	41' 01"
Eva Schulte	9439826	TK	2010	D	11,246	476' 02"	75' 06"	41' 01"
Everhard Schulte	9439838	TK	2010	D	11,246	476' 02"	75' 06"	41' 01"

Fleet Name / Vessel Name	Vessel IMO #	Vessel Type	Year Built	Engine Type	Cargo Cap. or Gross*	Overall Length	Vessel Breadth	Vessel Depth
BIGLIFT SHIPPING BV, AMSTERDAM, NETHERLANDS (bigliftshipping.com)								
Happy Ranger	9139311	HL	1998	D	10,990	452' 09"	74' 10"	42' 06"
Happy River	9139294	HL	1997	D	10,990	452' 09"	74' 10"	42' 06"
Happy Rover	9139309	HL	1997	D	10,990	452' 09"	74' 10"	42' 06"
Tracer	9204702	HL	2000	D	6,714	329' 09"	73' 06"	26' 11"
BLOUNT SMALL SHIP ADVENTURES, WARREN, RI (blountsmallshipadventures.com)								
Grande Caribe	8978631	PA	1997	D	97*	185' 10"	39' 00"	9' 09"
Built: Blount Industries Inc., Warren, RI								
Grande Mariner	8978643	PA	1998	D	97*	185' 10"	39' 00"	9' 09"
Built: Blount Industries Inc., Warren, RI								
BLYSTAD GROUP, OSLO, NORWAY (blystad.no)								
FOLLOWING VESSELS UNDER CHARTER TO SONGA SHIPMANAGEMENT								
Songa Challenge	9409510	TK	2009	D	11,623	477' 05"	77' 09"	43' 10"
Songa Emerald	9473937	TK	2009	D	11,259	472' 05"	74' 02"	41' 00"
Songa Opal	9473913	TK	2009	D	11,259	472' 05"	74' 02"	41' 00"
Songa Peace	9409522	TK	2009	D	11,623	477' 05"	77' 09"	43' 10"
(Global Peace '09-'13)								
BRIESE SCHIFFAHRTS GMBH & CO. KG, LEER, GERMANY (briese.de)								
BBC Alberta	9468102	HL	2010	D	9,611	452' 11"	68' 11"	36' 01"
*(Beluga Maturity '10-'10, Beluga Firmament '10-'11, **BBC Celina** '11-'15)*								
BBC Austria	9433327	GC	2009	D	7,002	393' 00"	66' 03"	32' 02"
BBC Balboa	9501667	GC	2012	D	6,310	393' 00"	66' 03"	32' 02"
BBC Elbe	9347059	GC	2006	D	12,936	469' 07"	75' 11"	43' 08"
(Horumersiel '06-'06)								
BBC Europe	9266308	GC	2003	D	7,002	392' 11"	66' 03"	32' 02"
BBC Fuji	9508419	GC	2011	D	8,255	412' 09"	72' 02"	35' 05"
BBC Germany	9297096	GC	2003	D	7,002	392' 11"	66' 03"	32' 02"
*(**BBC Germany** '03-'06, **Leda** '06-'08)*								
BBC Hudson	9435868	GC	2009	D	12,936	469' 07"	75' 11"	43' 08"
BBC Kibo	9508421	GC	2011	D	8,255	412' 09"	72' 02"	35' 05"
BBC Kwiatkowski	9436953	GC	2008	D	6,155	401' 09"	59' 09"	31' 02"
(Eugeniusz Kwiatkowski '08-'08)								
BBC Mississippi	9347061	GC	2006	D	12,936	469' 07"	75' 11"	43' 08"
(Greetsiel '06-'07)								
BBC Mont Blanc	9508433	GC	2011	D	8,255	412' 09"	72' 02"	35' 05"
BBC Olympus	9508457	GC	2012	D	8,255	412' 09"	72' 02"	35' 05"
BBC Polonia	9415325	GC	2010	D	6,155	401' 09"	59' 09"	31' 02"
BBC Rushmore	9508469	GC	2012	D	8,255	412' 09"	72' 02"	35' 05"
BBC Switzerland	9433315	GC	2008	D	7,002	393' 00"	66' 03"	32' 02"
BBC Utah	9468114	HL	2011	D	9,611	452' 11"	68' 11"	36' 01"
(Beluga Flashlight '11-'11, BBC Idaho '11-'14, Isakandar '14-'15, Idaho '15-'16)								
BBC Vesuvius	9508471	GC	2012	D	8,255	412' 09"	72' 02"	35' 05"
BBC Volga	9436329	GC	2009	D	12,936	469' 07"	75' 11"	43' 08"
(Ocean Breeze '09-'09)								
BBC Weser	9347047	GC	2006	D	12,936	469' 07"	75' 11"	43' 08"
(Westerdamm '06-'06, BBC Weser '06-'10, STX Bright '10-'14)								
BBC Xingang	9508483	GC	2013	D	8,255	412' 09"	72' 02"	35' 05"
CLI Pride	9513646	GC	2011	D	7,138	427' 02"	54' 02"	37' 09"
*(Brielle '11-'14, **BBC Luanda** '14-'18)*								

A Note About Saltwater Listings

Observers will likely spot saltwater vessels that are not included in this book. These may be newcomers to the Great Lakes/Seaway system, recent renames or new construction. This is not meant to be an exhaustive listing of every saltwater vessel that could potentially visit the Great Lakes and St. Lawrence Seaway. To attempt to do so, given the sheer number of world merchant ships, would be space and cost prohibitive. This list reflects vessels whose primary trade routes are on saltwater but which also regularly visit Great Lakes and St. Lawrence Seaway ports above Montreal. Fleets listed may operate other vessels worldwide than those included herein; additional vessels may be found on fleet websites, which have been included where available. Former names listed in **boldface** type indicate the vessel visited the Seaway under that name.

Fleet Name Vessel Name	Vessel IMO #	Vessel Type	Year Built	Engine Type	Cargo Cap. or Gross*	Overall Length	Vessel Breadth	Vessel Depth
Kurt Paul	9435856	GC	2009	D	12,936	469' 07"	75' 11"	43' 08"
Peter Ronna	9198628	GC	2002	D	3,198	324' 03"	49' 10"	24' 03"
(Peter Ronna '02-'03, Svend '03-'05)								
Sjard	9303314	GC	2007	D	12,936	469' 07"	75' 11"	43' 08"

BROSTROM AB, COPENHAGEN, DENMARK (brostrom.com)

Bro Agnes	9348302	TK	2008	D	12,164	472' 07"	75' 06"	40' 08"
Bro Alma	9356610	TK	2007	D	12,164	472' 07"	75' 06"	40' 08"
(Ganstar '07-'07)								
Bro Anna	9344435	TK	2008	D	12,164	472' 07"	75' 06"	40' 08"
(Gan Gesture '08-'08)								

C

CANADA FEEDER LINES BV, GRONINGEN, NETHERLANDS (cfl.nl)

Momentum Scan	9534432	GC	2010	D	6,693	381' 05"	58' 05"	34' 05"
Industrial More	9534482	GC	2013	D	6,693	381' 05"	58' 05"	34' 05"

CANFORNAV (CANADIAN FOREST NAVIGATION CO. LTD.), MONTREAL, CANADA (canfornav.com)

At press time, Canadian Forest Navigation Co. Ltd. had the following vessels under long-or short-term charter. Please consult their respective fleets for details: **Andean, Barnacle, Blacky, Bluebill, Bluewing, Brant, Cape, Chestnut, Cinnamon, Greenwing, Labrador, Maccoa, Mandarin, Mottler, Ruddy, Shoveler, Sunda, Torrent, Tufty, Tundra, Whistler** and **Wigeon.**

CARISBROOKE SHIPPING LTD., COWES, UNITED KINGDOM (carisbrooke.co)

Jacqueline C	9429754	BC	2009	D	9,530	453' 01"	68' 11"	36' 01"
Johanna C	9430131	BC	2009	D	9,530	453' 01"	68' 11"	36' 01"

CELSIUS SHIPPING APS, HELLERUP, DENMARK (celsiusshipping.com)

Celsius Mumbai	9304332	TK	2005	D	11,623	477' 05"	77' 09"	43' 10"
(Bum Eun '05-'13)								

CHEMBULK MARITIME LLC, SOUTHPORT, CT (chembulktankers.com)

Chembulk Kobe	9263136	TK	2002	D	11,590	477' 05"	77' 09"	43' 10"

CHEMFLEET SHIPPING LTD., ISTANBUL, TURKEY (chemfleet.org)

Mehmet A	9418822	TK	2011	D	13,000	530' 04"	73' 06"	34' 01"
(Aldemar '11-'11)								

CLEARWATER GROUP, ROTTERDAM, NETHERLANDS (clearwatergroup.nl)

Carolus Magnus	9298375	TK	2007	D	12,776	539' 02"	75' 06"	42' 00"
(MCT Breithorn '07-'15, SCT Breithorn '15-'17)								

Pia in the Welland Canal. (John C. Knecht)

Emanuel S.	9298363	TK	2007	D	12,776	539' 02"	75' 06"	42' 00"
(MCT Monte Rosa '07-'15, **SCT Monte Rosa** '15-'17)								
Rosy	9298387	TK	2008	D	12,776	539' 02"	75' 06"	42' 00"
(MCT Stockhorn '08-'15, **SCT Stockhorn** '15-'17)								

COASTAL SHIPPING LTD., GOOSE BAY, NEWFOUNDLAND, CANADA *(woodwards.nf.ca)*

Kitikmeot W.	9421219	TK	2010	D	13,097	491' 11"	75' 06"	42' 10"
(Icdas 09 '10-'18)								
Kivalliq W.	9187409	TK	2004	D	8,882	476' 08"	68' 03"	36' 09"
(Falcon '04-'09, **Sten Fjord** '09-'18)								
Qikiqtaaluk W.	9421221	TK	2011	D	13,097	491' 11"	75' 06"	42' 10"
(Icdas-11 '10-'18)								

C.O.E. SHIPPING GMBH & CO., BUXTEHUDE, GERMANY *(coeshipping.com)*
FOLLOWING VESSELS UNDER CHARTER TO SPLIETHOFF

COE Leni	9453793	HL	2010	D	9,627	454' 05"	68' 11"	36' 01"
(Marselisborg '10-'12, *Clipper Anne* '12-'14, **Marselisborg** '14-'16)								

COMPAGNIE DU PONANT S.A., MARSEILLES, FRANCE *(ponant.com)*

Le Champlain	9814038	PA	2018	D	9,976	431' 04"	59' 01"	59' 09"

CONTI REEDEREI MANAGEMENT GMBH & CO., MUNICH, GERMANY

Hamburg	9138329	PA	1997	D	15,067	472' 10"	70' 06"	33' 08"
Operated by Plantours Cruises, Bremen, Germany *(c. Columbus* '97-'12)								

COSCO SOUTHERN ASPHALT SHIPPING CO. LTD, GUANGZHOU, CHINA

Zhuang Yuan Ao	9650339	TK	2012	D	9,780	479' 00"	72' 02"	35' 05"

D-E

DUZGIT GEMI INSA SANAYI, ISTANBUL, TURKEY *(duzgit.com)*

Duzgit Dignity	9581019	TK	2014	D	5,770	390' 09"	56' 05"	30' 02"
Duzgit Endeavour	9581007	TK	2013	D	10,276	509' 09"	71' 02"	36' 05"

EASTERN PACIFIC SHIPPING, SINGAPORE

Ebony Ray	9363857	TK	2008	D	11,623	477' 05"	77' 09"	43' 10"
(Millennium Park '08-'14)								

ELBE SHIPPING GMBH, DROCHTERSEN, GERMANY *(reederei-elbe-shipping.de)*

BBC Thames	9368340	HL	2008	D	11,894	469' 02"	70' 06"	43' 08"
(Beluga Graduation '08-'09)								

Poland-registered bulk carrier Lubie on Lake Ontario. (Jeff Cameron)

Fleet Name Vessel Name	Vessel IMO #	Vessel Type	Year Built	Engine Type	Cargo Cap. or Gross*	Overall Length	Vessel Breadth	Vessel Depth
EMPIRE CHEMICAL TANKER HOLDINGS INC., PIRAEUS, GREECE								
Malmo	9373242	TK	2008	D	13,472	491' 11"	76' 01"	42' 10"

F-G

FAIRFIELD CHEMICAL CARRIERS, WILTON, CONNECTICUT, USA *(fairfieldchemical.com)*								
Fairchem Charger	9367401	TK	2009	D	11,623	477' 05"	77' 09"	43' 10"
Fairchem Colt	9304344	TK	2005	D	11,623	477' 05"	77' 09"	43' 10"
Fairchem Friesian	9367413	TK	2005	D	11,623	477' 05"	77' 09"	43' 10"
Fairchem Steed	9311256	TK	2005	D	11,623	477' 05"	77' 09"	43' 10"
FEDNAV, MONTREAL, CANADA *(fednav.com)*								
CANARCTIC SHIPPING CO. LTD. – DIVISION OF FEDNAV								
Arctic	7517507	BK	1978	D	20,236	727' 06"	75' 00"	50 00"
Built: Port Weller Dry Docks, Port Weller, ON								
Nunavik	9673850	BK	2014	D	22,622	619' 05"	87' 03"	51' 06"
Umiak I	9334715	BK	2006	D	22,462	619' 05"	87' 03"	51' 06"
FEDNAV INTERNATIONAL LTD. - DIVISION OF FEDNAV								
Federal Asahi {2}	9200419	BC	2000	D	20,659	656' 02"	77' 11"	48' 09"
Federal Baltic	9697806	BC	2015	D	20,789	656' 01"	77' 11"	48' 09"
Federal Barents	9697820	BC	2015	D	20,789	656' 01"	77' 11"	48' 09"
Federal Beaufort	9697818	BC	2015	D	20,789	656' 01"	77' 11"	48' 09"
Federal Bering	9697832	BC	2015	D	20,789	656' 01"	77' 11"	48' 09"
Federal Biscay	9697856	BC	2015	D	20,789	656' 01"	77' 11"	48' 09"
Federal Bristol	9697844	BC	2015	D	20,789	656' 01"	77' 11"	48' 09"
Federal Caribou	9671096	BC	2016	D	20,789	656' 01"	77' 11"	48' 09"

Americaborg at the Duluth Port Terminal. *(Chris Mazzella)*

Fleet Name / Vessel Name	Vessel IMO #	Vessel Type	Year Built	Engine Type	Cargo Cap. or Gross*	Overall Length	Vessel Breadth	Vessel Depth
Federal Cedar	9671101	BC	2016	D	20,789	656' 01"	77' 11"	48' 09"
Federal Champlain	9671058	BC	2016	D	20,789	656' 01"	77' 11"	48' 09"
Federal Churchill	9671060	BC	2016	D	20,789	656' 01"	77' 11"	48' 09"
Federal Clyde	9671072	BC	2016	D	20,789	656' 01"	77' 11"	48' 09"
Federal Columbia	9671084	BC	2016	D	20,789	656' 01"	77' 11"	48' 09"
Federal Danube {2}	9271511	BC	2003	D	22,654	652' 11"	78' 05"	50' 02"
Federal Dart	9805245	BC	2018	D	20,789	656' 01"	77' 11"	48' 09"
Federal Dee	9805269	BC	2018	D	20,789	656' 01"	77' 11"	48' 09"
Federal Delta	9805271	BC	2018	D	20,789	656' 01"	77' 11"	48' 09"
Federal Elbe	9230000	BC	2003	D	22,654	652' 11"	78' 05"	50' 02"
Federal Ems	9229984	BC	2002	D	22,654	652' 11"	78' 05"	50' 02"
Federal Hudson {3}	9205902	BC	2000	D	20,659	656' 02"	77' 11"	48' 09"
Federal Hunter {2}	9205938	BC	2001	D	20,659	656' 02"	77' 11"	48' 09"
Federal Katsura	9293923	BC	2005	D	19,165	624' 08"	77' 05"	49' 10"
Federal Kivalina	9205885	BC	2000	D	20,659	656' 02"	77' 11"	48' 09"
Federal Kumano	9244257	BC	2001	D	20,659	656' 02"	77' 11"	48' 09"
Federal Kushiro	9284702	BC	2003	D	19,165	624' 09"	77' 05"	49' 10"
Federal Leda	9229996	BC	2003	D	22,654	655' 10"	77' 09"	50' 02"
Federal Mackinac	9299460	BC	2004	D	18,825	607' 03"	77' 01"	46' 03"
Federal Margaree	9299472	BC	2005	D	18,825	607' 03"	77' 01"	46' 03"
Federal Mayumi	9529578	BC	2012	D	20,465	655' 06"	77' 11"	48' 09"
Federal Nagara	9805257	BC	2018	D	20,789	656' 01"	77' 11"	48' 09"
Federal Nakagawa	9278791	BC	2005	D	20,659	656' 02"	77' 11"	48' 09"
Federal Oshima	9200330	BC	1999	D	20,659	656' 02"	77' 11"	48' 09"
Federal Rhine {2}	9110925	BC	1997	D	20,837	656' 02"	77' 01"	48' 10"
Federal Rideau	9200445	BC	2000	D	20,659	656' 02"	77' 11"	48' 09"

Federal Elbe loading grain at the Richardson International Terminal in Thunder Bay, ON. (Gene Onchulenko)

Federal Saguenay {2}	9110913	BC	1996	D	20,837	656′ 02″	77′ 01″	48′ 10″
Federal Sakura	9288291	BC	2005	D	19,165	624′ 09″	77′ 05″	49′ 10″
Federal Satsuki	9529578	BC	2012	D	20,465	655′ 06″	77′ 11″	48′ 09″
Federal Schelde {3}	9118147	BC	1997	D	20,837	656′ 02″	77′ 01″	48′ 10″
Federal Seto	9267209	BC	2004	D	20,659	656′ 02″	77′ 11″	48′ 09″
Federal Shimanto	9218404	BC	2001	D	19,125	624′ 09″	77′ 05″	49′ 10″
Federal Welland	9205926	BC	2000	D	20,659	656′ 02″	77′ 11″	48′ 09″
Federal Weser	9229972	BC	2002	D	22,654	655′ 10″	77′ 09″	50′ 02″
Federal Yoshino	9218416	BC	2001	D	19,125	624′ 09″	77′ 05″	49′ 10″
Federal Yukon	9205897	BC	2000	D	20,659	656′ 02″	77′ 11″	48′ 09″

At press time, Fednav also had the following vessels under charter. Please consult their respective fleets for details: **Federal Alster, Federal Mosel, Federal Ruhr** and **Federal Yukina.**

FORESTWAVE NAVIGATION, HEERENVEEN, NETHERLANDS (forestwave.nl)

FWN Bonafide	9321108	BC	2006	D	7,767	477′ 09″	59′ 10″	33′ 10″
(UAL Antwerp '06-'12, UAL Nigeria '12-'15, Anna C '15-'15)								

FRANCO COMPANIA NAVIERA SA, ATHENS, GREECE (franco.gr)

Helena G.	9358369	BC	2007	D	22,792	655′ 10″	77′ 09″	50′ 02″
(Garganey '07-'17)								
Isabelle G.	9285938	BC	2004	D	22,792	655′ 10″	77′ 09″	50′ 02″
(Eider '04-'18)								
Johanna G.	9285940	BC	2005	D	22,792	655′ 10″	77′ 09″	50′ 02″
(Redhead '05-'18)								
Maria G.	9358383	BC	2007	D	22,792	655′ 10″	77′ 09″	50′ 02″
(Gadwall '07-'17)								

FREESE SHIPPING, STADE, GERMANY (freeseship.com)

BBC Kansas	9349291	HL	2006	D	9,611	453′ 00″	68′ 11″	36′ 01″
*(Beluga Foundation '06-'11, Opal Gallant '11-'11, Freya Scan '11-'13, Thorco Denmark '13-'15, **Amber** '15-'16)*								
Lisanna	9283954	HL	2004	D	9,618	453′ 00″	68′ 11″	36′ 01″
*(Beluga Efficiency '04-'06, BBC Carolina '06-'07, **Beluga Efficiency** '07-'11, Lilia '11-'11, Freese Scan '11-'12 BBC Washington '12-'15)*								
Pacific Huron	9546796	BC	2010	D	20,603	623′ 04″	77′ 11″	47′ 11″
(Seven Islands '10-'10)								
Three Rivers	9546784	BC	2010	D	20,603	623′ 04″	77′ 11″	47′ 11″

GEBRUDER AHRENS REEDEREI, GRUNENDEICH, GERMANY

Alina	9468085	HL	2010	D	9,611	452′ 11″	68′ 11″	36′ 01″
(Beluga Modification '10-'10, Beluga Faith '10-'11)								
Rike	9468097	HL	2010	D	9,611	452′ 11″	68′ 11″	36′ 01″
(Beluga Festival '10-'10)								

H

HANSA HEAVY LIFT GMBH, BREMEN, GERMANY (hansaheavylift.com)

HHL Amur	9435753	HL	2007	D	9,611	452′ 11″	68′ 11″	36′ 01″
(Beluga Fidelity '07-'11)								
HHL Elbe	9433262	HL	2008	D	9,627	454′ 05″	68′ 11″	36′ 01″
(BBC Alaska '08-'13, Elbe '13-'14)								
HHL Mississippi	9435765	HL	2009	D	9,611	452′ 11″	68′ 11″	36′ 01″
(Beluga Fantasy '09-'11, OXL Fantasy '11-'11)								
HHL Tyne	9433274	HL	2009	D	6,927	454′ 05″	68′ 11″	36′ 01″
(BBC Montana '09-'13, Tyne '13-'14)								
Josef	9467005	HL	2011	D	9,618	453′ 00″	68′ 11″	36′ 01″
*(Beluga Fealty '11-'11, **HHL Congo** '11-18)*								

HARREN & PARTNER GMBH, BREMEN, GERMANY (harren-partner.de)

Palabora	9501875	HL	2010	D	11,473	439′ 08″	75′ 06″	37′ 05″
Palmerton	9501863	HL	2009	D	11,473	439′ 08″	75′ 06″	37′ 05″
Pantanal	9316579	HL	2004	D	7,002	393′ 00″	66′ 03″	32′ 02″
Patras	9348297	TK	2007	D	12,164	472′ 07″	75′ 06″	40′ 08″

HARTMAN SEATRADE, URK, NETHERLANDS (hartmanseatrade.com)

Pacific Dawn	9558464	BC	2010	D	2,981	343′ 10″	52′ 06″	24′ 03″

Fleet Name Vessel Name	Vessel IMO #	Vessel Type	Year Built	Engine Type	Cargo Cap. or Gross*	Overall Length	Vessel Breadth	Vessel Depth
HERMANN BUSS GMBH, LEER, GERMANY								
BBC Carolina	9402043	HL	2007	D	9,618	453' 00"	68' 11"	36' 01"
(Beluga Fantastic '07-'11)								
BBC Manitoba	9384320	HL	2007	D	9,618	453' 00"	68' 11"	36' 01"
(Beluga Formation '07-'12, Formation '12-'14, Thorco Diamond '14-'15)								
HS SCHIFFAHRTS GMBH & CO, HAREN-EMS, GERMANY *(hs-schiffahrt.de)*								
DS Brazil	9535618	GC	2011	D	8,059	477' 10"	59' 10"	33' 10"
(Thorco Copenhagen '11-'16, BBC Brazil '16-'18)								
Onego Haren	9511636	GC	2010	D	7,878	477' 09"	59' 10"	33' 10"
(Beluga Loyalty '10-'11, BBC Haren '11-'12, Haren '12-'15, BBC Haren '15-'18)								
Onego Rotterdam	9631345	GC	2013	D	5,667	387' 07"	52' 02"	28' 10"
(Anna '13-'13)								
HUARONG HUIYIN LTD., HONG KONG, CHINA								
Chemical Aquarius	9576820	TK	2012	D	11,383	467' 06"	75' 06"	41' 04"

I-J-K

INTERMARINE, HOUSTON, TEXAS, USA *(intermarineusa.com)*								
Industrial Charger	9213959	GC	2000	D	7,252	393' 01"	65' 07"	37' 01"
(Virgo J '00-'00, Industrial Charger '00-'09, Ocean Charger '09-'15)								
Industrial Eagle	9407574	GC	2008	D	8,750	456' 00"	65' 07"	27' 03"
Ocean Crescent	9258193	GC	2002	D	7,252	393' 01"	65' 07"	37' 01"
(Pollux J. '02-'02, Industrial Crescent '02-'10)								
INTERSHIP NAVIGATION CO. LTD, LIMASSOL, CYPRUS *(intership-cyprus.com)*								
FOLLOWING VESSELS UNDER CHARTER TO FEDNAV LTD.								
Federal Alster	9766164	BC	2016	D	22,947	655' 10"	77' 09"	50' 03"
Federal Mosel	9766188	BC	2017	D	22,947	655' 10"	77' 09"	50' 03"
Federal Ruhr	9766176	BC	2017	D	22,947	655' 10"	77' 09"	50' 03"
INTREPID SHIPPING LLC. STAMFORD, CONNECTICUT, USA *(intrepidshipping.com)*								
Intrepid Republic	9466752	TK	2011	D	11,246	476' 02"	75' 06"	41' 00"
JOHANN M. K. BLUMENTHAL GMBH & CO., HAMBURG, GERMANY *(bluships.com)*								
Ida	9109536	BC	1995	D	11,193	486' 03"	74' 10"	40' 00"
Lita	9117416	BC	1995	D	11,193	486' 03"	74' 10"	40' 00"
JOHS THODE GMBH & CO., HAMBURG, GERMANY *(johs-thode.de)*								
Hanse Gate	9283540	BC	2004	D	18,825	607' 03"	77' 01"	46' 03"
(Federal Matane '04-'11, CL Hanse Gate '11-'15)								
JUMBO SHIPPING CO. SA, ROTTERDAM, NETHERLANDS *(jumbomaritime.nl)*								
Fairlane	9153654	HL	2000	D	7,971	362' 06"	67' 03"	44' 03"
Fairlift	8806905	HL	1990	D	6,953	330' 08"	68' 10"	43' 08"
JUNGERHANS MARITIME SERVICES GMBH & CO., HAREN EMS, GERMANY *(juengerhans.de)*								
BBC Kimberley	9407586	HL	2009	D	8,750	456' 00"	65' 07"	37' 01"
(Bellatrix J '09-'09, Industrial Egret '09-'12)								
KREY SCHIFFAHRTS GMBH & COMPANY KG, LEER, GERMANY *(krey-schiffahrt.de)*								
FOLLOWING VESSELS UNDER CHARTER TO SPLIETHOFF								
Erik	9435105	HL	2008	D	9,618	453' 00"	68' 11"	36' 01"
(BBC Louisiana '08-'17)								
Frieda	9435117	HL	2008	D	9,618	453' 00"	68' 11"	36' 01"
(BBC Colorado '08-'17)								
Pia	9384318	HL	2007	D	9,618	453' 00"	68' 11"	36' 01"
(BBC Alabama '07-'17)								

L-M

LAURANNE SHIPPING BV, GHENT, NETHERLANDS *(lauranne-shipping.com)*								
LS Evanne	9519614	TK	2010	D	4,808	390' 09"	55' 05"	27' 07"
(Kormel '10-'12)								

Fleet Name Vessel Name	Vessel IMO #	Vessel Type	Year Built	Engine Type	Cargo Cap. or Gross*	Overall Length	Vessel Breadth	Vessel Depth
LONGSHIP BV, GRONINGEN, NETHERLANDS *(longship.com)*								
Pride	9480277	BC	2008	D	10,784	497' 00"	68' 11"	39' 08"
(Qin Feng165 '08-'08, Avenue Pride '08-'13, Polaris Pride '13-'16)								
Senja	9516868	GC	2009	D	11,927	484' 01"	75' 06"	38' 09"
(Hagen '09-'16)								
Star II	9476068	BC	2008	D	10,784	497' 00"	68' 11"	39' 08"
(Avenue Star '08-'10, Polaris Star '10-'16)								
LUBECA MARINE GERMANY GMBH & CO., LUBECK, GERMANY *(lubeca-marine.de)*								
Gotland	9480136	GC	2011	D	12,772	471' 11"	74' 10"	43' 10"
(Rickmers Tianjin '11-'15)								
Lolland	9480124	GC	2011	D	12,772	471' 11"	74' 10"	43' 10"
(Rickmers Yokohama '11-'15)								
MASSOEL LTD., GENEVA, SWITZERLAND *(massoel.com)*								
Lugano	9244087	BC	2002	D	12,578	509' 00"	77' 09"	42' 08"
(DS Regent '02-'06)								
Martigny	9229867	BC	2002	D	12,578	509' 00"	77' 09"	42' 08"
(VOC Regal '02-'03, Clipper Regal '03-'06)								
MED MARITIME LTD., LONDON, ENGLAND								
Med Arctic	9410545	TK	2009	D	5,651	403' 10"	56' 05"	30' 02"
(Nordic Harmony '09-'09, Med Arctic '09-'15, Sea Dolphin '15-'15)								
MINERALIEN SCHIFFAHRT, SCHNAITTENBACH, GERMANY *(minship.com)*								
Harriett	9239458	BC	2002	D	17,665	590' 05"	75' 09"	45' 09"
Lady Doris	9459955	BC	2011	D	19,814	606' 11"	77' 09"	47' 11"
(Merganser '11-'11)								
Trudy	9415246	BC	2009	D	19,814	606' 11"	77' 09"	47' 11"
(Cresty '09-'09)								
Yulia	9459967	BC	2011	D	19,814	606' 11"	77' 09"	47' 11"
(Harlequin '11-'11)								
MTM SHIP MANAGEMENT LTD., SINGAPORE *(mtmshipmanagement.com)*								
MTM Antwerp	9291456	TK	2004	D	11,623	477' 05"	77' 09"	43' 10"
*(**Fairchem Stallion** '04-'14)*								
MTM Southport	9416032	TK	2008	D	11,930	481' 00"	77' 09"	42' 08"
(Golten '08-'10)								

N-O

NAVARONE SA MARINE ENTERPRISES, LIMASSOL, CYPRUS
FOLLOWING VESSELS UNDER CHARTER TO CANFORNAV

Andean	9413925	BC	2009	D	19,814	606' 11"	77' 09"	47' 11"

Tanker Chem Norma in the Welland Canal. (Matt Miner)

Fleet Name Vessel Name	Vessel IMO #	Vessel Type	Year Built	Engine Type	Cargo Cap. or Gross*	Overall Length	Vessel Breadth	Vessel Depth
Barnacle	9409742	BC	2009	D	19,814	607' 04"	77' 09"	47' 11"
Blacky	9393149	BC	2008	D	19,814	607' 04"	77' 09"	47' 11"
Bluebill	9263306	BC	2004	D	22,655	655' 10"	77' 09"	50' 02"
Brant	9393151	BC	2008	D	19,814	607' 04"	77' 09"	47' 11"
Chestnut	9477866	BC	2009	D	19,814	607' 04"	77' 09"	47' 11"
Labrador	9415222	BC	2010	D	19,814	606' 11"	77' 09"	47' 11"
Maccoa	9413913	BC	2009	D	19,814	606' 11"	77' 09"	47' 11"
Mottler	9477828	BC	2009	D	19,814	607' 04"	77' 09"	47' 11"
Ruddy	9459981	BC	2009	D	19,814	606' 11"	77' 09"	47' 11"
Shoveler	9459979	BC	2009	D	19,814	606' 11"	77' 09"	47' 11"
Torrent	9415210	BC	2010	D	19,814	606' 11"	77' 09"	47' 11"
Tufty	9393163	BC	2009	D	19,814	607' 04"	77' 09"	47' 11"
Tundra	9415208	BC	2009	D	19,814	606' 11"	77' 09"	47' 11"

NAVIGATION MARITIME BULGARE LTD., VARNA, BULGARIA (navbul.com)

Belasitza	9498262	BC	2011	D	19,906	610' 03"	77' 09"	48' 01"
Ludogorets	9415155	BC	2010	D	20,491	622' 02"	77' 04"	47' 11"
(Fritz '10-'15, MarBacan '15-'16)								
Lyulin	9498248	BC	2011	D	19,906	610' 03"	77' 09"	48' 01"
Oborishte	9415167	BC	2010	D	20,491	622' 02"	77' 04"	47' 11"
(Luebbert '10-'15, MarBioko '15-'16)								
Osogovo	9498250	BC	2010	D	19,906	610' 03"	77' 09"	47' 11"
Rodopi	9498274	BC	2012	D	19,906	610' 03"	77' 09"	47' 11"
Strandja	9564140	BC	2010	D	19,906	610' 03"	77' 09"	47' 11"
(Eastwind York '10-'10, Federal Yangtze '10-'10)								
Vitosha	9564138	BC	2010	D	19,906	610' 03"	77' 11"	47' 11"
(Eastwind Yates '10-'10, Federal Pearl '10-'10)								

NGM ENERGY S.A., PIRAEUS, GREECE

El Zorro	9344801	TK	2007	D	8,539	451' 11"	66' 11"	37' 09"

NORBULK SHIPPING CO. LTD., HAMILTON, BERMUDA (norbulkshipping.com)

Anuket Ruby	9393668	TK	2008	D	5,581	332' 08"	62' 06"	34' 05"

NOMADIC SHORT SEA SHIPPING, BERGEN, NORWAY (nomadic.no)

Nomadic Hjellestad	9452220	BC	2010	D	9,530	453' 01"	68' 11"	36' 01"
Nomadic Milde	9463554	BC	2011	D	9,530	453' 01"	68' 11"	36' 01"

NORDIC TANKERS MARINE A/S, COPENHAGEN, DENMARK (nordictankers.com)

Njord Clear	9230012	TK	2001	D	11,191	453' 01"	75' 06"	40' 02"
(Jo Chiara D '01-'04, Chiara '04-'06, Nora '06-'09, Harbour Clear '09-'15)								
Njord Cloud	9291066	TK	2004	D	11,191	453' 01"	75' 06"	40' 02"
(Phase D '04-'04, Phase '04-'09, Harbour Cloud '09-'15)								
Nordic Mari	9422677	TK	2009	D	11,930	481' 00"	77' 10"	42' 08"
(Clipper Mari '09-'14)								

Momentum Scan on Lake Ontario. (Jeff Cameron)

OCEAN CHALLENGE LTD., NICOSIA, CYPRUS
FOLLOWING VESSELS UNDER CHARTER TO CANFORNAV

Vessel	IMO	Type	Year	Eng	Cargo	Length	Breadth	Depth
Bluewing	9230919	BC	2002	D	18,311	611'08"	77'09"	46'0
Cinnamon	9239800	BC	2002	D	18,311	611'08"	77'09"	46'0
Greenwing	9230921	BC	2002	D	18,311	611'08"	77'09"	46'0
Mandarin	9239812	BC	2003	D	18,311	611'08"	77'09"	46'0

OCEANEX INC., MONTREAL, CANADA *(oceanex.com)*

Vessel	IMO	Type	Year	Eng	Cargo	Length	Breadth	Depth
Oceanex Avalon	9315044	CO	2005	D	14,639	481'11"	85'00"	45'1
Oceanex Connaigra	9649718	CO	2013	D	26,786	689'00"	97'01"	56'0
Oceanex Sanderling	7603502	RR	1977	D	21,849	364'01"	88'05"	57'0

(Rauenfels '77-'80, Essen '80-'81, Kongsfjord '81-'83, Onno '83-'87, ASL Sanderling '87-'08)

ONEGO SHIPPING & CHARTERING B.V., RHOON, NETHERLANDS *(onego.nl)*

Vessel	IMO	Type	Year	Eng	Cargo	Length	Breadth	Depth
Onego Rio	9258985	GC	2003	D	7,576	468'02"	59'09"	33'0

(Frida '03-'04, BBC England '04-'13, BBC Ecuador '13-'14, Thorco China '14-'16, BBC England '16-'17, England '17-'17

P

PARAKOU SHIPPING LTD., HONG KONG, CHINA *(parakougroup.com)*
FOLLOWING VESSELS UNDER CHARTER TO CANFORNAV

Vessel	IMO	Type	Year	Eng	Cargo	Length	Breadth	Depth
Whistler	9358371	BC	2007	D	22,792	655'10"	77'09"	50'02
Wigeon	9358395	BC	2007	D	22,792	655'10"	77'09"	50'02

PEARL SEAS CRUISES LLC, GUILFORD, CT *(pearlseascruises.com)*

Vessel	IMO	Type	Year	Eng	Cargo	Length	Breadth	Depth
Pearl Mist	9412701	PA	2009	D	5,109*	325'00"	52'00"	15'07

PHOENIX SHIPPING & TRADING SA, PIRAEAUS, GREECE *(phoenix-shipping.ro)*

Vessel	IMO	Type	Year	Eng	Cargo	Length	Breadth	Depth
Fearless	9228265	BC	2001	D	18,049	606'11"	77'05"	48'11

(Bright Laker '01-'13)

POLSTEAM (POLISH STEAMSHIP CO.), SZCZECIN, POLAND *(polsteam.com)*

Vessel	IMO	Type	Year	Eng	Cargo	Length	Breadth	Depth
Drawsko	9393450	BC	2010	D	20,603	623'04"	77'11"	47'11
Gardno	9767704	BC	2017	D	22,982	656'02"	77'09"	50'02

(Gardno '18-'18, Mont D'Iberville '18-'18)

Vessel	IMO	Type	Year	Eng	Cargo	Length	Breadth	Depth
Ina	9521875	BC	2012	D	17,096	492'00"	77'05"	41'00
Irma	9180396	BC	2000	D	21,387	655'10"	77'05"	50'02
Iryda	9180384	BC	1999	D	21,387	655'10"	77'05"	50'02
Isa	9180358	BC	1999	D	21,387	655'10"	77'05"	50'02
Isadora	9180372	BC	1999	D	21,387	655'10"	77'05"	50'02
Isolda	9180360	BC	1999	D	21,387	655'10"	77'05"	50'02
Juno	9422378	BC	2011	D	20,603	623'04"	77'11"	47'11
Lubie	9441984	BC	2011	D	20,603	623'04"	77'11"	47'11
Mamry	9496264	BC	2012	D	20,603	623'04"	77'11"	47'11
Miedwie	9393448	BC	2010	D	20,603	623'04"	77'11"	47'11
Narew	9521813	BC	2012	D	17,096	492'00"	77'05"	41'00
Olza	9521837	BC	2012	D	17,096	492'00"	77'05"	41'00
Prosna	9521849	BC	2012	D	17,096	492'00"	77'05"	41'00
Raba	9521825	BC	2012	D	17,096	492'00"	77'05"	41'00
Regalica	9521758	BC	2011	D	17,096	492'00"	77'05"	41'00
Resko	9393462	BC	2010	D	20,603	623'04"	77'11"	47'11
San	9521851	BC	2012	D	17,096	492'00"	77'05"	41'00
Skawa	9521863	BC	2012	D	17,096	492'00"	77'05"	41'00
Solina	9496252	BC	2012	D	20,603	623'04"	77'11"	47'11
Wicko	9393474	BC	2010	D	20,603	623'04"	77'11"	47'11

POT SCHEEPVAART BV, DELFZIJL, NETHERLANDS *(pot-scheepvaart.nl)*
FOLLOWING VESSELS UNDER CHARTER TO WAGENBORG SHIPPING

Vessel	IMO	Type	Year	Eng	Cargo	Length	Breadth	Depth
Kwintebank	9234288	GC	2002	D	6,378	433'09"	52'01"	36'07
Varnebank	9213739	GC	2000	D	6,130	433'09"	52'01"	36'07
Vikingbank	9604184	GC	2012	D	7,367	468'00"	52'01"	37'09

R

REDERI AB DONSOTANK, DONSO, SWEDEN *(donsotank.se)*

Solando	9428073	TK	2009	D	13,472	491' 11"	75' 06"	42' 10"

*(Messinia '09-'09, **Soley-1** '09-'13)*

REDERIET STENERSEN AS, BERGEN, NORWAY *(stenersen.com)*

Sten Arnold	9371610	TK	2007	D	11,935	472' 07"	75' 06"	40' 08"
Sten Baltic	9307671	TK	2005	D	11,935	472' 07"	75' 06"	40' 08"
Sten Bergen	9407988	TK	2009	D	11,935	472' 07"	75' 06"	40' 08"
Sten Hidra	9358931	TK	2002	D	11,935	472' 07"	75' 06"	40' 08"
Sten Idun	9261102	TK	2002	D	11,935	472' 07"	75' 06"	40' 08"
Sten Moster	9341184	TK	2006	D	11,935	472' 07"	75' 06"	40' 08"

REEDEREI FOROOHARI, STADE, GERMANY *(foroohari.com)*

BBC Fortune	9402067	HL	2008	D	9,611	455' 10"	68' 11"	36' 01"

*(Beluga Fortune '08-'11, **Fortune** '11-'18)*

Holandia	9312169	GC	2005	D	9,611	453' 00"	68' 11"	36' 01"

*(**Beluga Endurance** '05-'11, Martin '11-'13, Rickmers Mumbai '13-'14, **Nodana Emilie** '14-'16, Martin '16-'17, BBC Nebraska '17-'17)*

REEDEREI H. SCHULDT GMBH & CO., HAMBURG, GERMANY *(norddeutsche-reederei.de)*

Ocean Castle	9315537	BC	2005	D	18,825	607' 03"	77' 01"	46' 03"

(Federal Mattawa '05-'15)

REEDEREI HEINO WINTER, HAMBURG, GERMANY *(reederei-winter.de)*

Jule	9357999	HL	2005	D	9,611	453' 00"	68' 11"	36' 01"

(Beluga Expectation '05-'11, Jule '11-'13, OXL Avatar '13-'13, Clipper Anita '13-'15, Thorco Dolphin '15-'15)

REEDEREI HEINZ CORLEIS KG, STADE, GERMANY

Stade	9535620	BC	2011	D	8,059	477' 10"	59' 10"	33' 10"

REEDEREI NORD GMBH, HAMBURG, GERMANY *(reederei-nord.com)*

Nordisle	9457828	TK	2009	D	8,278	393' 08"	66' 11"	39' 00")

(Rio Daintree '09-'09)

RIGEL SCHIFFAHRTS GMBH, BREMEN, GERMANY *(rigel-hb.com)*

Amur Star	9480368	TK	2010	D	8,539	421' 11"	66' 11"	37' 05"
Colorado Star	9527609	TK	2010	D	8,539	421' 11"	66' 11"	37' 05"
Ganges Star	9496692	TK	2010	D	8,539	421' 11"	66' 11"	37' 05"
Mississippi Star	9527623	TK	2010	D	8,539	421' 11"	66' 11"	37' 05"

S

SAL HEAVY LIFT GMBH, HAMBURG, GERMANY *(sal-heavylift.com)*

Calypso	9512381	HL	2011	D	11,473	439' 08"	75' 06"	37' 05"
Imke	9501899	HL	2010	D	11,473	439' 08"	75' 06"	37' 05"

(Palau '10-'18)

SEAFARERS SHIPPING INC., MANILA, PHILIPPINES

AS Omaria	9363819	TK	2008	D	11,623	447' 05"	77' 09"	43' 10"

(Bow Omaria '08-'11)

SEASTAR SHIPMANAGEMENT LTD., ATHENS, GREECE

Cape	9498224	BC	2010	D	19,906	610' 03"	77' 09"	47' 11"

(Heloise '10-'15)

Sunda	9498236	BC	2010	D	19,906	610' 03"	77' 09"	47' 11"

(Emilie '10-'15)

SLOMAN NEPTUN SHIFFAHRTS, BREMEN, GERMANY *(sloman-neptun.com)*

Sloman Helios	9466740	TK	2011	D	11,246	476' 02"	75' 06"	41' 01"

(Intrepid Canada '10-'17)

Sloman Herakles	9466726	TK	2012	D	11,246	476' 02"	75' 06"	41' 01"
Sloman Hermes	9466738	TK	2012	D	11,246	476' 02"	75' 06"	41' 01"

SOUTH END TANKER MANAGEMENT, BARENDRECHT, NETHERLANDS *(se-tm.com)*

Selasse	9405320	TK	2008	D	7,776	426' 11"	64' 04"	35' 09"

(Selay-S '08-'17)

Fleet Name / Vessel Name	Vessel IMO #	Vessel Type	Year Built	Engine Type	Cargo Cap. or Gross*	Overall Length	Vessel Breadth	Vessel Depth
SPLIETHOFF, AMSTERDAM, THE NETHERLANDS *(www.spliethoff.com)*								
Eemsgracht	9081291	HL	1995	D	8,448	446' 02"	62' 00"	35' 11"
Fagelgracht	9428425	HL	2011	D	8,620	447' 10"	62' 00"	38' 03"
Flevogracht	9509956	HL	2011	D	8,620	447' 10"	62' 00"	38' 03"
Floragracht	9509968	HL	2011	D	8,620	447' 10"	62' 00"	38' 03"
Floretgracht	9507611	HL	2012	D	8,620	447' 10"	62' 00"	38' 03"
Florijngracht	9428413	HL	2010	D	8,620	447' 10"	62' 00"	38' 03"
Fortunagracht	9507609	HL	2012	D	8,620	447' 10"	62' 00"	38' 03"
Heemskerkgracht	9443669	HL	2009	D	9,618	453' 00"	68' 11"	36' 01"
(*Beluga Faculty* '09-'11, ***HHL Nile*** '11-'16)								
Marsgracht	9571507	HL	2007	D	9,524	464' 11"	62' 00"	38' 03"
Merwedegracht	9571519	HL	2011	D	9,524	464' 11"	62' 00"	38' 03"
Minervagracht	9571521	HL	2011	D	9,524	464' 11"	62' 00"	38' 03"
Muntgracht	9571545	HL	2012	D	9,524	464' 11"	62' 00"	38' 03"

At press time, Spliethoff also had the following vessels under charter. Please consult their respective fleets for details: **COE Leni, Erik, Frieda** and **Pia**.

Fleet Name / Vessel Name	Vessel IMO #	Vessel Type	Year Built	Engine Type	Cargo Cap. or Gross*	Overall Length	Vessel Breadth	Vessel Depth
SUNSHIP SCHIFFAHRTSKONTOR KG, EMDEN, GERMANY *(sunship.de)*								
Lake Ontario	9283538	BC	2004	D	18,825	607' 03"	77' 01"	46' 03"
(***Federal Manitou*** '04-'11)								
Lake St. Clair	9315549	BC	2004	D	18,825	607' 03"	77' 01"	46' 03"
(***Federal Miramichi*** '04-'16)								

T-V

Fleet Name / Vessel Name	Vessel IMO #	Vessel Type	Year Built	Engine Type	Cargo Cap. or Gross*	Overall Length	Vessel Breadth	Vessel Depth
TARBIT TANKERS B.V., DORDRECHT, NETHERLANDS *(tarbittankers.nl)*								
Stella Polaris	9187057	TK	1999	D	5,396	387' 02"	55' 09"	34' 05"
TB MARINE SHIPMANAGEMENT GMBH & CO., HAMBURG GERMANY *(tbmarine.de)*								
Harbour Fashion	9473080	TK	2011	D	11,880	473' 02"	75' 06"	40' 08"
Harbour Feature	9473092	TK	2011	D	11,880	473' 02"	75' 06"	40' 08"
(*Nordtank Lerner* '11-'11)								
Harbour First	9473119	TK	2011	D	11,880	473' 02"	75' 06"	40' 08"
Harbour Fountain	9473107	TK	2011	D	11,880	473' 02"	75' 06"	40' 08"
Harbour Pioneer	9572757	TK	2010	D	13,239	530' 05"	75' 06"	40' 09"
(*Harbour Pioneer* '10-'10, *Nordtank Franklin* '10-'10)								
Harbour Progress	9572745	TK	2010	D	13,239	530' 05"	75' 06"	40' 09"
TEAM TANKERS MANAGEMENT AS, HELLERUP, DENMARK *(teamtankers.com)*								
Sichem Beijing	9397042	TK	2007	D	8,539	421' 11"	66' 11"	37' 09"

Pochard S at anchor on Lake Ontario. (Jeff Cameron)

Fleet Name / Vessel Name	Vessel IMO #	Vessel Type	Year Built	Engine Type	Cargo Cap. or Gross*	Overall Length	Vessel Breadth	Vessel Depth
Sichem Challenge	9196448	TK	1998	D	7,228	382' 06"	62' 04"	33' 02"
*(Queen of Montreaux '98-'99, **North Challenge** '99-'06, Songa Challenge '06-'07)*								
Sichem Defiance	9244374	TK	2001	D	9,900	442' 11"	74' 10"	41' 00"
*(**North Defiance** '01-'06, **Songa Defiance** '06-'07)*								
Sichem Marseille	9378199	TK	2007	D	8,455	417' 04"	67' 00"	37' 09"
(Songa Onyx '07-'07)								
Sichem Melbourne	9376921	TK	2007	D	8,455	417' 04"	67' 00"	37' 09"
Sichem Mumbai	9322085	TK	2006	D	8,539	421' 11"	66' 11"	37' 09"
Sichem New York	9337834	TK	2007	D	8,455	417' 04"	67' 00"	37' 09"

TERAS BBC OCEAN NAVIGATION ENTERPRISES, HOUSTON, TEXAS

Houston	9331593	GC	2005	D	7,002	393' 00"	66' 03"	32' 02"
*(BBC Australia '05-'05, Wesier Hiede '05-'05, **BBC Australia** '05-'10, **BBC Houston** '10-'14)*								

TRADEWIND TANKERS, BARCELONA, SPAIN *(tradewindtankers.com)*

Tradewind Adventure	9485590	TK	2008	D	8,302	467' 06"	72' 02"	39' 04"

TRANSMARINE MANAGEMENT APS, COPENHAGEN, DENMARK *(transmarine.dk)*

Amarant	9260407	TK	2003	D	7,186	390' 09"	55' 05"	27' 07"

UNI-TANKERS A/S, MIDDELFART, DENMARK *(unitankers.com)*

Erria Swan	9347748	TK	2006	D	7,232	425' 08"	64' 04"	34' 01"
(Alaattin Bey '06-'07, Erria Helen '07-'12)								
Falstria Swan	9367217	TK	2006	D	3,933	337' 11"	52' 06"	28' 07"
(Ingrid Jakobsen '06-'12)								
Fionia Swan	9328974	TK	2005	D	10,810	485' 07"	70' 10"	37' 01"
Mona Swan	9371804	TK	2006	D	7,232	425' 08"	64' 04"	34' 01"
(M Can Bey '06-'08, Erria Ida '08-'12)								
Selandia Swan	9371787	TK	2008	D	11,711	438' 11"	73' 06"	41' 04"
Swan Baltic	9386249	TK	2007	D	8,198	426' 11"	64' 04"	35' 09"
(Ozay-5 '07-'14)								
Swan Biscay	9438444	TK	2008	D	8,198	426' 11"	64' 04"	35' 09"
(Ozay-6 '08-'14)								
Tasing Swan	9403891	TK	2007	D	7,232	425' 08"	64' 04"	34' 01"
(Hamza Efe Bey '07-'08, Erria Mie '08-'12)								

UNICORN TANKERS INTERNATIONAL LTD., LONDON, UNITED KINGDOM

Kowie	9382504	TK	2010	D	11,271	472' 05"	75' 06"	41' 00"
Umgeni	9382499	TK	2011	D	11,271	472' 05"	75' 06"	41' 00"
(Siyanda '11-'11, Umzimvubu '11-'11)								

Trudy and tugs greet the sunrise at Duluth, MN. *(Paul Scinocca)*

UNISEA SHIPPING B.V., SNEEK, NETHERLANDS

Beauforce	9526095	BC	2010	D	5,425	387' 07"	52' 02"	28' 10"

UTKILEN AS, BERGEN, NORWAY (utkilen.no)

Susana S	9406714	TK	2009	D	12,776	539' 02"	76' 01"	42' 00"

VBG DENIZCILIK SANAYI VE TICARET AS, ISTANBUL, TURKEY (vbgshipping.com)

Halit Bey	9410143	TK	2009	D	12,619	530' 04"	73' 06"	42' 00"
Nilufer Sultan	9410131	TK	2008	D	12,619	530' 04"	73' 06"	42' 00"

VICTORY CRUISE LINES, NEW ALBANY, IN (victorycruiselines.com)
  VESSELS OPERATED BY AMERICAN STEAMBOAT OPERATING CO., NEW ALBANY, IN

Victory I	9213129	PA	2001	D	4,954*	300' 00"	50' 00"	20' 00"

Built: Atlantic Marine Inc., Jacksonville, FL (**Cape May Light** '01-'09, Sea Voyager '09-'14, **Saint Laurent** '14-'16)

Victory II	9213131	PA	2004	D	4,954*	300' 00"	50' 00"	20' 00"

Built: Atlantic Marine Inc., Jacksonville, FL (**Cape Cod Light** '04-'07, Coastal Queen 2 '07-'08, Clipper Discoverer '08-'10, Sea Discoverer '10-'17)

VROON B.V., BREDA, NETHERLANDS (vroon.nl)

Iver Bright	9616759	TK	2012	D	6,105	367' 05"	59' 09"	32' 10"

W-Z

W. BOCKSTIEGEL REEDEREI KG, EMDEN, GERMANY (reederei-bockstiegel.de)

BBC Campana	9291963	HL	2003	D	9,618	453' 00"	68' 11"	36' 01"
BBC Florida	9433286	HL	2009	D	9,627	454' 05"	68' 11"	36' 01"
BBC Georgia	9357224	HL	2008	D	9,627	454' 05"	68' 11"	36' 01"
BBC Maine	9357200	HL	2007	D	9,627	454' 05"	68' 11"	36' 01"
BBC Plata	9291975	HL	2005	D	9,618	453' 00"	68' 11"	36' 01"
(Asian Voyager '05-'05)								
BBC Zarate	9337236	HL	2007	D	9,627	454' 05"	68' 11"	36' 01"

WAGENBORG SHIPPING BV, DELFZIJL, NETHERLANDS (wagenborg.com)

Adriaticborg	9546497	GC	2011	D	11,894	469' 02"	70' 06"	43' 08"
Alamosborg	9466348	GC	2011	D	11,894	469' 02"	70' 06"	43' 08"
Alaskaborg	9466374	GC	2012	D	11,894	469' 02"	70' 06"	43' 08"
Albanyborg	9466300	GC	2010	D	11,894	469' 02"	70' 06"	43' 08"
Amazoneborg	9333541	GC	2007	D	11,894	469' 02"	70' 06"	43' 08"
Americaborg	9365659	GC	2007	D	11,894	469' 02"	70' 06"	43' 08"

Fleet Name / Vessel Name	Vessel IMO #	Vessel Type	Year Built	Engine Type	Cargo Cap. or Gross*	Overall Length	Vessel Breadth	Vessel Depth
Amstelborg	9333527	GC	2006	D	11,894	469' 02"	70' 06"	43' 08"
Amurborg	9466336	GC	2011	D	11,894	469' 02"	70' 06"	43' 08"
Andesborg	9466324	GC	2011	D	11,894	469' 02"	70' 06"	43' 08"
Arneborg	9333539	GC	2006	D	11,894	469' 02"	70' 06"	43' 08"
Arubaborg	9466295	GC	2010	D	11,894	469' 02"	70' 06"	43' 08"
Atlanticborg	9466350	GC	2012	D	11,894	469' 02"	70' 06"	43' 08"
Avonborg	9466362	GC	2012	D	11,894	469' 02"	70' 06"	43' 08"
Azoresborg	9466051	GC	2010	D	11,894	469' 02"	70' 06"	43' 08"
Beatrix	9419280	GC	2009	D	8,911	507' 03"	56' 05"	37' 09"
(Fivelborg '09-'09)								
Ebroborg	9463451	GC	2010	D	7,196	452' 03"	52' 01"	36' 01"
Edenborg	9463449	GC	2010	D	7,196	452' 03"	52' 01"	36' 01"
Eeborg	9568328	GC	2012	D	7,680	474' 03"	52' 01"	36' 07"
Eemsborg	9225586	GC	2009	D	7,196	452' 03"	52' 01"	36' 01"
Elbeborg	9568249	GC	2011	D	7,680	474' 03"	52' 01"	36' 07"
Erieborg	9463437	GC	2009	D	7,196	452' 03"	52' 01"	36' 01"
Exeborg	9650482	GC	2011	D	7,680	474' 03"	52' 01"	36' 07"
Finnborg	9419321	GC	2011	D	8,911	507' 03"	56' 05"	37' 09"
Fivelborg	9419307	GC	2010	D	8,911	507' 03"	56' 05"	37' 09"
Flevoborg	9419292	GC	2010	D	8,911	507' 03"	56' 05"	37' 09"
Fraserborg	9419319	GC	2011	D	8,911	507' 03"	56' 05"	37' 09"
Fuldaborg	9559092	GC	2012	D	8,911	507' 03"	56' 05"	37' 09"
Jan van Gent	9456721	GC	2010	D	8,999	469' 00"	62' 00"	35' 11"
(Jan van Gent '10-'14, Nordana Madeleine '14-'16)								
Mississippiborg	9207508	GC	2000	D	6,540	441' 05"	54' 02"	32' 02"
Nassauborg	9248564	GC	2006	D	16,037	467' 03"	72' 06"	42' 00"
Reestborg	9592563	GC	2013	D	14,224	556' 11"	66' 11"	37' 11"
Reggeborg	9592575	GC	2014	D	14,224	556' 11"	66' 11"	37' 11"
Roerborg	9592599	GC	2014	D	14,224	556' 11"	66' 11"	37' 11"
Taagborg	9546461	GC	2013	D	14,695	565' 03"	70' 06"	43' 08"
Thamesborg	9546459	GC	2013	D	14,695	565' 03"	70' 06"	43' 08"
Trinityborg	9546485	GC	2013	D	14,695	565' 03"	70' 06"	43' 08"
Vaasaborg	9196242	GC	1999	D	6,130	433' 10"	52' 01"	31' 08"
(Vaasaborg '00-'03, Normed Hamburg '03-'04)								
Vancouverborg	9213741	GC	2001	D	6,361	433' 10"	52' 01"	31' 08"
Victoriaborg	9234276	GC	2001	D	6,361	433' 10"	52' 01"	31' 08"
Virginiaborg	9234290	GC	2001	D	6,361	433' 10"	52' 01"	31' 08"

Federal Schelde docked opposite Stewart J. Cort at Burns Harbor, IN. *(Roger LeLievre)*

Fleet Name / Vessel Name	IMO #	Vessel Type	Year Built	Engine Type	Cargo Cap. or Gross*	Overall Length	Breadth	Depth
Vlieborg	9554781	GC	2012	D	7,367	468′ 00″	52′ 01″	35′ 04″
Volgaborg	9631072	GC	2013	D	7,367	468′ 00″	51′ 09″	35′ 04″
Voorneborg	9179373	GC	1999	D	6,130	433′ 10″	52′ 01″	31′ 08″

FOLLOWING VESSELS UNDER CHARTER TO EGBERT A. K. BOS, WINTERSWIJK, NETHERLANDS

Anet	9456733	GC	2010	D	8,999	469′ 00″	62′ 00″	35′ 11″

(Anet '10-'10, Onego Bilbao '10-'11, Anet '11-'14, **Nordana Mathilde** '14-'15)

At press time, Wagenborg Shipping also had the following vessels under charter. Please consult their respective fleets for details: **Kwintebank, Morgenstond I, Morgenstond II, Varnebank** and **Vikingbank.**

WECO SHIPPING, RUNDSTED, DENMARK (wecobulk.com)

Billesborg	9488047	HL	2011	D	9,627	454′ 05″	68′ 11″	36′ 01″

(Billesborg '11-'11, Clipper Angela '11-'12)

WIJNNE BARENDS, DELFZIJL, NETHERLANDS (wijnnebarends.com)

Morgenstond I	9320506	BC	2006	D	8,999	469′ 00″	62′ 00″	35′ 11″

(Morgenstond I '06-'06, Beluga Locomotion '06-'08, Kent Locomotion '08-'08, Beluga Locomotion '08-'09, Morgenstond I '09-'10, **Kent Sunrise** '10-'12, Morgenstond I '12-'12, Clipper Athena '12-'14)

Morgenstond II	9367073	BC	2007	D	8,999	469′ 00″	62′ 00″	35′ 11″

(**Morgenstond II** '07-'07, Beluga Legislation '07-'07, Kent Legislation '07-'09, **Beluga Legislation** '09-'10, **Kent Sunset** '10-'13, **Morgenstond II** '13-'13, Clipper Aurora '13-'15)

YARDIMCI SHIPPING GROUP, ISTANBUL, TURKEY (yardimci.gen.tr)

Arsland	9395989	TK	2008	D	12,164	472′ 07″	75′ 06″	40′ 08″

(**CT Dublin** '08-'17)

Ayane	9395991	TK	2010	D	12,164	472′ 07″	75′ 06″	40′ 08″
Elevit	9466609	TK	2012	D	12,164	472′ 07″	75′ 06″	40′ 08″

YAWATAHAMA KISEN Y. K., YAWATAHAMA, JAPAN
FOLLOWING VESSEL UNDER CHARTER TO FEDNAV

Federal Yukina	9476977	BC	2010	D	20,465	655′ 06″	77′ 11″	48′ 09″

YILMAR SHIPPING & TRADING LTD., ISTANBUL, TURKEY (yilmar.com)

YM Jupiter	9291597	TK	2007	D	10,917	485′ 07″	70′ 10″	37′ 01″
YM Saturn	9362138	TK	2007	D	10,917	485′ 07″	70′ 10″	37′ 01″

ZEALAND SHIPPING BV, ALMERE, NETHERLANDS (zealand-shipping.nl)

Zealand Beatrix	9507087	BC	2010	D	9,514	441′ 11″	67′ 03″	36′ 01″
Zealand Delilah	9507075	BC	2011	D	9,514	441′ 11″	67′ 03″	36′ 01″

Saltie Rike overtakes the laker Mesabi Miner on the St. Marys River. (Roger LeLievre)

Photo credit: David Kaye

 FEDNAV

DELIVERING BULK CARGOES WORLDWIDE
FOR 75 YEARS

www.fednav.com

Sault Ste. Marie, Michigan

Museum Ship Valley Camp

20,000 sq. ft. Maritime Museum

- **Over 100 Exhibits**
- *Edmund Fitzgerald* **Lifeboats**

Tower of History

Breathtaking views from 210 ft. up

- **Museum Exhibits**
- **Express Elevator**

Located at
326 E. Portage Ave.

Open mid-May thru mid-October
888-744-7867 • saulthistoricsites.com

Steam tug Edna G. in service at Two Harbors, MN. She is now a museum at that port. (John Vournakis)

Marine Museums

MUSEUMS / Ship

Museum Name Vessel Name	Vessel Type	Year Built	Engine Type	Cargo Cap. or Gross*	Overall Length	Breadth	Depth
BUFFALO AND ERIE COUNTY NAVAL & MILITARY PARK, BUFFALO, NY (buffalonavalpark.org)							
Croaker	MU	1944	D	1,526*	311' 07"	27' 02"	33' 09"
Former U. S. Navy Gato class submarine IXSS-246; open to the public at Buffalo, NY							
Little Rock	MU	1945	T	10,670*	610' 01"	66' 04"	25' 00"
Former U. S. Navy Cleveland / Little Rock class guided missile cruiser; open to the public at Buffalo, NY							
The Sullivans	MU	1943	T	2,500*	376' 06"	39' 08"	22' 08"
Former U. S. Navy Fletcher class destroyer; open to the public at Buffalo, NY (Launched as USS Putnam)							
CITY OF KEWAUNEE, KEWAUNEE, WI							
Ludington	TB/MU	1943	D	249*	115' 00"	26' 00"	13' 08"
Built: Jakobson Shipyard, Oyster Bay, NY; former U.S. Army Corps of Engineers tug is open to the public							
as a marine museum at Kewaunee, WI (Major Wilbur F. Browder [LT-4] '43-'47)							
DOOR COUNTY MARITIME MUSEUM & LIGHTHOUSE PRESERVATION SOCIETY INC.,							
STURGEON BAY, WI (dcmm.org)							
John Purves	TB/MU	1919	D	436*	150' 00"	27' 06"	16' 08"
Built: Bethlehem Steel Co., Elizabeth, NJ; former Roen/Andrie Inc. tug has been refurbished as a museum							
display at Sturgeon Bay, WI (Butterfield '19-'42, LT-145 '42-'57)							
DULUTH ENTERTAINMENT CONVENTION CENTER, DULUTH, MN (decc.org/william-a-irvin)							
William A. Irvin	BC/MU	1938	T	14,050	610' 09"	60' 00"	32' 06"
Built: American Shipbuilding Co., Lorain, OH; former United States Steel Corp. bulk carrier last operated							
Dec. 16, 1978; open to the public at Duluth, MN							
ERIE MARITIME MUSEUM, ERIE, PA (flagshipniagara.org)							
Niagara	MU/2B	1988	W	295*	198' 00"	32' 00"	10' 06"
Reconstruction of Oliver Hazard Perry's U. S. Navy brigantine from the War of 1812							
FRIENDS OF KEEWATIN, PORT McNICOLL, ON (sskeewatin.com)							
Keewatin {2}	PA/MU	1907	Q	3,856*	346' 00"	43' 08"	26' 06"
Built: Fairfield Shipbuilding and Engineering Co. Ltd., Govan, Scotland; former Canadian Pacific Railway Co.							
passenger vessel last operated Nov. 29, 1965; now a marine museum at Port McNicoll, ON							
GREAT LAKES NAVAL MEMORIAL & MUSEUM, MUSKEGON, MI (silversidesmuseum.org)							
McLane	MU	1927	D	289*	125' 00"	24' 00"	12' 06"
Built: American Brown Boveri Electric Co., Camden, NJ; former U.S. Coast Guard Buck & A Quarter class							
medium endurance cutter; on display at Muskegon, MI (USCGC McLane '27-'70, Manatra II '70-'93)							
Silversides	MU	1941	D/V	1,526*	311' 08"	27' 03"	33' 09"
Built: Mare Island Naval Yard, Vallejo, CA; former U.S. Navy Albacore (Gato) class submarine AGSS-236;							
open to the public at Muskegon, MI							
GREAT LAKES SCIENCE CENTER, CLEVELAND, OH (greatscience.com)							
William G. Mather {2}	BC/MU	1925	T	13,950	618' 00"	62' 00"	32' 00"
Built: Great Lakes Engineering Works, Ecorse, MI; former Cleveland-Cliffs Steamship Co. bulk carrier last							
operated Dec. 21, 1980; open to the public at Cleveland, OH							
H. LEE WHITE MARINE MUSEUM, OSWEGO, NY (hleewhitemarinemuseum.com)							
LT-5	MU	1943	D	305*	115' 00"	28' 00"	14' 00"
Built: Jakobson Shipyard, Oyster Bay, NY; former U.S. Army Corps of Engineers tug last operated in 1989;							
open to the public at Oswego, NY (Major Elisha K. Henson '43-'47, U.S. Army LT-5 '47-'47, Nash '47-'95)							
HMCS HAIDA NATIONAL HISTORICAL SITE, HAMILTON, ON (hmcshaida.com)							
Haida	MU	1943	T	2,744*	377' 00"	37' 06"	15' 02"
Former Royal Canadian Navy Tribal class destroyer G-63 / DDE-215; open to the public at Hamilton, ON							
ICEBREAKER MACKINAW MARITIME MUSEUM INC., MACKINAW CITY, MI (themackinaw.org)							
Mackinaw [WAGB-83]	IB/MU	1944	D	5,252*	290' 00"	74' 00"	29' 00"
Built: Toledo Shipbuilding Co., Toledo, OH; former U.S. Coast Guard icebreaker was decommissioned in 2006;							
open to the public at Mackinaw City, MI (Launched as USCGC Manitowoc [WAG-83])							
LAKE COUNTY HISTORICAL SOCIETY, TWO HARBORS, MN (lakecountyhistoricalsociety.org)							
Edna G.	TB/MU	1896	R	154*	102' 00"	23' 00"	14' 06"
Built: Cleveland Shipbuilding Co., Cleveland, OH; former Duluth, Missabe & Iron Range Railroad tug last							
operated in 1981; open to the public at Two Harbors, MN							
LAKEHEAD TRANSPORTATION MUSEUM SOCIETY, THUNDER BAY, ON (ltms.ca)							
Alexander Henry	IB/MU	1959	D	1,674*	210' 00"	44' 00"	17' 09"
Built: Port Arthur Shipbuilding Co., Port Arthur, ON; former Canadian Coast Guard icebreaker was retired in							
1985; formerly at Kingston, ON, open to the public at Thunder Bay, ON							

Continued on Page 123

More than 500 breathtaking photographs,
250 incredible artifacts, 45 interactive exhibits and
a 617' iron-ore freighter tell the awe-inspiring history of
the Great Lakes and provide an entertaining, educating
and enjoyable experience for families of all ages.

New in 2019 - The newly restored Tug *Ohio*
will open for tours this summer.

Check our website or call for opening date.

1701 Front Street • Toledo, OH 43605 • 419.214.5000 • NMGL.org

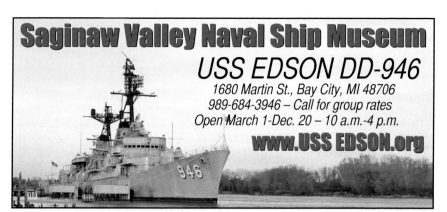

Saginaw Valley Naval Ship Museum

USS EDSON DD-946

1680 Martin St., Bay City, MI 48706
989-684-3946 – Call for group rates
Open March 1-Dec. 20 – 10 a.m.-4 p.m.

www.USS EDSON.org

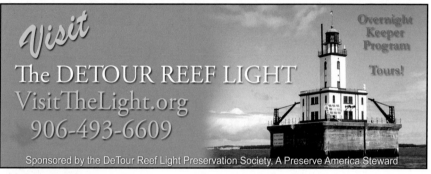

Visit

The DETOUR REEF LIGHT
VisitTheLight.org
906-493-6609

Overnight Keeper Program Tours!

Sponsored by the DeTour Reef Light Preservation Society, A Preserve America Steward

PORT HURON MUSEUMS

Make your day *unforgettable*
at one of our
four unique locations!

Thomas Edison DEPOT

Huron LIGHTSHIP

Carnegie CENTER

Fort Gratiot LIGHT STATION

810-982-0891 ext 118
www.phmuseum.org

VISIT PORT HURON · MICHIGAN

LE SAULT DE SAINTE MARIE HISTORIC SITES INC., SAULT STE. MARIE, MI (saulthistoricsites.com)

Valley Camp {2}	BC/MU	1917	R	12,000	550′ 00″	58′ 00″	13′ 00″

Built: American Shipbuilding Co., Lorain, OH; former Hanna Mining Co./Wilson Marine Transit Co./Republic Steel Corp. bulk carrier last operated in 1966; open to the public at Sault Ste. Marie, MI (Louis W. Hill '17–'55)

MARATHON DISTRICT HISTORICAL MUSEUM, MARATHON, ON (marathondistrictmuseum.weebly.com)

Peninsula	TB/MU	1944	D	261*	111′ 00″	27′ 00″	22′ 06″

Built: Montreal Drydock Ltd., Montreal, QC; former Gravel & Lake Services tug is open to the public at Marathon, ON (HMCS Norton [W-31] '44–'45, W.A.C. 1 '45–'46)

MUSÉE MARITIME DU QUÉBEC, L' ISLET, QC (mmq.qc.ca)

Ernest Lapointe	MU	1941	R	1,179*	185′ 00″	36′ 00″	22′ 06″

Built: Davie Shipbuilding Co., Lauzon, QC; former Canadian Coast Guard icebreaker; open to the public at L'Islet, QC

NATIONAL MUSEUM OF THE GREAT LAKES, TOLEDO, OH (inlandseas.org)

Col. James M. Schoonmaker	BC/MU	1911	T	15,000	617′ 00″	64′ 00″	33′ 01″

Built: Great Lakes Engineering Works, Ecorse, MI; former Shenango Furnace Co./Republic Steel Co./Cleveland-Cliffs Steamship Co. bulk carrier last operated in 1980; open to the public at Toledo, OH (Col. James M. Schoonmaker 1911–'69, Willis B. Boyer '69–'11)

Ohio	TB/MU	1903	D	194*	101′ 02″	26′ 00″	13′ 07″

Built: Great Lakes Towing Co., Chicago, IL; veteran tug is the latest addition to the National Museum's growing collection (M.F.D. No. 15 '03–'52, Laurence C. Turner '52–'73)

PORT HURON MUSEUM, PORT HURON, MI (phmuseum.org)

Huron	MU	1920	D	392*	96′ 05″	24′ 00″	10′ 00″

Built: Charles L. Seabury Co., Morris Heights, NY; former U.S. Coast Guard lightship WLV-526 was retired Aug. 20, 1970; open to the public at Port Huron, MI (Lightship 103 – Relief [WAL-526] '20–'36)

SAGINAW VALLEY NAVAL SHIP MUSEUM, BAY CITY, MI (ussedson.org)

Edson [DD-946]	MU	1958	T	4,050*	418′ 03″	45′ 03″	22′ 00″

Built: Bath Iron Works, Bath, ME; Forrest Sherman class destroyer was decommissioned in '88; from '89–'04 on display at the Intrepid Sea, Air & Space Museum, New York, NY; declared a U.S. National Historic Landmark in '90; returned to U.S. Navy in '04; open to the public at Bay City, MI

S.S. CITY OF MILWAUKEE – NATIONAL HISTORIC LANDMARK, MANISTEE, MI (carferry.com)

Acacia	BT/MU	1944	DE	1,025*	180′ 00″	37′ 00″	17′ 04″

Built: Marine Iron and Shipbuilding Corp., Duluth, MN; former U.S. Coast Guard buoy tender/icebreaker was decommissioned in '06 (Launched as USCGC Thistle [WAGL-406])

City of Milwaukee	MU	1931	R	26 cars	360′ 00″	56′ 03″	21′ 06″

Built: Manitowoc Shipbuilding Co., Manitowoc, WI; train ferry sailed for the Grand Trunk Railroad '31–'78 and the Ann Arbor Railroad '78–'81; open to the public at Manistee, MI

S.S. COLUMBIA PROJECT, NEW YORK, NY (sscolumbia.org)

Columbia {2}	PA/MU	1902	R	968*	216′ 00″	60′ 00″	13′ 06″

Built: Detroit Dry Dock Co., Wyandotte, MI; former Detroit to Bob-Lo Island passenger steamer last operated Sept. 2, 1991; moved to Buffalo, NY, Sept. 2, 2015, for further restoration and possible return to service

Continued on Page 125

Museum ship William A. Irvin on the move at Duluth, MN, in 2018. (Nick Stenstrup)

S.S. CITY OF MILWAUKEE & USCGC ACACIA
NATIONAL HISTORIC LANDMARK

MUSEUM SHIP / BED & BREAKFAST
NATIONAL HISTORIC LANDMARK

Stay Aboard a Steamship From a Bygone Era
Restored Rooms • Tours • USCG Acacia

CARFERRY.COM
Manistee, Michigan • 231-723-3587

40 Mile Point Lighthouse
7323 U.S.23 North • Rogers City, Mich.
Open Memorial Day Weekend – Mid-October
Tuesday-Saturday 10 a.m.-4 p.m., Sunday Noon- 4 p.m.
Closed Monday • (989) 734-4907

Tour an 1896 Great Lakes lighthouse and museum and visit the restored pilothouse of the 1912 steamer *Calcite*

See our website for
Guest Lighthouse Keeper Program information

www.40milepointlighthouse.org

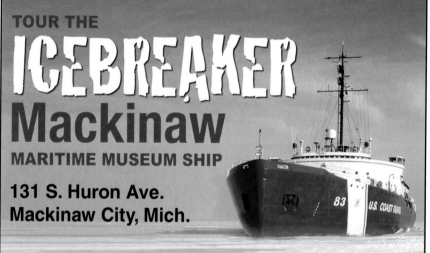

TOUR THE
ICEBREAKER
Mackinaw
MARITIME MUSEUM SHIP

131 S. Huron Ave.
Mackinaw City, Mich.

83 U.S. COAST GUARD

Visit Our Website For Details On Our Great Lakes Freighter Trip Raffle

Open Mid-May~Mid-October   231-436-9825
www.themackinaw.org

Museum Name Vessel Name	Vessel Type	Year Built	Engine Type	Cargo Cap. or Gross*	Overall Length	Breadth	Depth

S.S. METEOR WHALEBACK SHIP MUSEUM, SUPERIOR, WI *(superiorpublicmuseums.org/s-s-meteor-2)*

Meteor {2}	TK/MU	1896	R	40,100	380' 00"	45' 00"	26' 00"

Built: American Steel Barge Co., Superior, WI; former ore carrier/auto carrier/tanker is the last vessel of whaleback design surviving on the Great Lakes; Cleveland Tankers vessel last operated in 1969; open to the public at Superior, WI (Frank Rockefeller 1896-'28, South Park '1928-'43)

S.S. MILWAUKEE CLIPPER PRESERVATION INC., MUSKEGON, MI *(milwaukeeclipper.com)*

Milwaukee Clipper	PA/MU	1904	Q	4,272	361' 00"	45' 00"	28' 00"

Built: American Shipbuilding Co., Cleveland, OH; rebuilt in '40 at Manitowoc Shipbuilding Co., Manitowoc, WI; former Wisconsin & Michigan Steamship Co. passenger/auto carrier last operated in 1970; undergoing restoration and open to the public at Muskegon, MI (Juniata '04-'41)

ST. MARYS RIVER MARINE CENTRE, SAULT STE. MARIE, ON *(norgoma.org)*

Norgoma	PA/MU	1950	D	1,477*	188' 00"	37' 06"	22' 06"

Built: Collingwood Shipyards, Collingwood, ON; former Ontario Northland Transportation Commission passenger vessel last operated in 1974; open to the public at Sault Ste. Marie, ON

USS COD SUBMARINE MEMORIAL, CLEVELAND, OH *(usscod.org)*

Cod	MU	1943	D/V	1,525*	311' 08"	27' 02"	33' 09"

Built: Electric Boat Co., Groton, CT; former U.S. Navy Albacore (Gato) class submarine IXSS-224 open to the public at Cleveland, OH

USS LST 393 PRESERVATION ASSOCIATION, MUSKEGON, MI *(lst393.org)*

LST-393	MU	1942	D	2,100	328' 00"	50' 00"	25' 00"

Built: Newport News Shipbuilding and Dry Dock Co., Newport News, VA; former U.S. Navy/Wisconsin & Michigan Steamship Co. vessel last operated July 31, 1973; open to the public at Muskegon, MI (USS LST-393 '42-'47, Highway 16 '47-'99)

WISCONSIN MARITIME MUSEUM, MANITOWOC, WI *(wisconsinmaritime.org)*

Cobia	MU	1944	D/V	1,500*	311' 09"	27' 03"	33' 09"

Built: Electric Boat Co., Groton, CT; former U. S. Navy Gato class submarine AGSS-245 is open to the public at Manitowoc, WI

Continued on Page 126 with Museums Ashore

Great Lakes Museum Ship Stack Markings

**Museum Ship
City of Milwaukee**
Manistee, MI

**Museum Ship Col.
James M. Schoonmaker**
Toledo, OH

**Museum Ship
Keewatin**
Port McNicoll, ON

**Museum Ship
Alexander Henry**
Thunder Bay, ON

**Museum Ship
HMCS Haida**
Hamilton, ON

**Museum Ships
USS Little Rock
USS The Sullivans**
Buffalo, N.Y.

**Museum Ship
Meteor**
Superior, WI

**Museum Ship
Milwaukee Clipper**
Muskegon, MI

**Museum Ship
Norgoma**
Sault Ste. Marie, ON

**Museum Ship
Valley Camp**
Sault Ste. Marie, MI

**Museum Ship
William A. Irvin**
Duluth, MN

**Museum Ship
William G. Mather**
Cleveland, OH

**Museum Ship
USCG Mackinaw**
Mackinaw City, MI

**Museum Tug
John Purves**
Sturgeon Bay, WI

**Museum Tug
Edna G.**
Two Harbors, MN

**Museum Tug
Peninsula**
Marathon, ON

125

Where History is *Fun!*

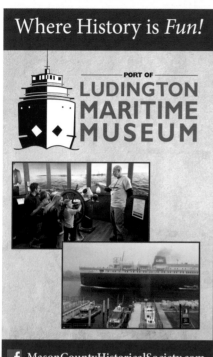

PORT OF
LUDINGTON
MARITIME
MUSEUM

f MasonCountyHistoricalSociety.com

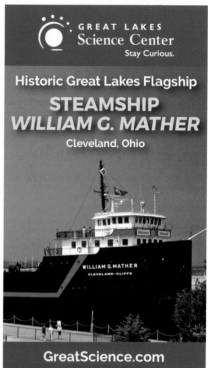

GREAT LAKES
Science Center
Stay Curious.

Historic Great Lakes Flagship

STEAMSHIP
WILLIAM G. MATHER

Cleveland, Ohio

WILLIAM G. MATHER
CLEVELAND-CLIFFS

GreatScience.com

st. catharines
museum
& WELLAND CANALS CENTRE

EXPLORE THE CITY'S HERITAGE AND ENJOY THE DAY WATCHING SHIPS TRANSIT THE WELLAND CANAL IN A TRANQUIL PARK-LIKE SETTING.

OPEN DAILY YEAR ROUND

FOR HOURS PLEASE VISIT:

🐦 @StCMuseum
f /stcatharinesmuseum

st. catharines museum
& WELLAND CANALS CENTRE

St. Catharines

stcatharinesmuseum.ca

Museums Ashore

Information can change without notice. Call ahead to verify location and hours.

ALGONAC CLAY MARITIME MUSEUM, 1240 ST. CLAIR RIVER DR., ALGONAC, MI – (810) 794-9015: Features many models of pleasure boats built by Chris-Craft, and includes pieces from local freighters and sailor paraphernalia. *(achistory.com)*

ANTIQUE BOAT MUSEUM, 750 MARY ST., CLAYTON, NY – (315) 686-4104: A large collection of freshwater boats and engines. Annual show is the first weekend of August. Seasonal. *(abm.org)*

ASHTABULA MARITIME & SURFACE TRANSPORTATION MUSEUM, 1071 WALNUT BLVD., ASHTABULA, OH – (440) 964-6847: Housed in the 1871/1898-built former lighthouse keeper's residence, the museum includes models, paintings, artifacts, photos, the world's only working scale model of a Hullett ore unloading machine, a Titanic display, a display of the 1876 Ashtabula Train Bridge Disaster and the pilothouse from the steamer *Thomas Walters*. Seasonal.

BUFFALO HARBOR MUSEUM, 66 ERIE ST., BUFFALO, NY – (716) 849-0914: Exhibits explore local maritime history. Open all year, Thursday and Sunday only. *(llmhs.org)*

DOOR COUNTY MARITIME MUSEUM & LIGHTHOUSE PRESERVATION SOCIETY INC., 120 N. MADISON AVE., STURGEON BAY, WI – (920) 743-5958: Many excellent models help portray the role shipbuilding has played in the Door Peninsula. Open all year. *(dcmm.org)*

DOSSIN GREAT LAKES MUSEUM, 100 THE STRAND, BELLE ISLE, DETROIT, MI – (313) 833-5538: Models, interpretive displays, the smoking room from the 1912 passenger steamer *City of Detroit III*, an anchor from the *Edmund Fitzgerald* and the pilothouse from the steamer *William Clay Ford* are on display. *(detroithistorical.org/main/dossin)*

ELGIN MILITARY MUSEUM, 30 TALBOT ST., ST. THOMAS, ON – (519) 633-7641: *HMCS Ojibwa*, a Cold War Oberon-class submarine, is open to the public at Port Burwell, ON. *(theelginmilitarymuseum.ca)*

ERIE MARITIME MUSEUM, 150 E. FRONT ST., ERIE, PA – (814) 452-2744: Displays depict the Battle of Lake Erie and more. Open all year. *(flagshipniagara.org)*

FAIRPORT HARBOR LIGHTHOUSE & MARINE MUSEUM, 129 SECOND ST., FAIRPORT, OH – (440) 354-4825: Located in the Fairport Lighthouse, displays include the pilothouse from the *Frontenac* and the mainmast of the first *USS Michigan*. Seasonal. *(fairportharborlighthouse.org)*

Continued on Page 128

Former U.S. Navy destroyer Edson, now a museum at Bay City, MI. *(Gordy Garris)*

GREAT LAKES LORE MARITIME MUSEUM, 367 N. THIRD ST., ROGERS CITY, MI – (989) 734-0706: The generations of men and women who sailed and made their livings on the Great Lakes are remembered here, as are their uniforms, personal possessions and navigational and other maritime tools. *(gllmm.com)*

GREAT LAKES SHIPWRECK MUSEUM, WHITEFISH POINT, MI – (906) 635-1742 or (800)-635-1742: Museum includes lighthouse and shipwreck artifacts, a shipwreck video theater, the restored lighthouse keeper's quarters and an *Edmund Fitzgerald* display that features the ship's bell. Seasonal. *(shipwreckmuseum.com)*

LAKE SUPERIOR MARITIME VISITOR CENTER, 600 CANAL PARK DRIVE, DULUTH, MN – (218) 720-5260: Museum provides displays, historic artifacts and programs that explain the roles of Duluth and Superior in Great Lakes shipping, as well as the job of the U.S. Army Corps of Engineers in maintaining the nation's waterways. Many excellent models and other artifacts are on display. Open all year. *(lsmma.com)*

LE SAULT DE SAINTE MARIE HISTORICAL SITES INC., 501 E. WATER ST., SAULT STE. MARIE, MI – (906) 632-3658: The 1917-built steamer *Valley Camp* is the centerpiece of this museum. The ship's three cargo holds house artifacts, models, aquariums, photos and other memorabilia, as well as a tribute to the *Edmund Fitzgerald* that includes the ill-fated vessel's lifeboats. Seasonal. *(saulthistoricsites.com)*

LUDINGTON MARITIME MUSEUM, 217 S. LAKESHORE DRIVE, LUDINGTON, MI – (231) 843-4808): Diverse, interactive exhibits tell the stories of schooners, railroad carferries, the U.S. Coast Guard and the many other maritime activities of the region. *(ludingtonmaritimemuseum.org)*

MARINE CITY PRIDE & HERITAGE MUSEUM, 405 S. MAIN ST., MARINE CITY, MI – (810) 765-5446: Displays explore the ship and shipbuilding history of the area. Seasonal. *(marinecitymuseum.com)*

MARITIME MUSEUM OF SANDUSKY, 125 MEIGS ST., SANDUSKY, OHIO – (419) 624-0274: Exhibits explore local maritime history. Open all year. *(sanduskymaritime.org)*

MARQUETTE MARITIME MUSEUM, 300 N. LAKESHORE BLVD., MARQUETTE, MI – (906) 226-2006: Museum re-creates the offices of the first commercial fishing / passenger freight companies. Displays also include photos, models and maritime artifacts. Seasonal. *(mqtmaritimemuseum.com)*

MICHIGAN MARITIME MUSEUM, 260 DYCKMAN AVE., SOUTH HAVEN, MI – (269) 637-8078: Exhibits are dedicated to the U.S. Lifesaving Service / Coast Guard. The tall ship *Friends Good Will* operates during the summer. Open all year. *(michiganmaritimemuseum.org)*

MUSKOKA BOAT AND HERITAGE CENTRE, 275 STEAMSHIP BAY ROAD, GRAVENHURST, ON – (705) 687-2115: Visiting this museum, which includes many models of the early steamships to serve the area, is a great complement to a trip on the *RMS Segwun*, moored adjacent. *(realmuskoka.com/discovery-centre)*

Continued on Page 130

The always-photogenic Col. James M. Schoonmaker museum ship at Toledo, OH. The veteran steamer Alpena is passing by. (Aaron J. Border)

Where Great Lakes maritime history comes alive!

DOOR COUNTY maritime museum

One history...
three ports of call:

- Door County Maritime Museum - Sturgeon Bay
- Cana Island Lighthouse - Baileys Harbor
- Death's Door Maritime Museum - Gills Rock

920.743.5958 • www.DCMM.org • Find us on social media - #dcmaritime

Lake Superior Marine Museum Gift Shop

Maritime Books and Gifts
Toys • Puzzles • Clothing • Postcards
Lake Superior & Duluth Mementos

**At the foot of the Aerial Lift Bridge
Canal Park in Duluth, Minnesota**

(218) 727-1521 • LSMMA.COM

GALES OF NOVEMBER

Nov. 1 & 2 – Join Us in Duluth!

Roger LeLievre relates the 60-year history of *Know Your Ships.*
 + Hear a History of the U.S. Coast Guard
 + Meet the Guardsman who helped find the *Edmund Fitzgerald*
 + Hear Joel Stone, senior curator of the Detroit Historical Society
 + Cruise of a Lifetime Drawing • Exhibitors • Silent Auction

LAKE SUPERIOR MARINE MUSEUM ASSOCIATION

Keep our maritime heritage alive!

Join the Lake Superior Marine Museum Association
www.LSMMA.com or call 218-727-2497

PORT COLBORNE HISTORICAL & MARINE MUSEUM, 280 KING ST., PORT COLBORNE, ON – (905) 834-7604: Wheelhouse from the tug *Yvonne Dupre Jr.* is among the museum's displays. Seasonal. (*portcolborne.com/page/museum*)

RUDY NAUTICAL MUSEUM, 23650 VAN DYKE DRIVE, CENTERLINE, MI – (586) 206-2791: Exhibits include nautical artifacts, models, paintings and research summaries. (*rudynauticalmuseum.com*)

SOMBRA MUSEUM, 3470 ST. CLAIR PARKWAY, SOMBRA, ON – (519) 892-3982: Marine room includes nautical equipment, Great Lakes and St. Clair River photos, and the Alan Mann Collection. (*sombramuseum.webs.com*)

STRAITS OF MACKINAC SHIPWRECK MUSEUM, OLD MACKINAC POINT LIGHT, MACKINAC CITY, MI – (231) 436-4100: Houses artifacts recovered from the sunken *Cedarville* as well as others that tell the story of the many shipwrecks that dot the Straits of Mackinac. Seasonal. (*mackinacparks.com*)

U.S. ARMY CORPS OF ENGINEERS MUSEUM, SOO LOCKS VISITOR CENTER, SAULT STE. MARIE, MI – (906) 632-7020: Exhibits include a working model of the Soo Locks, historic photos and a 25-minute film. Free; open Mother's Day weekend through mid-October. Check at the Visitor Center information desk for a list of vessels expected at the locks.

WELLAND CANALS CENTRE & ST. CATHARINES MUSEUM, THOROLD, ON – (905) 984-8880: Museum at Lock 3 traces the development of the Welland Canal. Museum and adjacent gift shop open year-round. Observation deck open during the navigation season. Check at the information desk for vessels expected at Lock 3. (*infoniagara.com*)

WILLIAM PURVIS MARINE CENTRE, 40 WATER ST., GORE BAY, ON – (705-282-0190): Museum and archive is open Victoria Day-Thanksgiving Day (Canadian). (*gorebaymuseum.com/marine-museum*)

WISCONSIN MARITIME MUSEUM, 75 MARITIME DRIVE, MANITOWOC, WI – (866) 724-2356: Displays explore the history of area shipbuilding and also honor submariners and submarines built in Manitowoc. One of the engines of the Straits of Mackinac trainferry *Chief Wawatam* is on display. The World War II sub *Cobia* is adjacent to the museum and open for tours. Open all year. (*wisconsinmaritime.org*)

S.S. WILLIAM CLAY FORD PILOT HOUSE

The **Dossin Great Lakes Museum** showcases 300 years of our region's maritime history on the shores of Belle Isle.

Summer Hours:
Wednesday – Sunday, 10 am – 4 pm

Year-Round Hours:
Friday – Sunday, 10 am – 4 pm

Free Admission

DOSSIN GREAT LAKES MUSEUM

detroithistorical.org

Ashtabula
Maritime & Surface Transportation Museum

Visit the former lightkeeper's home, which overlooks a working port. Step inside the pilothouse of the *Thomas Walters.* View a 4-foot scale model of a Hulett unloader as well as lakeboat models and a train display of the Ashtabula Harbor docks.

Website / Webcam

AshtabulaMaritimeMuseum.org

Stacks
and
Flags

Ashley & Dustin Steamer Line stack on the passenger vessel Put-In-Bay prior to 1953.
(Hal Jackson)

COLORS OF THE GREAT LAKES

Abaco Marine Towing
Clayton, NY

Algoma Central Corp.
St. Catharines, ON

American Steamship Co.
Williamsville, NY

Andrie Inc.
Muskegon, MI

Ashton Marine Co.
North Muskegon, MI

Bay City Boat Lines
Bay City, MI

Bay Shipbuilding Co.
Fincanteri Marine Group
Sturgeon, Bay, WI

Beaver Island Boat Co.
Charlevoix, MI

Blue Heron Co.
Tobermory, ON

Buffalo Dept.
of Public Works
Buffalo, N.Y.

Busch Marine Inc.
Carrollton, MI

Calumet River Fleeting
Chicago, IL

Canada Steamship Lines
Div. CSL Group
Montreal, QC

Canada Steamship Lines
Div. CSL Group
Montreal, QC

Canadian Coast Guard
Ottawa, ON

Carmeuse North America
(Erie Sand & Gravel)
Erie, PA

Causley Marine
Contracting LLC
Bay City, MI

Central Marine Logistics Inc.
Operator for ArcelorMittal
Griffith, IN

Chicago Fire Dept.
Chicago, IL

Cleveland Fire Dept.
Cleveland, OH

Cooper Marine Ltd.
Selkirk, OH

Coopérative de Transport
Maritime et Aérien (C.T.M.A.)
Cap-aux-Meules, QC

Croisières AML Inc.
Québec, QC

Dann Marine Towing
Chesapeake City, MD

Dean Construction Co.
Windsor, ON

Detroit City Fire Dept.
Detroit, MI

Diamond Jack's
River Tours
Detroit, MI

Duc D'Orleans Cruise Boat
Corunna, ON

Durocher Marine
Cheboygan, MI

Eastern Upper Peninsula
Transportation Authority
Sault Ste. Marie, MI

Fraser Shipyards Inc.
Superior, WI

G3 Canada Ltd.
Algoma Central – Mgr
Winnipeg, MB

Gaelic Tugboat Co.
Detroit, MI

Gananoque Boat Line
Gananoque, ON

Genesis Energy
Houston, TX

Geo. Gradel Co.
Toledo, OH

Goodtime Cruise Line
Cleveland, OH

Grand Portage /
Isle Royale Trans. Line
Superior, WI

Great Lakes Dock
& Materials
Muskegon, MI

Great Lakes Fleet Inc.
Key Lakes Inc.– Mgr.
Duluth, MN

Great Lakes & International
Towing & Salvage
Burlington, ON

Great Lakes
Maritime Academy
Traverse City, MI

Great Lakes Science Center
Ann Arbor, MI

Great Lakes Towing Co.
Cleveland, OH

Groupe Desgagnés Inc.
Québec City, QC

Groupe Desgagnés Inc.
Québec City, QC

Groupe Desgagnés Inc.
Québec City, QC

Groupe Océan Inc.
Québec, QC

AND SEAWAY SMOKESTACKS

Hamilton Port Authority
Hamilton, ON

Heritage Marine
Two Harbors, MN

Inland Lakes Management
Alpena, MI

Inland Tug and Barge
Brockville, ON

Interlake Steamship Co.
Middleburg Heights, OH

J.W. Westcott Co.
Detroit, MI

Kindra Lake Towing
Chicago, IL

The King Company
Holland, MI

Lafarge North America Inc.
Southfield, MI

Lake Erie Island Cruises
Sandusky, OH

Lakehead Tugboats Inc.
Thunder Bay, ON

Lake Michigan Carferry Service Inc.
Ludington, MI

Les Barges De Matane Inc.
Matane, QC

Lower Lakes Towing
Lower Lakes Transportation
Port Dover, ON / Williamsville, NY

Luedtke Engineering
Frankfort, MI

MCM Marine Inc.
Sault Ste. Marie, MI

MacDonald Marine Ltd.
Goderich, ON

Madeline Island Ferry Line Inc.
LaPointe, WI

Malcolm Marine
St. Clair, MI

Manitou Island Transit
Leland, MI

Mariposa Cruise Line
Toronto, ON

McAsphalt Marine Transportation
Hamilton, ON

McInnis Cement
Montreal, QC

McKeil Marine Ltd.
Burlington, ON

McKeil Marine Ltd.
Burlington, ON

McNally International
Hamilton, ON

Midwest Maritime Corp.
Franklin, WI

Miller Boat Line
Put-in-Bay, OH

Ministry of Transportation
Downsview, ON

Montreal Port Authority
Montreal, QC

Muskoka Steamship & Historical Society
Gravenhurst, ON

Nadro Marine Services
Port Dover, ON

New York State Marine Highway Transportation
Troy, NY

North Shore Marine Terminal and Logistics
Escanaba, MI

NovaAlgoma Cement Carriers Ltd.
St. Catharines, ON

Open Lake Group LLC.
Detroit, MI

Owen Sound Transportation Co. Ltd.
Owen Sound, ON

Pere Marquette Shipping
Ludington, MI

Port City Cruise Lines
Muskegon, MI

Port City Steamship
Port City Tug Inc.
Muskegon, MI

Purvis Marine Ltd.
Sault Ste. Marie, ON

Reinauer Transportation Companies
Staten Island, NY

Roen Salvage Co.
Sturgeon Bay, WI

Ryba Marine Construction
Cheboygan, MI

Sea Service LLC
Superior, WI

Selvick Marine Towing Corp.
Sturgeon Bay, WI

Shoreline Sightseeing Co.
Chicago, IL

Société des Traversiers Du Québec
Québec, QC

133

Soo Locks Boat Tours
Sault Ste. Marie, MI

St. James Marine Co.
Beaver Island, MI

St. Lawrence Cruise Lines Inc.
Kingston, ON

St. Lawrence Seaway Development Corp.
Massena, NY

St. Lawrence Seaway Management Corp.
Cornwall, ON

St. Marys Cement Group
Toronto, ON

Star Line Mackinac Ferry
St. Ignace, MI

Sterling Fuels Ltd.
Hamilton, ON

Thousand Islands & Seaway Cruises
Brockville, ON

Thunder Bay Tug Services Ltd.
Thunder Bay, ON

Toronto Drydock Ltd.
Toronto, ON

Toronto Fire Services
Toronto, ON

Toronto Port Authority
Toronto, ON

United States Army Corps of Engineers
Cincinatti, OH

United States Coast Guard 9th Coast Guard District
Cleveland, OH

United States Fish & Wildlife Service
Elmira, MI

U.S. Oil Div. U.S. Venture Inc.
Appleton, WI

VanEnkevort Tug & Barge
Escanaba, MI

SALTWATER FLEETS ON THE SEAWAY

ABC Maritime
Nyon, Switzerland

Ace Tankers CV
Amsterdam, Netherlands

Alliance Tankers
Hamilton, Bermuda

Ardmore Shipping Ltd.
Cork, Ireland

Armador Gemi Isletmeciligi Ticaret Ltd.
Istanbul, Turkey

ARA Group
Werkendam, Netherlands

Atlantik Denizcilik Ticaret Ve Sanayi A.S.
Istanbul, Turkey

Atlantska Plovidba
Dubrovnik, Croatia

Auerbach Schifffahrt GMBH & Co. KG
Hamburg, Germany

Bernhard Schulte Group
Hamburg, Germany

BigLift Shipping
Amsterdam, Netherlands

Blystad Group
Oslo, Norway

Briese Schiffahrts GMBH & Co. KG
Leer, Germany

Brostrom AB
Copenhagen, Denmark

Canada Feeder Lines BV
Groningen, Netherlands

Canfornav Inc.
Montreal, QC, Canada

Carisbrooke Shipping Ltd.
Cowes, United Kingdom

Chemfleet Shipping
Istanbul, Turkey

Coastal Shipping Ltd. (Div. Woodward Group)
Goose Bay, NL, Canada

Conti Reederei Management
Munich, Germany

C.O.E. Shipping GMBH & Co.
Buxtehude, Germany

Cosco Southern Asphalt Shipping Co.
Guangzhou, China

Duzgit Gemi Insa Sanayi
Istanbul, Turkey

Eastern Pacific Shipping
Singapore

Egbert A.K. Bos
Winterswijk, Netherlands

Elbe Shipping GMBH
Drochtersen, Germany

Empire Chemical Tankers
Piraeus, Greece

Fairfield Chemical Carriers
Wilton, CT, USA

Fednav
Montreal, QC, Canada

Fednav
Montreal, QC, Canada

Franco Compania Naviera SA
Athens, Greece

Freese Reederei Group
Stade, Germany

Gebruder Ahrens Reederei
Grunendeich, Germany

Hansa Heavy Lift GMBH
Bremen, Germany

Harren & Partner Schiffahrts GMBH
Bremen, Germany

Hermann Buss GMBH
Leer, Germany

HS Schiffahrts
Haren-Ems, Germany

Huarong Huiyin LTD.
Hong Kong, China

Intership Navigation Co.
Limassol, Cyprus

Johann M.K. Blumenthal GMBH & Co.
Hamburg, Germany

Johs Thode & Company
Bremen, Germany

Jumbo Shipping Co. SA
Rotterdam, Netherlands

Krey Schiffahrts GMBH & Co.
Leer, Germany

Lauranne Shipping BV
Ghent, Netherlands

Longship BV
Groningen, Netherlands

Lubeca Marine Management GmbH & Co. KG
Lübeck, Germany

Mineralien Schiffahrt Spedition
Schnaittenbach, Germany

MTM Ship Management LTD.
Singapore

Navigation Maritime Bulgare Ltd.
Varna, Bulgaria

Nomadic Short Sea Shipping
Bergen, Norway

Nordic Tankers Marine A/S
Copenhagen, Denmark

Oceanex Inc.
Montreal, QC, Canada

Parakou Shipping Ltd.
Hong Kong, China

Pearl Seas Cruises LLC.
Guilford, CT

Peter Dohle Schiffahrts
Hamburg, Germany

Phoenix Shipping and Trading SA
Piraeus, Greece

Polsteam Polish Steamship Co.
Szczecin, Poland

Pot Scheepvaart BV
Delfzijl, Netherlands

Rederi AB Donsotank
Donso, Sweden

Reederei Heino Winter
Hamburg, Germany

Rederiet Stenersen AS
Bergen, Norway

Reederei H. Schuldt GMBH & Co. KG
Hamburg, Germany

Reederei Nord GMBH
Hamburg, Germany

Rigel Schiffahrts GMBH
Bremen, Germany

Sloman Neptun Shiffahrts
Bremen, Germany

Spliethoff
Amsterdam, Netherlands

Sunship Schiffahrtskontor KG
Emden, Germany

Tarbit Tankers B.V.
Dordrecht, Netherlands

TB Marine Shipmanagement GMBH & Co.
Hamburg, Germany

Team Tankers Management AS
Hellerup, Denmark

Thorco
Copenhagen, Denmark

Tradewind Tankers
Barcelona, Spain

Transmarine Management APS
Copenhagen, Denmark

Uni-Tankers International
Middelfart, Denmark

Unicorn Tankers International Ltd.
London, United Kingdom

VBG Denizcilik Sanaya VE Ticaret AS
Istanbul, Turkey

Victory Cruise Lines
New Albany, IN

Vroon B.V.
Breda, Netherlands

W. Bockstiegel Reederei KG
Emden, Germany

Wagenborg Shipping
Delfzijl, Netherlands

Yardimci Shipping Group
Istanbul, Turkey

Yilmar Shipping & Trading Ltd.
Istanbul, Turkey

Zealand Shipping BV
Almere, Netherlands

TRANSLATIONS: The terms **REEDERI** and **SCHIFFFAHRT** mean shipping in German. **SCHEEPVAART** means shipping in Dutch. The acronym **GmbH** designates a company as a private, or limited liability company in Germany. **TICKARET** is Arabic for commerce or trade.

FLAGS OF REGISTRY

Barbados

Belgium

Bermuda

Bulgaria

Canada

Bahamas

China

Croatia

Cyprus

Denmark

Finland

France

Germany

Greece

Hong Kong

India

Ireland

Israel

Italy

Japan

Liberia

Lithuania

Malta

Monaco

Netherlands

Norway

Panama

Philippines

Poland

Russia

Singapore

Spain

St.Vincent and The Grenadines

Sweden

Switzerland

Taiwan

Turkey

Ukraine

United Kingdom

United States

Vanuatu

Yugoslavia

FLEET HOUSEFLAGS

Algoma Central Corp.
St. Catherines, ON

American Steamship Co.
Williamsville, NY

Andrie Inc.
Muskegon, MI

**ArcelorMittal
Central Marine Logistics**
Griffith, IN

Beaver Island Boat Co.
Charlevoix, MI

**Canada Steamship
Lines Inc. (CSL)**
Montreal, QC

**Canadian Coast
Guard**
Ottawa, ON

Canfornav Inc.
Montreal, QC

Fednav
Montreal, QC

**G3 Canada Ltd.
Algoma Central – Mgr**
Winnipeg, MB

**Gaelic Tugboat Co.
Diamond Jack's River Tours**
Detroit, MI

**Great Lakes Fleet Inc.
Key Lakes Inc. - Mgr.**
Duluth, MN

**Great Lakes
Maritime Academy**
Traverse City, MI

Great Lakes Towing Co.
Cleveland, OH

Groupe Desgagnés Inc.
Québec City, QC

Groupe Océan Inc.
Québec, QC

**Inland Lakes
Management Inc.**
Alpena, MI

Interlake Steamship Co
Middleburg Heights, OH

J.W. Westcott Co.
Detroit, MI

**Key Lakes Inc.
Great Lakes Fleet - Mgr.**
Duluth, MN

LaFarge Inc.
Southfield, MI

**Lake Michigan
Carferry Service Inc.**
Ludington, MI

**Lower Lakes Towing Ltd.
Lower Lakes Transportation Co.**
Port Dover, ON / Williamsville, NY

**McAsphalt Marine
Transportation Ltd.**
Hamilton, ON

McKeil Marine Ltd.
Burlington, ON

**Pere Marquette
Shipping Co.**
Ludington, MI

**Polsteam
Polish Steamship Co.**
Szczecin, Poland

Purvis Marine Ltd.
Sault Ste. Marie, ON

Spliethoff
Amsterdam, Netherlands

**St.Lawrence Seaway
Development Corp.**
Massena, NY

**St.Lawrence Seaway
Management Corp.**
Cornwall, ON

St. Marys Cement Group
Toronto, ON

**U.S. Army Corps
of Engineers**
Cincinnati, OH

**U.S. Coast
Guard**
Cleveland, OH

Wagenborg Shipping
Delfzijl, Netherlands

**VanEnkevort
Tug & Barge**
Escanaba, MI

Victory Cruise Lines
New Albany, IN

Other Flags of Note

Dangerous Cargo
On Board

Pilot On Board

Diver Down

RIVER CRUISING

Experience the 1000 Islands, the remarkable International Seaway locks, museums, mansions, historic villages & world-class capital cities. 4,5,6,7 night cruises on calm, inland waters aboard the nostalgic replica steamboat CANADIAN EMPRESS

ST. LAWRENCE & OTTAWA RIVERS

CANADIAN VACATIONS

Quebec City, Ottawa, Kingston Departures

1-800-267-7868
StLawrenceCruiseLines.com

Great Lakes Aquarium

Witness THE WONDER

OPEN DAILY
10 A.M. - 6 P.M.

218.740.FISH

353 HARBOR DRIVE, DULUTH
EXIT 256B ON I-35

WWW.GLAQUARIUM.ORG

Connect To The North
CHI-CHEEMAUN

Relax on open-air decks...

Enjoy a sunset dinner cruise...

Cruise across Georgian Bay...

TOBERMORY-SOUTH BAYMOUTH
ONTARIOFERRIES.COM
800.265.3163

Ontario
An Agency of the
Province of Ontario

Extra Tonnage

Ports • Cargoes
Locks • Canals

On board the veteran tug Wisconsin at Monroe, MI. (Neil Schultheiss)

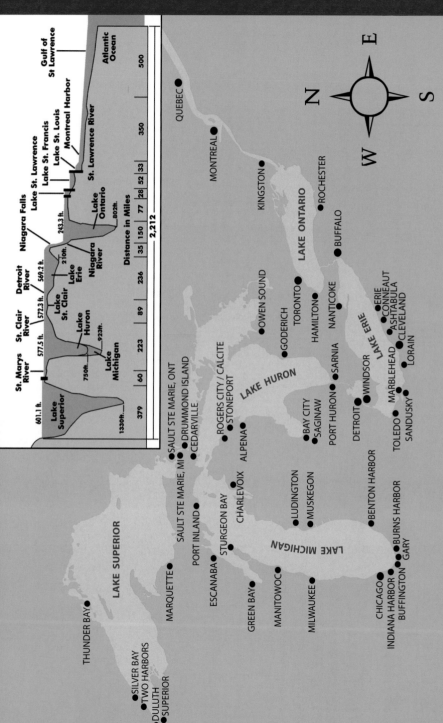

Taconite ore is loaded for delivery to lower lakes steel mills at Duluth, Two Harbors, Taconite Harbor and Silver Bay, MN, as well as Superior, WI, and Marquette, MI. Limestone-loading ports are Port Inland, Cedarville, Drummond Island, Calcite, Rogers City and Stoneport, MI, and Marblehead, OH. Coal ports are Superior, WI, S. Chicago, IL, and the Ohio ports of Toledo, Sandusky, Ashtabula and Conneaut. Petroleum is loaded aboard vessels at Sarnia, ON, and E. Chicago, IN. Grain export ports include Duluth, MN; Milwaukee and Superior, WI; and the Ontario ports of Thunder Bay, Sarnia and Owen Sound.

The primary U.S. iron ore and limestone receiving ports are Cleveland and Chicago, along with Gary, Burns Harbor and Indiana Harbor, IN; Detroit, MI; and Toledo, Lorain, Ashtabula and Conneaut, OH. In Canada, Nanticoke, Hamilton and Sault Ste. Marie, ON, are major ore-receiving ports. Coal is carried by self-unloaders to power plants in the United States and Canada. Most grain loaded on the lakes is destined for export via the St. Lawrence Seaway, although some is carried to Toledo, OH, and Buffalo, NY. Cement from Alpena and Charlevoix, MI, is delivered to terminals from Lake Superior to Lake Ontario. Tankers bring petroleum products to cities as diverse in size as Cleveland, OH, Green Bay, WI, and Cheboygan and Detroit, MI. Self-unloaders carry limestone, coal, road salt and sand to cities throughout the region.

John G. Munson loading stone at Drummond Island, MI. (Robert Prusak)

AVERAGE RUNNING TIMES

Times listed are for downbound passages. Reverse for upbound times. Times vary with speed / weather / traffic.

LAKE SUPERIOR
Duluth/Superior – Soo Locks .... 24 hrs
Marquette or Thunder Bay – Soo Locks .... 12 hrs

ST. MARYS RIVER
Soo Locks – DeTour, MI .... 6 hrs
DeTour – Port Huron .... 19 hrs

LAKE HURON
DeTour – Mackinac Bridge .... 2 hrs
DeTour – Port Huron .... 19 hrs
Harbor Beach – Port Huron .... 4 hrs

LAKE MICHIGAN
Gray's Reef Light – Gary, IN .... 22 hrs

LAKE ERIE
Detroit River Light – Toledo .... 1.75 hrs
Detroit River Light – Southeast Shoal .... 3 hrs
Southeast Shoal – Long Point .... 9 hrs
Long Point – CIP 15 (off Port Weller) .... 3 hrs
Detroit River Light – Port Colborne piers – CIP 16
   (Welland Canal) .... 15 hrs

LAKE ONTARIO
Welland Canal (Port Weller) – Hamilton .... 2 hrs
Welland Canal (Port Weller) – Cape Vincent, NY
   (call-in points at Newcastle, mid-lake and
   Sodus Point) .... 12 hrs

AGRICULTURAL PRODUCTS – Wheat, grain, soybeans, canola, flax and oats are shipped on the Great Lakes. Some is used domestically, but most is shipped to international markets.

BLAST FURNACE TRIM – Raw crushed taconite.

BUNKER C – A special grade of heavy fuel oil, also known as No. 6 fuel.

CEMENT CLINKER – A material, made by heating ground limestone and clay, that is ground up to a fine powder to produce cement.

CLINKER – The incombustible residue that remains after the combustion of coal.

COAL – Both eastern (high sulfur, used in industry) and western (low sulfur, burned at power plants) coal are shipped aboard Great Lakes vessels.

Algoma Transport at Lorain, OH. *(Roger Durfee)*

COKE – A byproduct of blended coals baked in ovens until mostly pure carbon is left. Coke is used to generate the high heat necessary to make steel in blast furnaces.

COKE BREEZE – Byproduct of coke production.

DOLOMITE – Rock similar to limestone but somewhat harder and heavier.

FLUXSTONE – Taconite pellets premixed with limestone, so no limestone needs to be added in a blast furnace.

IRON FINES – Fines (ore less than 6mm in diameter) are created as a result of mining, crushing and processing the larger pieces of ore. See **SINTER**.

LIMESTONE – Common sedimentary rock consisting mostly of calcium carbonate used as a building stone and in the manufacture of lime, carbon dioxide and cement.

LIQUID ASPHALT – The last product taken from an oil refinery. The thick, black product is mixed with small stones to make asphalt pavement material.

MILL SCALE – Byproduct of the shaping of iron and steel.

PETROLEUM COKE – Petroleum coke (petcoke) is the bottom end of oil refining – the parts of crude oil that will not vaporize in the refining process. It is mostly used as fuel (often blended with coal) in power plants.

PIG IRON – Crude iron that is the direct product of the blast furnace and is refined to produce steel, wrought iron or ingot iron.

POTASH – A compound used for fertilizer.

SALT – Most salt shipped on the Great Lakes is used on roads and highways during the winter to melt ice.

SINTER – Broken taconite pellets, a.k.a. taconite pellet chips and fines. Small, but still useful in the blast furnace.

SLAG – Byproduct of the steelmaking process is used in the production of concrete and as seal coat cover, a base for paving, septic drain fields and railroad ballast.

TACONITE – A low-grade iron ore, containing about 27 percent iron and 51 percent silica, found as a hard rock formation in the Lake Superior region. It is pelletized for shipment to steel mills (see below).

TRAP ROCK – Rock, usually ground fairly fine, for use as foundations and roads or walkways. It is mined near Bruce Mines, ON, and loaded there.

About taconite pellets

The high-grade iron ore (around 60 percent pure) that was mined on the ranges around Lake Superior was mostly exhausted in the tremendous mining efforts of World War II through the early 1950s. There was still plenty of iron ore in the ground, but it was only about 20-30 percent pure. To mine and ship that ore in its natural form would have been expensive, so engineers developed the taconite pelletization process to increase the iron content of the product coming off the ranges.

Pellets have a number of positive attributes. Their iron content (and the content of other elements) can be precisely controlled, so the steel mills know exactly what they are getting. Pellets are relatively moisture free compared with raw iron ore, so they are less prone to freeze in rail cars, storage piles or dock pockets. This means the pellets can be shipped for a much longer season than natural iron ore, so companies need fewer rail cars and ships to carry the same amount of pellets, thus saving money on labor and infrastructure. Pellets are also uniform in size, shape and mass, making them very easy to handle on conveyor belt systems, which makes for speedy, precise ship loading and unloading using a shipboard self-unloading system, again cutting down on costs.

A self-unloader's system of belts moves cargo from the holds to the dock via a movable boom that swing to either side.

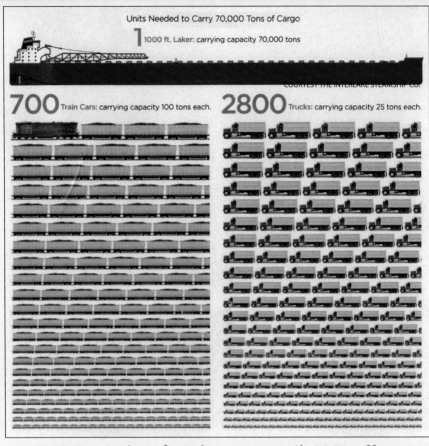

Units Needed to Carry 70,000 Tons of Cargo

1 1000 ft. Laker: carrying capacity 70,000 tons

COURTESY THE INTERLAKE STEAMSHIP CO.

700 Train Cars: carrying capacity 100 tons each.

2800 Trucks: carrying capacity 25 tons each.

A Great Lakes freighter can sail **607 miles** on **1 gallon** of fuel per ton of cargo.
A 1,000-footer can haul as much as **3 million tons** of cargo in a single shipping season.

Erie Trader and Walter J. McCarthy Jr. meet in Soo Harbor. (Scott Tomlinson)

SOO LOCKS BOAT TOURS

800-432-6301 • soolocks.com
Sault Ste. Marie, Michigan

Lock Tour · Dinner · Themed · Lighthouse

The Soo Locks at Sault Ste. Marie, MI, on the St. Marys River, overcome a 21-foot difference in water levels between Lake Superior and lakes Huron, Michigan and Erie. The first canal on the U.S. side was built from 1853-55. Several larger locks followed, spurred by the building of even larger ships.

Under the jurisdiction of the U.S. Army Corps of Engineers, the locks operate on gravity, as do all locks in the St. Lawrence Seaway system. No pumps are used to empty or fill the lock chambers; valves are opened, and water is allowed to seek its own level. All traffic passes through the locks toll-free. Traffic is directed by radio to the appropriate lock according to size, other vessels in the locks area and the time the captain first calls in to the lockmaster. All vessels longer than 730 feet and /or wider than 76 feet are restricted by size to the **Poe**, or second, lock. Smaller vessels go to the **MacArthur Lock**, closest to the viewing platform. Vessels are under engine and thruster control at all times, with crews ready to drop mooring lines over bollards on the lock wall to stop their movement.

As soon as the vessel is in position, the engines are stopped and mooring lines are made fast. If the vessel is being lowered, valves at the lower end of the lock chamber are opened to allow the water inside to flow out. If the vessel is being raised, valves at the upper end of the chamber are opened to allow water to enter. When the water reaches the desired level, the valves are closed, the protective boom is raised, and the gates are opened, and the vessel leaves the lock.

MacArthur Lock

Named after World War II Gen. Douglas MacArthur, the MacArthur Lock is 800 feet long (243.8 meters) between inner gates, 80 feet wide (24.4 meters) and 31 feet deep (9.4 meters) over the sills. The lock was built in 1942-43 and opened to traffic on July 11, 1943. Vessel size is limited to 730 feet long (222.5 meters) by 76 feet wide (23 meters).

Poe Lock

The Poe Lock is 1,200 feet long (365.8 meters) and 110 feet wide (33.5 meters), and has a depth over the sills of 32 feet (9.8 meters). Named after Col. Orlando M. Poe, it was built in the years 1961-68. The lock's vessel size limit is 1,100 feet long (335.3 meters) by 105 feet wide (32 meters).

Davis and Sabin locks

Dating from the first two decades of the 20th century, these two locks are scheduled to be replaced with one lock.

Canadian Lock

The Canadian Lock at Sault Ste. Marie, ON, has its origin in a canal constructed from 1887-95. The present lock, operated by Parks Canada, is used by pleasure craft, tugs and tour boats.

Thanks to higher water levels, cargo records were smashed at the Soo Locks on Sept. 24, 2017, when the 1,000-foot-long *American Integrity* broke the all-time record for the largest load through the locks by carrying 75,095 tons of iron ore pellets. Her cargo added up to 150,190,000 pounds. Assuming each taconite pellet weighed 0.1 oz. (per info provided by the U.S. Army Corps of Engineers) that's more than 24 billion taconite pellets.

Federal Yukon heads into the Poe Lock. The MacArthur Lock is at left. (Roger LeLievre)

At long last, a new lock is coming to the Soo

The Soo Locks may soon look like the top photo, taken in 1965 during the construction of the current Poe Lock.
(Ruth Stevens, courtesy Bob Campbell)
Inset shows a finished new lock at left.

The U.S. Army Corps of Engineers' 2019 work plan to Congress includes $32 million as an initial outlay for the design and construction of a new lock at Sault Ste. Marie, MI.

The total cost of the new lock is estimated at $1 billion, with construction expected to take seven years. Additionally, $20.7 million has been allocated for repairs to the former Carbide Dock and other infrastructure in the Soo to accommodate the lock project.

The new lock, which was authorized by Congress in 1986 but never funded, will be a twin to the existing Poe Lock. With 100 percent of the iron ore used by U.S. industry moving through the Soo Locks, a backup lock has been deemed essential to national security. At present, 86 percent of all traffic is restricted to the Poe Lock due to vessel size. A failure at the Soo Locks would have a significant impact on manufacturing throughout the U.S. and Canada.

Saginaw departs the Soo Locks headed upbound. *(Keith Norling)*

The St. Marys River flows out of the southeast corner of Lake Superior in a southeasterly direction to Lake Huron. Vessels transiting the St. Marys River system are under the jurisdiction of Soo Traffic, part of the U.S. Coast Guard at Sault Ste. Marie, MI, and must radio their positions on VHF Ch. 12 (156.600 MHz) at predetermined locations. Vessels in the vicinity of the Soo Locks fall under the jurisdiction of the lockmaster, who must be contacted on VHF Ch. 14 (156.700 MHz) for lock assignments.

Call-in points (bold type on map) are not the same for upbound and downbound traffic. Approximate running times between call-in points are at left; times may vary due to other traffic and weather. Because of their size, 1,000-footers take more time to transit than smaller vessels.

Arrival times at the Soo Locks are available at the Information Center located in the locks park. Upbound vessels must make a pre-call to Soo Traffic one hour before entering the river at DeTour, and downbound traffic is required to make a one-hour pre-call above Ile Parisienne.

Upbound traffic passes Neebish Island on the east side. Downbound traffic passes the island to the west through the Rock Cut, a channel dynamited out of solid rock in the early 1900s.

WHITEFISH BAY

CANADA

U.S.A.

ILE PARISIENNE
DOWNBOUND ONLY

GROS CAP
UPBOUND ONLY

WEST PIER SAULT STE. MARIE, ON
EAST PIER

SAULT STE MARIE, MI

SOO LOCKS
BIG POINT

MISSION POINT

SUGAR ISLAND

LAKE GEORGE

NINE MILE POINT

LAKE NICOLET

BARBEAU
ROCK CUT

NEEBISH ISLAND

STRIBLING POINT

JOHNSONS POINT

WINTER POINT

MUNUSCONG LAKE

ST. JOSEPH ISLAND

MUD LAKE
JUNCTION BUOY

LIME ISLAND

RABER

DETOUR VILLAGE

DETOUR →
REEF LIGHT

DRUMMOND ISLAND

LAKE HURON

UPBOUND	J'ct. Buoy	Nine Mile	Miss. Point	Clear Locks	Gros Cap
DeTour	1:35	3:35	4:20	5:50	7:25
Junction Buoy		1:50	2:45	4:15	5:50
Nine Mile Point			0:55	2:25	4:00
Mission Point*				1:30	3:05
Clear of Locks					1:35

DOWNBOUND	Gros Cap	Big Point	Clear Locks	Nine Mile	J'ct Buoy	DeTour
Ile Parisienne	0:45	1:55	3:25	4:20	6:20	8:00
Gros Cap		1:10	2:40	3:35	5:35	7:15
Big Point*			1:30	2:25	4:25	6:05
Clear of Locks				0:55	2:55	4:35
Nine Mile Point					2:00	3:40
Junction Buoy						1:40

* Lockmaster only

147

Vessels transiting the St. Clair River, Lake St. Clair and the Detroit River are under the jurisdiction of Sarnia Traffic and must radio their positions at predetermined locations. Call-in points (bold type on map) are not the same for upbound and downbound traffic. Average running times between call-in points are below. *

UPBOUND	Buoys 1&2	Black River	Stag Isl.	Salt Dock	X-32	Crib Light	Grassy Isl.
Detroit River Lt.	8:10	7:50	7:20	6:00	4:20	4:00	1:35
Grassy Island	6:45	6:25	5:55	4:35	2:55	2:35	
St. Clair Crib	4:10	3:50	3:20	2:00	0:25		
Light X-32	3:50	3:30	3:00	1:35			
Salt Dock	2:10	1:50	1:20				
Stag Isl. Upper	0:50	0:35					
Black River	0:20						

DOWNBOUND	Det. River	Grassy Isl.	Belle Isl.	Crib Light	Light 23	Salt Dock	Black River	7&8
30 min. above buoys 11 & 12	9:05	7:35	6:25	5:10	3:55	3:10	1:20	0:40
Buoys 7 & 8	8:15	6:55	5:45	4:30	3:15	2:30	0:40	
Black River	7:45	6:15	5:05	3:50	2:35	1:50		
Salt Dock	5:55	4:25	3:15	2:00	0:45			
Light 23	5:10	3:40	2:30	1:10				
St. Clair Crib	3:55	2:25	1:10					
USCG Belle Isle	2:40	1:10						
Grassy Isl.	1:30							

* Times can change if vessels stop for fuel or are delayed by other traffic.

Map labels:

BUOYS 11&12 DOWNBOUND ONLY
BUOYS 7&8 DOWNBOUND ONLY
BUOYS 1&2 UPBOUND ONLY
BLACK RIVER
STAG ISLAND UPPER UPBOUND ONLY
LAKE HURON
PORT HURON
SARNIA
IMPERIAL FUEL DOCK
SHELL FUEL DOCK
ST. CLAIR
ST. CLAIR EDISON POWER PLANT RECOR POINT
MARINE CITY
SALT DOCK
ALGONAC
HARSENS ISLAND
LIGHT 23 DOWNBOUND ONLY
X(RAY) 32 UPBOUND ONLY
ST. CLAIR CRIB LIGHT
LAKE ST. CLAIR
USCG BELLE ISLE DOWNBOUND ONLY
J.W. WESTCOTT MAILBOAT
DETROIT
MISTERSKY FUEL
WINDSOR
ROUGE RIVER
STERLING FUEL
GRASSY ISLAND
FIGHTING ISLAND
GROSSE ILE
LIVINGSTONE CHANNEL
AMHERSTBURG CHANNEL
DETROIT RIVER LIGHT
N
W
E
S
POINT PELEE
PELEE PASSAGE
MONROE
LAKE ERIE
PELEE ISLAND
SOUTHEAST SHOAL

Frontenac about to pass under the Ambassador Bridge between Detroit and Windsor. (Neil Schultheiss)

FRONTENAC

Detroit River Light is the first call-in point when entering the Detroit River upbound. The Fermi II nuclear generating plant is in the background.
(Roger LeLievre)

The **28-mile (44 km) Welland Canal** is the fourth version of a waterway link between Lake Ontario and Lake Erie, first built in 1829. The present canal was completed in 1932, deepened in the 1950s as part of the Seaway project and further straightened in 1973. Today its eight locks, all Canadian, lift ships 326 feet (100 meters) over the Niagara Escarpment.

Each of the seven Welland Canal locks has an average lift of 46.5 feet (14.2 meters). All locks (except Lock 8) are 859 feet (261.8 meters) long, 80 feet (24.4 meters) wide and 30 feet (9.1 meters) deep. Lock 8 measures 1,380 feet (420.6 m) long.

The largest vessel that may transit the canal is 740 feet (225.5 meters) long, 78 feet (23.8 meters) wide and 26.5 feet (8.08 meters) in draft. **Locks 1, 2** and **3** are at Port Weller and St. Catharines, ON, on the Lake Ontario end of the waterway. At Lock 3, the Welland Canals Centre and St. Catharines Museum also houses an information desk (which posts a list of vessels expected at the lock), a gift shop and restaurant.

At Thorold, ON, **Locks 4, 5** and **6**, twinned to help speed passage of vessels, are controlled with an elaborate interlocking system for safety. These locks (positioned end to end, they resemble a short flight of stairs) have an aggregate lift of 139.5 feet (42.5 meters). Just south of locks **4, 5** and **6** is **Lock 7**. **Lock 8**, 7 miles (11.2 km) upstream at Port Colborne, ON, completes the process, making the final adjustment to Lake Erie's level.

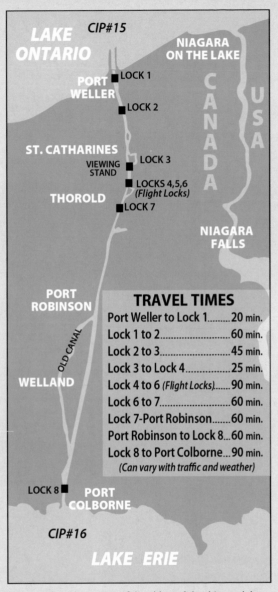

TRAVEL TIMES

Port Weller to Lock 1	20 min.
Lock 1 to 2	60 min.
Lock 2 to 3	45 min.
Lock 3 to Lock 4	25 min.
Lock 4 to 6 *(Flight Locks)*	90 min.
Lock 6 to 7	60 min.
Lock 7-Port Robinson	60 min.
Port Robinson to Lock 8	60 min.
Lock 8 to Port Colborne	90 min.

(Can vary with traffic and weather)

In 1973, a new channel was constructed to replace the section of the old canal that bisected the city of Welland. The Welland Bypass eliminated long delays for canal navigation and for road and rail traffic. Two tunnels allow auto and train traffic to pass beneath the canal.

The average passage time for the canal is 8-11 hours, with the majority of the time spent transiting Locks 4-7. All vessel traffic though the Welland Canal is regulated by a control center, Seaway Welland, which also remotely operates the locks and the traffic bridges over the canal. Vessels passing through the Welland Canal and St. Lawrence Seaway must carry a qualified pilot at all times.

Cedarglen has just left the Welland Canal flight locks. (Paul Beesley)

Algoma Central Corp. Equinox-class vessels meet in the Welland Canal. From this vantage point, it's easy to see why the waterway is nicknamed "The Ditch." (Marine Delivers)

Tug Ocean K. Rusby and grain carrier G3 Marquis at Quebec City, QC. (Mac Mackay)

The St. Lawrence Seaway is a waterway extending some 2,038 miles (3,701.4 km) from the Atlantic Ocean to the head of the Great Lakes at Duluth, Minn., including Montreal harbor and the Welland Canal. More specifically, it is a system of locks and canals (U.S. and Canadian), built between 1954 and 1958 at a cost of $474 million and opened in 1959, that allows vessels to pass from Montreal to the Welland Canal at the western end of Lake Ontario. For the Montreal-Lake Ontario section, the average transit time is 24 hours upbound and 22 hours downbound. The difference is mainly due to the current in the St. Lawrence River. The vessel size limit within this system is 740 feet (225.6 meters) long, 78 feet (23.8 meters) wide and 26 feet (7.9 meters) draft. It takes 8-10 days for a ship to go from Lake Superior to the Atlantic Ocean.

BY THE NUMBERS

The 2018 season was the best year for St. Lawrence Seaway shipping in more than a decade.

Top 3 Cargoes

Grain: 12.1 million metric tons, a 20 percent increase compared to the same time last year

Dry Bulk: 10.7 million metric tons, a three percent increase

Liquid Bulk: 4.5 million metric tons, a 22 percent increase

Closest to the ocean is the **St. Lambert Lock**, which lifts ships some 15 feet (4.6 meters) from Montreal harbor to the level of the Laprairie Basin, through which the channel sweeps in a great arc 8.5 miles (13.7 km) long to the second lock. The **Côte Ste. Catherine Lock**, like the other six St. Lawrence Seaway locks, is built to the dimensions shown in the table above. The Côte Ste. Catherine lifts ships from the level of the Laprairie Basin 30 feet (9.1 meters) to the level of Lake Saint-Louis, bypassing the Lachine Rapids. Beyond it, the channel runs 7.5 miles (12.1 km) before reaching Lake Saint-Louis.

The **Lower Beauharnois Lock**, bypassing the Beauharnois Power House, lifts ships 41 feet (12.5 meters) and sends them through a short canal to the **Upper Beauharnois Lock**, where they are lifted 41 feet (12.5 meters) to reach the Beauharnois Canal. After a 13-mile (20.9 km) trip in the canal and a 30-mile (48.3 km) passage through Lake Saint Francis, vessels reach the U.S. border and the **Snell Lock**, which has a lift of 45 feet (13.7 meters) and empties into the 10-mile (16.1 km) Wiley-Dondero Canal.

After passing through the Wiley-Dondero, ships are raised another 38 feet (11.6 meters) by the **Dwight D. Eisenhower Lock**, after which they enter Lake St. Lawrence, the pool upon which nearby power-generating stations draw for their turbines located a mile to the north.

At the western end of Lake St. Lawrence, the **Iroquois Lock** allows ships to bypass the Iroquois Control Dam. The lift here is only about 1 foot (0.3 meters). Once in the waters west of Iroquois, the channel meanders through the Thousand Islands to Lake Ontario, the Welland Canal and beyond.

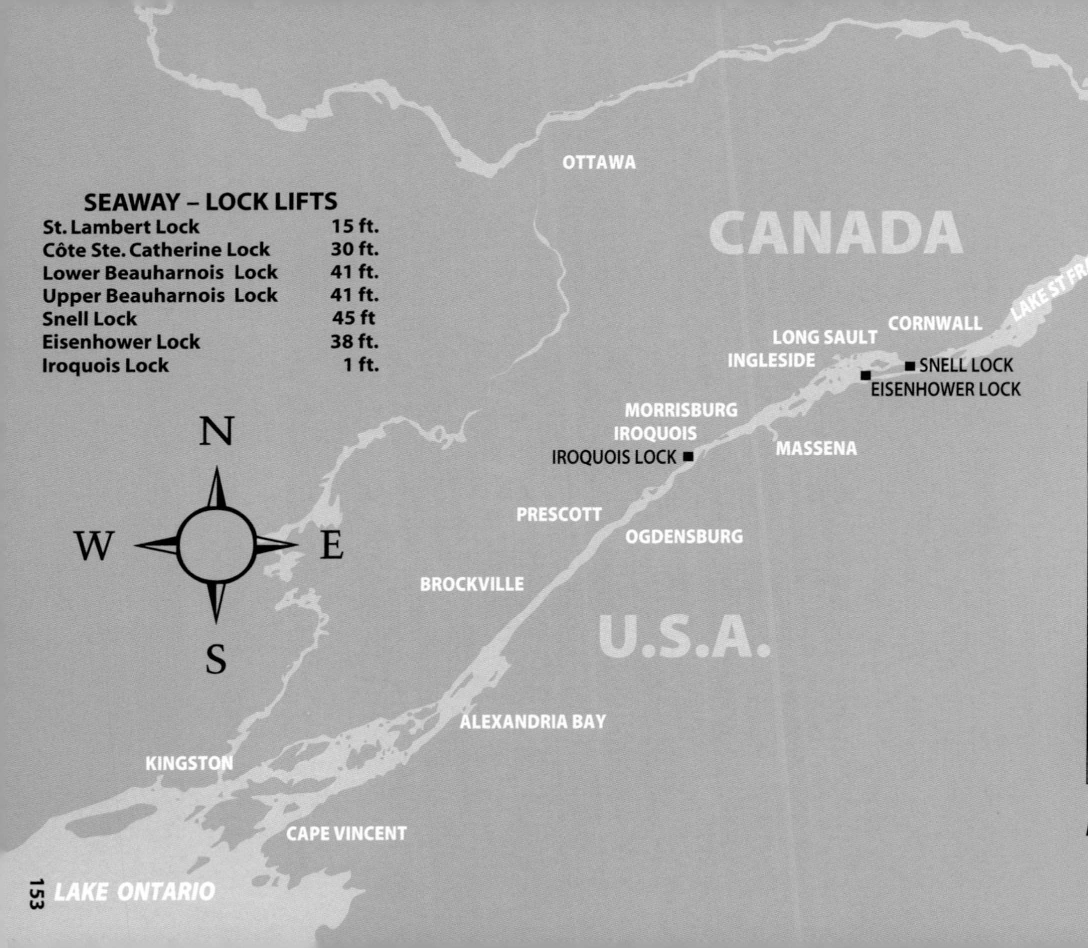

The St. Lawrence Seaway turns 60 in 2019. Here, Canada Steamship Lines' flag-bedecked Lemoyne makes an early 1960 passage through the St. Lambert Lock at Montreal. (Press Photo, Roger LeLievre Collection)

SEAWAY – LOCK LIFTS

St. Lambert Lock	15 ft.
Côte Ste. Catherine Lock	30 ft.
Lower Beauharnois Lock	41 ft.
Upper Beauharnois Lock	41 ft.
Snell Lock	45 ft.
Eisenhower Lock	38 ft.
Iroquois Lock	1 ft.

ST LAMBERT

ST LAMBERT LOCK

MONTREAL

CÔTE STE CATHERINE LOCK

LAKE ST-LOUIS

BEAUHARNOIS LOCKS

BEAUHARNOIS CANAL

LAKE ST-FRANCOIS

CANADA

OTTAWA

CORNWALL

LONG SAULT

SNELL LOCK

EISENHOWER LOCK

INGLESIDE

MASSENA

MORRISBURG

IROQUOIS

IROQUOIS LOCK

OGDENSBURG

U.S.A.

PRESCOTT

BROCKVILLE

ALEXANDRIA BAY

KINGSTON

CAPE VINCENT

LAKE ONTARIO

N E W S

153

Lake Carriers' Association

Helping the U.S. fleet navigate the Great Lakes since 1880

Proudly representing:
American Steamship Company
Andrie Inc.
Armstrong Steamship Company
Bell Steamship Company
Central Marine Logistics, Inc.
Great Lakes Fleet
Inland Lakes Management, Inc.
The Interlake Steamship Company
Lake Michigan Carferry Service
Pere Marquette Shipping
Port City Marine Services, Inc.
Soo Marine Supply, Inc.
VanEnkevort Tug & Barge, Inc.

(440) 333-4444 | www.LCAShips.com | @LCAShips

The Great Lakes shipping season runs from March 25 to January 15, when most vessels tie up for the winter.

A vessel traveling from the Atlantic Ocean to Lake Superior through the St. Lawrence Seaway and the Soo Locks rises nearly 600 feet. The first lift, a total of 224 feet, is provided by the seven St. Lawrence Seaway locks that begin at Montreal. The Welland Canal raises vessels an additional 326 feet. The Soo Locks complete the process with a 21-foot lift.

One short blast of a vessel's whistle while in the lock means "cast off lines."

A red-and-white flag flying from a vessel's mast indicates a pilot is on board. Saltwater vessels must pick up Great Lakes pilots at various points in their voyage.

No tolls are charged at the Soo Locks. However, tolls are charged for the Welland Canal and St. Lawrence Seaway locks.

In the spring and fall, a small fleet of icebreakers operated by the U.S. and Canadian coast guards, as well as commercial tugs, help keep navigation channels open.

There are about 130 major cargo carriers, including tug/barge combinations, engaged in regular Great Lakes / Seaway trade. They are supplemented by a variety of saltwater visitors, also known as salties, from all over the world.

The St. Marys River, running 80 miles (128.7 km) from Ile Parisienne at its north end to DeTour Reef Light at its south end, connects Lake Superior with Lake Huron. It includes two engineering marvels, the Soo Locks at Sault Ste. Marie, MI, and the West Neebish Cut at Barbeau, MI, a channel dynamited out of solid rock that allows traffic to pass to the west side of Neebish Island.

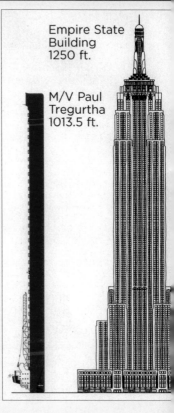

Empire State Building 1250 ft.

M/V Paul Tregurtha 1013.5 ft.

Plimsoll and other hull markings

The Plimsoll line is a reference mark located on a ship's hull that indicates the maximum depth to which the vessel may be safely immersed when loaded with cargo. This depth varies with a ship's dimensions, type of cargo, time of year and the water densities encountered in port and at sea. In the 1860s, after increased loss of ships due to overloading, government regulations were proposed by Samuel Plimsoll, a British Member of Parliament. The Plimsoll mark, or Plimsoll line, was adopted in 1876. Since that time every vessel has been required to have a line painted amidships on both sides of the hull to act as a visual indicator of the limit to which ships could be loaded. It is a circle with a horizontal line drawn through it. This has, over time, been adopted worldwide.

Left symbol warns of a bow or stern thruster below. The one at right indicates a bulbous bow and how far it extends in front of the hull.

Plimsoll mark (center), with draft markings in meters and feet at left. Symbols at right indicate draft markings in saltwater (SW) and freshwater (FW).

FOLLOWING THE FLEET

AIS (Automatic Identification System): All major vessels are now equipped with AIS, an automatic tracking system. With sites such as **MarineTraffic.com** or **ais.boatnerd.com**, it's possible to find vessel positions and see other information including speed and destimation.

With an inexpensive VHF scanner, boatwatchers can tune to ship-to-ship and ship-to-shore traffic using the following frequency guide.

Calling/distress only	**Ch. 16 – 156.800 MHz**	Calling/distress only
Commercial vessels only	**Ch. 06 – 156.300 MHz**	Working channel
Commercial vessels only	**Ch. 08 – 156.400 MHz**	Working channel
DeTour Reef – Lake St. Clair Light	**Ch. 11 – 156.550 MHz**	Sarnia Traffic - Sect. 1
Long Point Light – Lake St. Clair Light	**Ch. 12 – 156.600 MHz**	Sarnia Traffic - Sect. 2
Montreal – Mid-Lake St. Francis	**Ch. 14 – 156.700 MHz**	Seaway Beauharnois – Sect. 1
Mid-Lake St. Francis – Bradford Island	**Ch. 12 – 156.600 MHz**	Seaway Eisenhower – Sect. 2
Bradford Island – Crossover Island	**Ch. 11 – 156.550 MHz**	Seaway Iroquois – Sect. 3
Crossover Island-Cape Vincent	**Ch. 13 – 156.650 MHz**	Seaway Clayton – Sect. 4 St. Lawrence River portion
Cape Vincent – Mid-Lake Ontario	**Ch. 12 – 156.600 MHz**	Seaway Sodus – Sect. 4 Lake Ontario portion
Seaway Pilot Office – Cape Vincent	**Ch. 14 – 156.700 MHz**	Pilotage traffic
Mid-Lake Ontario – Welland Canal	**Ch. 11 – 156.550 MHz**	Seaway Newcastle – Sect. 5
Welland Canal	**Ch. 14 – 156.700 MHz**	Seaway Welland – Sect. 6
Welland Canal to Long Point Light	**Ch. 11 – 156.550 MHz**	Seaway Long Point – Sect. 7
Montreal traffic	**Ch. 10 – 156.500 MHz**	Vessel traffic
Soo Traffic	**Ch. 12 – 156.600 MHz**	Vessel control, Sault Ste. Marie, MI
Lockmaster, Soo Locks	**Ch. 14 – 156.700 MHz**	Soo Lockmaster (WUE-21)
Coast Guard traffic	**Ch. 21 – 157.050 MHz**	United States Coast Guard
Coast Guard traffic	**Ch. 22 – 157.100 MHz**	United States Coast Guard
U.S. mailboat, Detroit, MI	**Ch. 10 – 156.500 MHz**	Mailboat *J. W. Westcott II*

The following prerecorded messages help track vessel arrivals and departures

Boatwatcher's Hotline	**(218) 722-6489**	Superior, Duluth, Two Harbors, Taconite Harbor and Silver Bay
CSX coal docks/Torco dock	**(419) 697-2304**	Toledo vessel information
Eisenhower Lock	**(315) 769-2422**	Eisenhower Lock vessel traffic
Michigan Limestone dock	**(989) 734-2117**	Calcite, MI, vessel information
Michigan Limestone dock	**(906) 484-2201**	Press 1 – Cedarville, MI, passages
Presque Isle Corp.	**(989) 595-6611**	Stoneport vessel information ext. 7
Seaway Vessel Locator	**(450) 672-4115**	
Soo Locks Visitor Center Hotline	**(906) 253-9290**	Current Soo Locks traffic information
Superior Midwest Energy	**(715) 395-3559**	Superior, WI, vessel information
Thunder Bay Port Authority	**(807) 345-1256**	Thunder Bay, ON, vessel information
Welland Canal Traffic	**(905) 688-6462**	Welland Canal traffic

MEANINGS OF BOAT WHISTLES

1 SHORT: I intend to leave you on my port side (answered by same if agreed upon).

2 SHORT: I intend to leave you on my starboard side (answered by same if agreed upon). (Passing arrangements may be agreed upon by radio. If so, no whistle signal is required.)

1 PROLONGED: Vessel leaving dock.

3 SHORT: Operating astern propulsion.

1 PROLONGED, SOUNDED AT INTERVALS OF NOT MORE THAN 2 MINUTES: Vessel moving in restricted visibility.

1 SHORT, 1 PROLONGED, 1 SHORT: Vessel at anchor in restricted visibility (optional). May be accompanied by the ringing of a bell on the forward part of the ship and a gong on the aft end.

3 PROLONGED & 2 SHORT: Salute (formal)

1 PROLONGED & 2 SHORT: Salute (commonly used)

3 PROLONGED & 1 SHORT: International Shipmasters' Association member salute

5 OR MORE SHORT BLASTS SOUNDED RAPIDLY: Danger

Spotlight

- **Ships**
- **Sailors**
- **Adventures**

Lights ablaze on the Paul R. Tregurtha just before dawn. (Logan Vasicek)

Ancestor Harry Groh (circled) aboard the tug Peter Reiss. (Groh Collection)

Groh-ing Up Sailors

Brothers are sixth-generation Great Lakes mariners

By CHRIS WINTERS

Rocky Groh with sons Brendan and Peter aboard the Medusa Challenger in 1992.
(Groh Collection)

Old timers say sailing on the Great Lakes gets into your blood. Evidently, it leaks into the DNA, and before you know it, there are whole families who sail for lake shipping lines from one generation to the next. George Groh Sr. delivered his brood to the raw frontier port of Sheboygan, WI – by boat – and promptly shipped out on Lake Michigan in the ancient mists of 1841. There has been a Groh treading the deck of one lake vessel or other ever since.

George Sr.'s eldest son, Ole Groh, honed his marlinspike skills on fish tugs as a boy, graduated to harbor tugs and then joined the wooden ships and iron men aboard the vast lake schooner fleet of the era. Within a generation of landing at Sheboygan, the Groh family had moved into vessel ownership, keeping three harbor tugs and an array of dredging and marine construction equipment in partnership with Clemens Reiss, founder of the C. Reiss Coal Co. and its eventual steamship line. Ole Groh became Sheboygan's first harbormaster, and opened the settlement's lifesaving station in 1876, serving as its first keeper. Ole Groh's brother, William, caught steamboat fever, shipped out and had a son – Harry T. Groh – who followed in his father's footsteps. Harry Groh skippered the steam tug *Peter Reiss* – a carved facsimile of which his grandson Ray "Rocky" Groh happened upon in an octagon tavern window five decades later. Sailing had already seeped into Rocky Groh's blood via his pop, Harry F. Groh, a career wheelsman for the Reiss fleet, but his chance encounter with that tavern window influenced a unique mutation of the lake sailor gene.

"I was over wheeling on the *Raymond H. Reiss* in 1970. Me and my roommate Carl Schirel were up the street in Green Bay, and we walked by a bar … I remember it had an octagon window on the street. We stopped, and I said to Carl: 'That's the tug *Green Bay* in the window. My grandpa was skipper.'" Groh tried to buy the tug model from the bar's proprietor, but the fellow wouldn't part with it. When Groh and his shipmate returned to the *Reiss* "I kept talking about that model. Finally, Carl says: "Why don't you just carve one?" Suitably inspired, Groh had the cook save the fruit crates that were brought aboard to provision the galley. "Peach crates in particular used to be exactly a quarter inch slab, the sides were three-quarter inch, says Groh. "Always nice, clear pine. And strawberries came in little boxes of real fine wood strips." Groh's first model, cobbled together out of the Reiss' fruit crates, fell short of his expectations and wound up in the ashcan.

Peter Groh lays up the Lee A. Tregurtha in early 2019. *(Chris Winters)*

By the middle 1970s, Groh had installed a fully outfitted workshop in his cabin aboard the *Medusa Challenger*. The rhythm of steamboat life paid out gradually over 44 years for this fifth-generation lake sailor. There was plenty of time to fill between watches, and an off-season perfect for honing a craft like scale model shipbuilding. Groh estimates he has built 70-plus models since that first attempt, including no less than 13 1/16 scale models of his old ship *Medusa Challenger* thus far.

Extending the Groh family's presence on the working waterfront to an unprecedented sixth generation, Rocky Groh's oldest boy, Brendan Groh, now 34, shipped out aboard Hannah Marine's tug/barge combo *Susan W. Hannah/Medusa Conquest* at the tender age of 16. "My Dad ordered me to shape up and ship out," he said. The crack is especially apt, because that was the advice Rocky Groh – who wanted to pursue a career in commercial art – got from his no-nonsense father in the 1960s. "Sailing is my normal," Brendan continues. "I grew up around it, it's something that has always flowed naturally for me."

In spite of the spartan accommodations, extreme weather, long stretches away from home and setbacks the once-powerful industry has suffered since the 1980s, Brendan Groh is still positive about the profession. "I feel like I'm in a unique position, having learned the trade from the old guard like my dad and grandpa. My dad, especially, saw a lot of change during his career, and not all of it was good."

Rocky Groh with one of his handmade Medusa Challenger models in 1976. *(Groh Collection)*

Reflecting over a beer in hometown Sheboygan after laying up the *Stewart J. Cort* at the Port of Milwaukee, Brendan Groh continued: "I've watched a new type of professional taking up the tradition – better educated, more comfortable with information technology, more comfortable with the accelerated pace of change in the industry. We've become aware of things like the fleet's carbon footprint and overall environmental impact, and the

Continued on Page 160

Merchant marine ID cards for Harry Francis Groh, Rocky Groh's dad (top left). Left is Harry T. Groh's 1918 waterfront pass. Above, an 11-year-old Peter Groh tries his hand at Edward L. Ryerson's wheel. (Groh Collection and Chris Winters)

value of good public relations. The stereotype of the drunken sailor – an outcast unable to adjust to life ashore – is long gone."

After completing high school and one year at the Great Lakes Maritime Academy, Brendan Groh worked his way up the hawsepipe from ordinary seaman to able-bodied seaman with the Oglebay Norton fleet, crewing on the vanished postwar classics *Middletown*, *Reserve* and *Armco*. Like many lake sailors of that era, his career was dealt a major seniority setback when the 150-year-old Oglebay fleet was broken up and sold off in 2004. Groh landed with the short-lived Wisconsin and Michigan Steamship Co., then did a stretch with Central Marine Logistics aboard the *Joseph L. Block* and *Wilfred Sykes*. In 2010, he signed on with the Interlake Steamship Co. and shipped out aboard their 1,000-footer *Stewart J. Cort*. (It's interesting to note that the *Cort* is commanded by another dynamic Great Lakes family duo, Capt. and Chief Engineer Greg and Mark Sipper.) Brendan wrote his third mate's license aboard the *Cort* in 2012, got a towing endorsement on his license aboard the ATB *Pathfinder*, (Harry T. Groh would be pleased, no doubt) and he now spends the lion's share of the shipping season aboard Interlake's *Hon. James L. Oberstar*. "It's become something of a niche trade, and you can expect the unexpected. But if you look at the investment in fleet renewal Interlake and others are making, you know lake shipping is going to be around for a long time," he says.

Brendan Groh in the Cort's pilothouse. (Chris Winters)

The sailing life has also charmed Brendan's younger brother. Peter Groh, 28, spent his adolescence as a relentless Boatnerd shutterbug, collector of Great Lakes maritime ephemera, and apprentice model shipbuilder. He held down a shoreside job at a local big box after high school, then shipped out in the family trade as an ordinary seaman aboard the *James R. Barker* in May 2012. "I tried college three times, and struggled," he says candidly. "I knew myself – I learn better by doing, and I knew I could have a better future if I went sailing." He punched his AB ticket in 2014 and since then has crewed aboard virtually every boat in Interlake's nine-vessel fleet. He admits shipping out full-time has taken some of the shine off his Boatnerd hobby. "I don't think I've taken a picture since July, he laughs in January. "Some days, I still get up and

Brendan, Rocky and Peter Groh pose at the wreck of the Lottie Cooper, a three-masted schooner dredged out of Sheboygan harbor in 1992 and now on display on the waterfont. The vessel was owned by Ole Groh when it sank in 1896. (Chris Winters)

think, 'This is pretty amazing,' but now it's a job, like any other." His most recent permanent assignment is as an AB/wheelsman aboard the venerated World War II-era tanker convert *Lee A. Tregurtha*. As a connoisseur of sorts, he prefers Interlake's river-class double-enders to its big boats for practical, as well as aesthetic, reasons: "The runs are usually shorter, so time passes more quickly. I like the different ports of call and the sense of connection to the old days on the '50s-era boats."

Still handy with a camera, Peter Groh continues to fire away when inspiration strikes and as his daily responsibilities aboard the *Lee A. Tregurtha* allow. Under the tutelage of Digital Shipyard creator John Belliveau, he has also perfected a method of rendering full-color vessel profiles with Photoshop software, an avocation he practices during his idle time between watches, "like Dad used to with his models, I guess."

Peter Groh, in his bunk aboard ship, points to one of his photos published in Know Your Ships. (Chris Winters)

And what does the "Old Man," as the boys refer to him, who lived through the terrible hollowing out of the industry in the 1980s, think of the fact that his sons have followed him into the family business? Rocky Groh is matter-of-fact in his assessment: "To be honest with you, in spite of everything, I was pretty proud. Especially Peter. I figured Brendan would go sailing. But now Peter is doing well, too. They complain about the cold and the time away from home, but when spring comes, they're down on the dock waiting for fit-out, like I always was."

When spring returns in 2019, and the ice goes out of the quiet bays and connecting rivers, two sailors will make their way back to their respective boats, to an old way of life that has become new again for brothers of a sixth generation. Somewhere over the horizon and for the 178th shipping season, a Groh will be treading the deck of a Great Lakes boat.

ALGOVERSARY
120 Years of Smooth Sailing for Algoma

When it comes to anniversaries, 120 years in business is a pretty major milestone. Founded in 1899, the Algoma Central Corp. now owns and operates the largest fleet of dry and liquid bulk carriers operating on the Great Lakes-St. Lawrence Seaway, including self-unloading dry-bulk carriers, gearless dry-bulk carriers and product tankers. Algoma has also expanded into global short-sea markets through a 50 percent interest in NovaAlgoma Cement Carriers and NovaAlgoma Short Sea Carriers.

The fleet's beginning can be traced to August 11, 1899, when the Algoma Central Railway Co. was incorporated in Sault Ste. Marie, ON. It was founded to construct a railway from Sault Ste. Marie to a main Canadian Pacific Railway line for the transport of iron ore and timber. Under the Land Grant Aid Act (Ontario) of 1900, and as a result of its commitment to build the rail line, the Algoma Central Railway received more than 1.6 million acres of forest lands in the Algoma region where Sault Ste. Marie is located.

Paliki, built in 1889 in England, was one of Algoma's first steamers. *(Peter B. Worden Collection, MHSD)*

Conditions attached to the land grant included an obligation to "maintain a Great Lakes fleet of four steel vessels of at least 2,000 tons carrying capacity." On Feb. 16, 1900, the board of directors of Algoma Central Railway met and approved the "purchase of four steam vessels to be used for freight and passenger service in connection with the company's railway." That was how the Algoma Central fleet was born. Those early vessels were *Monkshaven, Paliki,*

J. Frater Taylor, added to the fleet in 1913, became the first Algosoo. *(Peter B. Worden Collection, MHSD)*

Theano and *Agawa. Thomas Drummond, W.C. Franz* and *J.A. McKee* were also early members of the fleet.

Although the pace of investment in the railway and fleet was initially rapid, within a few years, the corporation began to suffer from lack of funds. In 1903, it entered into a long period of financial restructuring, during which the railway and the fleet of Great Lakes vessels continued to operate. In 1913, the steamer *J. Frater Taylor* was purchased and renamed *Algosoo*. She would serve Algoma until in 1967. *Home Smith*, added in 1917, would become *Algorail*.

Algoway in the early 1960s, likely on the St. Clair River. (Emory A. Massman Jr.)

The mid-1930s found the company seeking more tonnage, which it found by buying two vessels from the Postal Steamship Co. *John J. Barlum* would become *Algocen* in 1934, while *Thomas Barlum* would become *Algosteel* one year later.

In 1940, the fleet expanded again with the purchase of *John J. Boland Jr.* from the American Steamship Co. She was renamed *Algoway* and sailed until sold for scrap in 1964. By 1953, Algoma was ready to build its own vessel. The 560-foot-long *E.B. Barber,* a product of the Port Arthur Shipbuilding Co., entered service in 1953. Ten years later, she was converted to a self-unloader, another important milestone for the company.

In 1958, the corporation felt it was on sufficiently secure financial footing to consider a refinancing proposal that would clear Algoma's old debt and enable it to emerge from court protection and seek a public listing on the Toronto Stock Exchange. On May 21, 1958, the corporation, previously named the Algoma Central and Hudson

Self-unloader E.B. Barber in 1976. (Roger LeLievre)

Bay Railway, was granted a listing by the exchange and the corporation officially completed its refinancing on Nov. 14, 1958.

In the mid-1960s, the company embarked on an ambitious fleet renewal program, starting in 1965 with the building of a new *Algocen*, followed by a new *Algorail* in 1967, *Agawa Canyon*

Continued on Page 164

Nearly new Agawa Canyon in 1971. (Roger LeLievre)

Algosoo of 1974 was theGreat Lakes last vessel built with the pilothouse in the front. (Jim Hoffman)

Tanker Algocanada in the Detroit River. (Wade P. Streeter)

in 1970, another *Algoway* in 1972 and *Algolake* in 1977.

Algoma also purchased several vessels from other fleets, including *A.S. Glossbrenner* in 1972 (renamed *Algogulf* and later *Algosteel*), *V.W. Scully* in 1973 (later *Algosound*), *Lake Manitoba* in 1986 (renamed *Algomarine*) and *John A. France* and *J.N. McWatters* in 1994 (renamed *Algoriver* and *Algogulf* respectively). Other acquisitions followed in the 1980s, including *Capt. Henry Jackman*, *Algowest* (later *Peter R. Cresswell*) and *John B. Aird*.

Since becoming a public company, Algoma has held interests in many aspects of the transportation industry, including trucking, helicopter and air expediting services, while maintaining its focus on the marine fleet. In 1995, Algoma Central Railway was sold, followed in 1997 by the sale of the corporation's large forest land holdings. In 1998, Algoma expanded its domestic shipping operations, acquiring from Imperial Oil Ltd. that company's fleet of domestic product tankers and forming Algoma Tankers Ltd.

Since 1990, Algoma has grown its domestic dry-bulk operations, beginning with the establishment of Seaway Bulk Carriers in 1990 and Seaway Self-Unloaders in 1993. Those two pools eventually came together to form Seaway Marine Transport. Algoma closed the circle in 2011 by buying out its partner to become the sole owner of the domestic dry-bulk business. In 1997, Algoma acquired an interest in Marbulk Canada Inc. in order to broaden its interests in dry-bulk shipping and, in particular, in self-unloader trades. This led to the formation of Algoma Shipping Ltd. and the corporation's entry into the international dry-bulk shipping business.

The fleet's current domestic dry-bulk vessels carry cargoes of raw materials such as iron ore, grain, salt and aggregates, and operate throughout the Great Lakes-St. Lawrence waterway. Seven new vessels have recently been added to the company's fleet as part of its Equinox-class vessels that are 45 percent more energy efficient than earlier vessels. That domestic dry-bulk fleet renewal program was led by the 2013 commissioning of *Algoma Equinox*. Others of the class are *Algoma Strongfield, Algoma Harvester, Algoma Sault, Algoma Niagara* and *Algoma Innovator*. Expected to join them in 2019 is *Algoma Conveyor*.

The product tankers marine transportation segment includes ownership and management of the operational and commercial activities of six Canadian-flagged tankers operating on the Great Lakes, St. Lawrence Seaway and the east coast of North America. A seventh tanker, *Algonorth*, was added in late 2018.

The ocean self-unloaders segment includes ownership of five oceangoing self-unloading vessels, a 50 percent interest in a sixth self-unloader and a 25 percent interest in a specialized ocean vessel. These vessels are engaged in carrying dry-bulk commodities worldwide.

The global short sea shipping segment focuses on niche markets featuring specialized equipment or services. The NACC fleet comprises pneumatic cement carriers servicing large global manufacturers that support infrastructure investment; the fleet is now the second largest in the world. *NACC Argonaut* and *NACC Quebec* are now familiar sights in the Lake Ontario cement trade. NASC manages a short sea mini-bulker fleet that comprises owned

ships, chartered vessels, and vessels under third-party management contracts. The NASC fleet moves approximately 15 million tons annually in support of the agricultural, cement, construction, energy and steel industries worldwide.

Algoma Central's first 120 years were pretty spectacular, and with its ongoing fleet renewal program and expansion into the world marketplace, the company is clearly poised for whatever challenges the next decades might bring.

Algoma Sault passes Detroit. *(Peter Groh)*

Algoma Equinox during 2013, her first season. *(Roger LeLievre)*

G-tug Cleveland assists Joseph H. Thompson at her namesake port. (Roger Durfee)

Great Lakes Towing, Fednav also mark milestones

G-tug Florida during a Detroit River tug race circa 1950. (Press Photo, Roger LeLievre Collection)

Not only are *Know Your Ships* and the St. Lawrence Seaway celebrating anniversaries in 2019, so are The Great Lakes Towing Co. and Fednav. The busy red and green G-tugs are familiar sights at nearly every port on the Great Lakes, while the bright red Fednav vessels are frequent visitors at ports from western Lake Superior to Montreal and beyond.

The Great Lakes Towing Co. was the first company of the Cleveland, Ohio-based The Great Lakes Group, founded 120 years ago in New Jersey on July 7, 1899. The company began full operation on the Great Lakes (except Lake Ontario and the St. Lawrence River) in 1900, starting its first navigating season with over 150 tugboats.

Widely referred to as "The Towing Company," it is the largest U.S.-flagged tugboat company engaged in towing on the Great Lakes. Its tugs – most of which are named after states – provide harbor towing, docking / undocking, interport towing and icebreaking, as well as rescue and assistance to grounded or damaged ships with a fleet of nearly 40 tugboats stationed around U.S. Great Lakes ports.

Throughout its history, The Great Lakes Towing Co, has always operated a Cleveland shipyard. Over the years, it constructed many of the fleet's tugs

G-tug Wisconsin, built in 1897 and the oldest commercially operating tug in the world, assists the new U.S. Navy combat ship Wichita at Detroit in 2018. (Paul C. LaMarre III)

Federal Clyde, built in 2016, on the St. Lawrence Seaway. (Ron Beaupre)

One of Fednav's early vessels, Federal Voyager.

and repaired all of the towing company's tugs and barges. Great Lakes Shipyard is located in the Old River Channel on the Cuyahoga River in Cleveland. In 2007, the shipyard began construction of new tugboats, recently completing the tugs *Ohio* and *Cleveland* for the fleet.

On July 29, 2011, the shipyard debuted its new mobile vessel hoist, named *America* after one of the company's original tugboats (still in service as *Wisconsin*). The 770-ton hoist, manufactured by Marine Travelift, is the largest of its kind on the Great Lakes and third largest in the world.

The Great Lakes Group also includes Tugz International LLC, which designs, constructs, and owns tractor and tractor-type tugs for charter and operation by affiliated companies, and for charter to third parties for use throughout the United States. Soo Linehandling Services Inc. provides assistance to vessels transiting the Soo Locks.

The Montreal-based Fednav fleet, traces its origins back 75 years, to Sept. 7, 1944, when the Federal Commerce & Navigation Co. was founded in Toronto, ON. It now comprises close to 100 owned, long-term chartered and spot-chartered vessels and includes a significant number of St. Lawrence Seawaymax-sized bulk carriers and Supramax and Panamax vessels. The rest of Fednav's roster – with names all beginning with the word Federal – consists of 20-40 short-and long-term charters, depending on the time of year.

Federal Schelde upbound for grain. (Sam Hankinson)

Many of the ships in the fleet are strengthened for navigation in ice. Three vessels – the 1978-built *Arctic*, 2006-built *Umiak I*, and 2014-built *Nunavik* – are fitted with icebreaker bows and have enough ice-strengthening and installed power to operate independently in Arctic ice conditions. In 2018, Fednav ordered a fourth icebreaking cargo vessel to eventually replace the *Arctic*, scheduled for delivery in 2020.

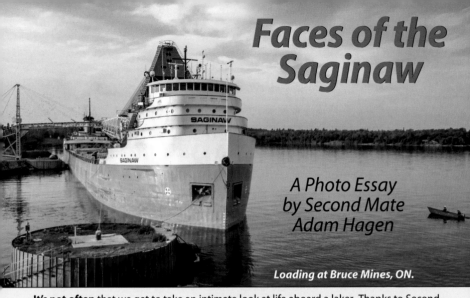

Faces of the Saginaw

A Photo Essay by Second Mate Adam Hagen

Loading at Bruce Mines, ON.

It's not often that we get to take an intimate look at life aboard a laker. Thanks to Second Mate Adam Hagen, we are able to present this superb selection of images from the 2018 season aboard Lower Lakes Towing Co.'s *Saginaw*. What would a vessel be without the hard-working folks who make her sail? Thank you, Adam, for this behind-the-scenes look.

Left: *Training Mate Austin Moore.* **Center:** *Capt. Colin Lozon on the bridge wing.*
Right: *Wheelsman Bill Sly.* **Below:** *The tunnel crew – Paul Lomond, Dwayne Munden, Eric Chislett and Gary Taylor – takes a break after unloading at Cleveland.*

Top: *Brandon Cleary and Jay Shaw touch up the name on Saginaw's superstructure.*

Above left: *Deckhand Todd McBride.* **Above center:** *Bill Sly and First Officer Jesse Vickers.*
Above right: *Fourth Engineer Joe Brawley, Cadet Andrew Armata and Third Engineer Nigel D'silva in the engine room.* **Below:** *Deckhand Evan Urquhart after a day unloading coal.*

Above left: *Fourth Engineer Kyle Araujo, Third Engineer Nigel D'Silva and Engineer Assistant Dillon Organ at the the gangway door.* **Upper right:** *Wheelsman Brandon Cleary and Trainng Mate Austin Moore.* **Lower right:** *Head Cargo Maintenance Man Rob MacDonald.*

Above left: *Gary Taylor.* **Above middle:** *First Officer Jesse Vickers.* **Above right:** *Deckhand Jason Shaw.* **Below left:** *Todd McBride.* **Below right:** *Brenden Conboy and Brandon Cleary.*

AB Nick Tabone, OS Tyler Quinn, OS Jason Shaw, OS Jay Hall and OS Evan Urquhart

Left: First Officer Jesse Vickers. **Middle:** OS Jay Hall. **Right:** Haircuts on deck with Brandon Cleary and Adam Hagen. **Below:** Deckhands Brenden Conboy, Jason Shaw and Evan Uruquart.

Photographer Adam Hagen

River And Lake Cruises Aboard GOODTIME III

Narrated Tours
Dance Cruises
Rush Hour Cruises
Lunch / Dinner Cruises
Private Charters
Tickets Online
May – September

888-916-SHIP

The Best Way to See Cleveland

goodtimeiii.com

Cruising PORT HURON aboard the HURON LADY II

Public Sightseeing Cruises
One and a half-hour cruises of the St. Clair River. See the Blue Water Bridge, Fort Gratiot Lighthouse, Lake Huron and the Sarnia and Port Huron areas from the water

810-984-1500
www.HuronLady.com

May – September

Uncharted. Unexpected.

Located on Niagara's South Coast, **Port Colborne** offers a thriving festival and entertainment scene, white sand beaches, culinary favourites, Sugarloaf Marina, fishing, golfing, and unique shopping districts along the historic Welland Canal.

PORT COLBORNE
Niagara's South Coast

niagara original

www.PortColborne.ca • 1.888.PORT.FUN

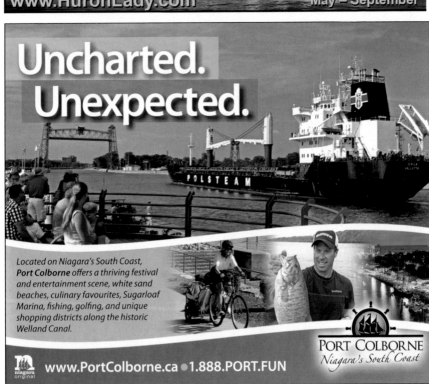

Historic Gallery

Midland Prince loading grain,
possibly at Fort William, ON.
(John Leonard Collection)

Ruth Hindman meets Frankcliffe Hall on the St. Marys River, June 1974. *(Roger LeLievre)*

Hosing down on the Kinsman Enterprise after loading grain. *(Bob Campbell)*

Michigan loading at Marquette, MI, in 1959. (Jeff Cameron Collection)

Buckeye Steamship Co.'s veteran Buckeye Monitor in the Soo Locks. She was scrapped in the early 1970s. (Bob Campbell)

Pere Marquette 22 backing into the Jones Island slip at Milwaukee. (Skip Meier Collection)

S.T. Crapo at Manitowoc, WI, in April 1971, under tow of Lauren Castle. (Roger LeLievre)

USS Great Lakes Fleet's Irvin L. Clymer in 1990. She was scrapped three years later. (Jim Hoffman)

Passenger liner City of Detroit III on the Detroit River. (Fr. Peter VanderLinden Collection)

GREAT LAKES/ST. LAWRENCE SEAWAY

DIGITAL DATELINE

Don't miss out on System news

- *No gossip.*
- *No fluff.*
- *Just real news hand-picked by our editor.*
- *Delivered to your inbox every week!*

SIGN UP TODAY! IT'S FREE!

Email us at **harbor@harborhouse.com**

GREAT LAKES SEAWAY REVIEW

(800) 491-1760
greatlakes-seawayreview.com

Thirsty for Stories About Michigan's History?

Fill up on the Great Lakes State's past with *Michigan History* magazine.

hsmichigan.org • (800) 366-3703

Crew of the schooner Lucia A. Simpson at Milwaukee in1929. At that time, there were only four commercial schooners left sailing the Great Lakes. Capt. Hans Simensen is the gentleman in the white hat. (Press Photo, Roger LeLievre Collection)

Willis B. Boyer shows off her Bicentennial colors. (Skip Meier Collection)

Heron Bay and tug Louisiana in the Rouge River at Detroit in 1975. (Paul C. LaMarre Jr.)

Mantadoc in St. Clair River ice, 1984. (Bob Campbell)

USCG Woodrush and Cason J. Callaway in winter ice at Duluth, MN. (Tom Manse Collection)

World War II Maritime-class steamer Ashland at the Soo Locks in 1977. (Bob Campbell)

Detroit River passenger steamer Columbia in 1997. (William A. Hoey)

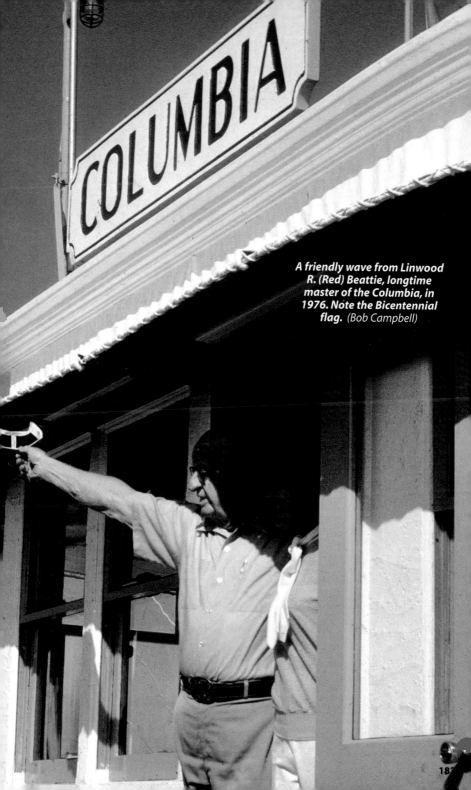

COLUMBIA

A friendly wave from Linwood R. (Red) Beattie, longtime master of the Columbia, in 1976. Note the Bicentennial flag. (Bob Campbell)

Get a FREE Copy of <u>THE</u> Ship History Magazine

PowerShips

PowerShips *is the ultimate source for stories about powerful ships, spirited passengers and hardworking crews, published quarterly by the nation's favorite ship history organization.*

Email info@sshsa.org
or call 1-401-463-3570

and we'll send you a FREE copy and tell you how to subscribe.

STEAMSHIP HISTORICAL SOCIETY OF AMERICA

INFO@SSHSA.ORG • WWW.SSHSA.ORG

Daniel J. Morrell passes docked John J. Boland at Detroit, October 1966. The Morrell would sink in late November. (Hal Jackson)

G.A. Tomlinson unloading coal at Duluth, MN, in 1936. (Press Photo, Roger LeLievre Collection)

Unloading coal from Cleveland Cliffs' Cadillac at Marquette, MI, in the 1970s. (Tom Manse)

French Line saltie Kurt Arlt passing through the gate in the new dike at Cornwall, ON, in 1957. The gate was closed permanently on July 1, 1958, and Lake St. Lawrence was formed. (Press Photo, Roger LeLievre Collection)

Wilson Marine Transit Co.'s Ben Moreell on the St. Marys River in 1971. (Roger LeLievre)

BEN MOREELL

Buckeye in tight quarters, 1976. (Skip Meier Collection)

BUCKEYE

Canada Steamship Lines' Tarantau in 1976. She was scrapped in 1999. (Roger LeLievre)

Silverdale (1926-1984) on Lake Ontario. (Jim Hoffman)

William J. De Lancey unloads at the Lorain Pellet Terminal in 1982. She sails today as Paul R. Tregurtha. (Press Photo, Roger LeLievre Collection)

U.S. Steel's steamer D.M. Clemson, bow detail, 1974. (Skip Meier Collection)

Seaway visitor Fro at Detroit in 1965. Mailboat J.W. Westcott II is alongside. *(Hal Jackson)*

A Great Lakes captain in his pilothouse, unknown vessel and year. *(Erhard Peters)*

'A Passenger Ship Empire'

Long known for its large fleet of cargo carriers, Canada Steamship Lines once operated a fleet of passenger steamers so vast that a maritime historian called it "a passenger ship empire." These steamers could be found in ports all the way from Duluth, Minnesota, to the lower St. Lawrence River in Quebec, where CSL owned two fine hotels and even a shipyard that built some of its best passenger ships. In *Great White Fleet*, a handsome book with plentiful pictures and polished prose, journalist and author John Henry revisits a passenger fleet that had no peer.

Hardcover 8 ½" x 11 3/8" – 142 pages, 120 illustrations
$30. Available at Amazon.com, Amazon.ca

GREAT LAKES GLOSSARY

AAA CLASS – Vessel design popular on the Great Lakes in the early 1950s. *Arthur M. Anderson* is one example.

AFT – Toward the back, or stern, of a ship.

AMIDSHIPS – The middle point of a vessel, referring to either length or width.

ARTICULATED TUG/BARGE (ATB) – Tug-barge combination. The two vessels are mechanically linked in one axis but with the tug free to move, or articulate, on another axis.

BACKHAUL – The practice of carrying a revenue-producing cargo (rather than ballast) on a return trip from hauling a primary cargo.

BARGE – Vessel with no engine, either pushed or pulled by a tug.

BEAM – The width of a vessel at its widest point.

BILGE – Lowest part of a hold or compartment, generally where the rounded side of a ship curves from the keel to the vertical sides.

BOW THRUSTER – Propeller mounted transversely in a vessel's bow under the waterline to assist in moving sideways. A stern thruster may also be installed.

BRIDGE – The platform above the main deck from which a ship is steered/navigated. Also: PILOTHOUSE or WHEELHOUSE.

BULK CARGO – Goods, loose or in mass, that generally must be shoveled, pumped, blown or scooped out of a vessel.

BULKHEAD – Wall or partition that separates rooms, holds or tanks within a ship's hull.

BULWARK – The part of the ship that extends fore and aft above the main deck to form a rail.

DATUM – Level of water in a given area, determined by an average over time.

DEADWEIGHT TONNAGE – The actual carrying capacity of a vessel, equal to the difference between the light displacement tonnage and the heavy displacement tonnage, expressed in long tons (2,240 pounds or 1,016.1 kilograms).

DECK SPRINKLERS – The reason for water spraying on a vessel's deck is to help cool the upper part of a boat and prevent hogging (bending due to temperature differences above and below the waterline). With decks exposed to the sun all day, the surface can get very hot. The hull of the boat underwater stays cooler. Hogging can affect cargo capacity and the depth to which a boat can load.

DISPLACEMENT TONNAGE – The actual weight of the vessel and everything aboard her, measured in long tons. The displacement is equal to the weight of the water displaced by the vessel. Displacement tonnage may be qualified as light – indicating the weight of the vessel without cargo, fuel and stores – or heavy, indicating the weight of the vessel loaded with cargo, fuel and stores.

DRAFT – The depth of water a ship needs to float. Also, the distance from keel to waterline.

FIT OUT – The process of preparing a vessel for service after a period of inactivity.

FIVE-YEAR INSPECTION – U.S. Coast Guard survey, conducted in a drydock every five years, of a vessel's hull, machinery and other components.

FLATBACK – Lakes slang for a non-self-unloader.

FOOTER – Lakes slang for 1,000-foot vessel.

FOREPEAK – The space below the forecastle.

FREEBOARD – The distance from the waterline to the main deck.

GEARLESS VESSEL – One that is not a self-unloader.

GROSS TONNAGE – The internal space of a vessel, measured in units of 100 cubic feet (2.83 cubic meters) = a gross ton.

HATCH – An opening in the deck through which cargo is lowered or raised. A hatch is closed by securing a hatch cover over it.

IMO # – Unique number issued by International Maritime Organization, or IMO, to ships for identification. Not all vessels have an IMO number.

INTEGRATED TUG/BARGE (ITB) – Tug-barge combination in which the tug is rigidly mated to the barge. *Presque Isle* is one example.

IRON DECKHAND – Mechanical device that runs on rails on a vessel's main deck and is used to remove and replace hatch covers.

JONES ACT – A U.S. law that mandates that cargoes moved between American ports be carried by U.S.-flagged, U.S.-built and U.S.-crewed vessels.

KEEL – A ship's steel backbone. It runs along the lowest part of the hull.

LAID UP or **LAY-UP** – Out of service.

MARITIME CLASS – Style of lake vessel built during World War II as part of the nation's war effort. *Mississagi* is one example.

NET REGISTERED TONNAGE – The internal capacity of a vessel available for carrying cargo. It does not include the space occupied by boilers, engines, shaft alleys, chain lockers or officers' and crew's quarters. Net registered tonnage is usually referred to as registered tonnage or net tonnage and is used to calculate taxes, tolls and port charges.

PLIMSOLL LINE – A reference mark located on a ship's hull that indicates the maximum depth to which the vessel may be safely immersed when loaded with cargo.

RIVER CLASS – Group of vessels built in the 1970s to service smaller ports and negotiate narrow rivers.

SELF-UNLOADER – Vessel able to discharge its own cargo using a system of conveyor belts and a movable boom.

STEM – The extreme forward end of the bow.

STEMWINDER – Vessel with all cabins aft.

STERN – The back of the ship.

STRAIGHT-DECKER – Non-self-unloading vessel.

STEM – The extreme forward end of the bow.

TACONITE – Processed, pelletized iron ore. Easy to load and unload, this is the primary type of ore shipped on the Great Lakes and St. Lawrence Seaway. Also known as pellets.

TOLL – Fee charged against a ship, cargo and passengers for a complete or partial transit of a waterway covering a single trip in one direction.

TURKEY TRAIL – Route from North Channel (above Manitoulin Island) into the St. Marys River, named for the many courses which zigzag through the area's islands, shoals and ports.

Shipwatcher's Favorite for Over 20 Years!

DIAMOND JACK'S

RIVER TOURS

2 Hour Narrated Detroit River Tours
Detroit and Wyandotte

www.diamondjack.com

VESSEL LOG / *Record your own ship spottings*

Date	Vessel Name	Location

Date	Vessel Name	Location

ADVERTISER INDEX *Thank you!*

Thanks to these advertisers, we have been able to keep our cover price the same for 10 years.

Algoma Central Corp. 3
Ashtabula Maritime & Surface
   Transportation Museum.......................... 130
Best Aerial Photos 23
Blue Water Convention Center 88
Canada Steamship Lines .... Inside Front Cover
Captain Spicer's Gallery...............................28
Celebrating Canada Steamship
   Lines Passenger Ships 191
Central Marine Logistics............................. 18
City of Milwaukee Marine Museum 124
DeTour Reef Lighthouse 122
Detroit Historical Society.......................... 130
Diamond Jack's River Tours 193
Don Lee Cartoons 31
Door County Maritime Museum.................... 129
Dre Designs..32
Duluth Seaway Port Authority 24
40 Mile Point Lighthouse 124
Fednav.. 117
Georgian Centre 25
Goodtime III 172
Great Lakes Aquarium 138
Great Lakes Fleet.....................................20
Great Lakes Lighthouse
   Keepers Association 27
Great Lakes Maritime Academy 200
Great Lakes Science Center 126
Great Lakes Shipwreck
   Museum .... Inside Back Cover
Great Lakes Towing Co. 8
Historical Society of Michigan 178
Huron Lady II 172
Icebreaker Mackinaw Museum.................... 124
Inn at Lock 7 4
Interlake Steamship Co. 93
J.W. Westcott Co. 4

Lake Carriers' Association.......................... 154
Lake Freighter Minis LLC 32
Lake Michigan Carferry.............................29
Lake Superior Magazine 21
Lake Superior Marine Museum Association ...129
Lake Superior Marine Museum Gift Shop ... 129
Lee Murdock 27
Lighthouse Digest 22
Ludington Maritime Museum 126
Marine Artist Anthony Strublic 30
Marine Artist Ed Labernic 97
Mike's Voyageur 199
National Museum of the Great Lakes 121
Owen Sound Transportation Co. 138
Plets Express 30
Port Colborne Tourist Centre 172
Port Huron Museum 122
Port of Monroe 8
PowerShips 184
Rand Logistics...89
Saginaw Valley Marine Museum 122
Sault Historic Sites (Valley Camp) 118
Sault Ste. Marie
   Convention & Visitor's Bureau 1
Seaway Review 178
Sip N' Sail Cruises 88
Soo Locks Boat Tours 144
South Pier Inn 2
St. Catharines Museum/Welland
   Canals Centre 126
St. Clair Inn 198
St. Clair Rotary 199
St. Lawrence Cruise Lines 138
VanEnkevort Tug & Barge 18
Visit Duluth 26
Whistles on the Water 199
Yooper Gifts 88

Fireworks at Cleveland as Herbert C. Jackson arrives. (Logan Vasicek)

MORE KYS PHOTOS ONLINE

Every year, *Know Your Ships* gets nearly 1,000 great photo submissions. Unfortunately, there isn't room in the book for them all, so we've created galleries of some of these images at **knowyourships.com**. Please stop by and take a look.

Paul H. Townsend at Port Colborne, ON, for scrapping. (Gordy Garris)

THE St.CLAiR INN

OPENING SUMMER 2019

Newly Restored Historic Hotel in St. Clair, Michigan

Located on the banks of the St. Clair River, this unique property has a rich history dating back to its opening in 1926, as the area's first hotel. The Inn is the ideal spot to relax and watch ships cruising up and down this active waterway. The St. Clair Inn exists to create immersive experiences and promote self-discovery through a superior time away. It is home to history and stories that do not end at your destination but begin there.

Experience the St. Clair Inn - Where Every Stay Has a Story

- Picture-perfect riverfront location designed for your comfort & relaxation
- 7 distinctive locations to dine and drink while enjoying local and seasonable selections
- Unique event venues, featuring spectacular views and unparalleled service
- Full service spa, workout facilities and outdoor pool for your wellness, beauty and recreation

St.C

THE ST. CLAIR INN, A TRIBUTE PORTFOLIO HOTEL
500 North Riverside Ave, St Clair, MI 48079 | 810.637.8554 | StClairInn.com

St. Clair Rotary Club's
2019 Great Lakes Freighter Raffle

You could be the fortunate winner of a one-of-a-kind round-trip summer cruise on a working Great Lakes freighter *(for 4-6 adults, depending on the vessel)*.

The trip will be scheduled by the Interlake Steamship Company for the 2020 Navigation Season.

Raffle sales are limited to 2,500 tickets. They can be purchased by mailing a check for $10/each along with a self-addressed, stamped envelope to:

St. Clair Rotary Club
P. O. Box 441
St. Clair, MI 48079

The drawing will be held at *Whistles on the Water*
Saturday, September 28, 2019
You need not be present to win

For more information visit www.stclairrotary.org

A Steam Whistle Event
re-creating sounds of the past

September 28, 2019

9 a.m. to 4 p.m.
Palmer Park in St. Clair, Michigan

On the banks of
the St. Clair River and
the United States/Canada border

www.stclairontheriver.com/
whistles-on-the-water-2

Riverview Dining

The Voyageur

"Why Go Anywhere Else?"

The Voyageur restaurant, flanking the St. Clair River, grants an elegant view of the waterway, with fine cuisine that compliment the fresh landscape.

Whether you come for lunch, dinner or a drink with friends, you'll enjoy a breathtaking view (great from any table, thanks to The Voyageur's large picture windows) as huge ocean-faring freighters glide by, only a matter of yards from your table!

Be accompanied by live singing and piano music starting at 6pm every Tuesday, Thursday, Friday, Saturday and Sunday. And on the street side, The Voyageur Sports Bar adds bits of revelry, featuring Keno, several large screen televisions to view all the big games and a great menu.

Come by today. Our friendly staff is waiting to serve you. -

(810) 329-3331 • thevoyageur.com • 525 South Riverside Ave • St Clair, MI 48079

Sports Bar & Grill   *Bowling*

Michigan's Maritime College

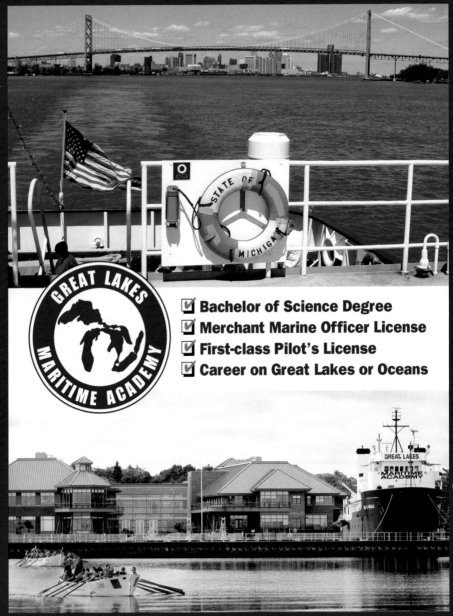

- ☑ Bachelor of Science Degree
- ☑ Merchant Marine Officer License
- ☑ First-class Pilot's License
- ☑ Career on Great Lakes or Oceans

GREAT LAKES
MARITIME ACADEMY

nmc.edu/maritime • 877-824-7447